S^{The}YNOPTIC GOSPEL™

The Story of The Life of Jesus

I0150499

®

STANDARD EDITION

.

The SYNOPTIC GOSPEL™

The Story of The Life of Jesus

STANDARD EDITION

Using the *New American Standard Bible* (NASB) Edition

of FIVE COLUMN: The SYNOPTIC GOSPEL

Compiled by: Daniel John

Smart Publishing Ltd.

Surrey, British Columbia, Canada

synpoticgospel.com

The Synoptic Gospel:
The Story of The Life of Jesus
** A reprint of the Fifth Column of FIVE COLUMN: The Synoptic Gospel **

Standard Edition - Paperback   3.7 - 2025
ISBN 978-1-988271-30-9
Copyright © 2009, 2014, 2017, 2021

Smart Publishing Ltd.
Surrey, British Columbia   Canada
synopticgospel.com

Compiled by: Daniel John
Cover design: Daniel John
Cover image: *La Última Cena*, by Juan de Juanes (*c. 1562)*
The *Jesus Logo* trademark is owned by Smart Publishing Ltd. ® 2012.

Printed by Amazon.

*   *   *   *   *   *   *

Other formats of **The Synoptic Gospel**
Kindle: ISBN 978-0-9939140-3-4   ePub: ISBN 978-1-988271-49-1
Standard PDF: ISBN 978-1-988271-29-7   *Complete* PDF: ISBN 978-1-988271-41-5
Complete Edition - Paperback: ISBN 978-1-988271-44-6
Complete Edition - Hard Cover: ISBN 978-1-988271-83-5
Audiobook Download (.m4b): ISBN 978-1-988271-00-2

Editions of **The Red Letter Gospel***: All the Words of Jesus Christ in Red*
Kindle: ISBN 978-1-988271-07-1
ePub: ISBN 978-1-988271-10-1   PDF: ISBN 978-1-988271-06-4
Standard Edition - Paperback: ISBN 978-1-988271-89-7
Complete Edition - Paperback: ISBN 978-1-988271-90-3
Complete Edition - Hard Cover: ISBN 978-1-988271-84-2

Editions of **FIVE COLUMN - Verse-By-Verse** *(Four Gospel Harmony + Merger)*
PDF: ISBN 978-1-998271-72-9
Paperback: ISBN 978-1-988271-79-8   Hard Cover: ISBN 978-1-988271-93-4

Editions of **FIVE COLUMN - Word-For-Word** *(554 pages)*
PDF: ISBN 978-0-993914-06-5   Paperback: ISBN 978-1-988271-01-9
are available at: synopticgospel.com/purchase

The Synoptic Gospel:
The Story of The Life of Jesus

Copyright Statement With Permissions of Use and To Quote
synopticgospel.com/copyright

All Rights Reserved Worldwide. No part of this publication may be copied, printed, reproduced or transmitted in any form, for any purpose, with the exception of the following specific permissions:

1. Use of The Synoptic Gospel Verses

A) Use of Up To Nine Verses - In exception to the above Reservation of Rights, and Fair Dealing (see Part 3. on the following page), short quotations of up to nine Verses from the text of this book may be quoted, reproduced, or otherwise used without the written permission of Smart Publishing Ltd. for **non-commercial use** in worship or for educational purposes, as when read aloud during a service, sermon or study, or when printed in a lesson, missive or newsletter, etc.

Acknowledgement: All Verses that are read aloud or quoted verbally should be acknowledged as: *"The Synoptic Gospel, verse xxx.y"*, where *xxx* is the *scene reference number* and *y* is the *Verse(s)*. When quoted in print the acknowledgement (as on the Copyright Page) should read "*The Synoptic Gospel* © 2009 by Smart Publishing Ltd. synopticgospel.com" and the individual Verse references can be shortened to *TSG xxx.y*.

Commercial Use or Reproduction: For permission or license to reproduce TSG Verses for any commercial reproduction or use please request permission at:
synopticgospel.com/copyright/permission-request-form/

B) Use of Ten Or More Verses - Up to and including one hundred (100) Verses from the text of this book may be quoted, reproduced, or otherwise used for **non-commercial use** without the written permission of Smart Publishing Ltd. provided that the quoted Verses amount to less than 30% of the total work in which they are used, and that the reference to each *Synoptic Gospel* Verse or set of Verses is notated as *The Synoptic Gospel xxx.y*, or *TSG xxx.y*, or simply as *xxx.y* for acknowledgement types i) and ii) below - where *xxx* is the *scene reference number* and *y* is the *verse(s)*.

Acknowledgement: The use of ten or more Verses requires that acknowledgement is included on the copyright page of the completed work, or where it is appropriate, of the most applicable of the following statements:

i) All Scriptures are from *The Synoptic Gospel* © 2009. Used by permission of Smart Publishing Ltd. All rights reserved. synopticgospel.com

ii) Unless otherwise noted, all Scriptures are from *The Synoptic Gospel* © 2009. Used by permission of Smart Publishing Ltd. All rights reserved. synopticgospel.com

iii) Scripture quotations marked *The Synoptic Gospel* (or *TSG*) are from *The Synoptic Gospel* © 2009. Used by permission of Smart Publishing Ltd. All rights reserved. synopticgospel.com

Commercial Use or Reproduction: For permission or license to reproduce TSG Verses for any commercial reproduction or use please request permission at:
synopticgospel.com/copyright/permission-request-form/

Permissions continued >

The Synoptic Gospel: *The Story of The Life of Jesus*

Copyright Statement With Permissions of Use and To Quote - *continued*

C) Use of More Than One Hundred Verses - For permission to quote or reproduce more than one hundred (100) Verses in a single commercial or non-commercial work, or fewer Verses if they exceed 30% of the total length of a short work, please obtain permission from the publisher and copyright owner Smart Publishing Ltd., using the form at: *synopticgospel.com/copyright/permission-request-form/*

2. Use of Other Content

The following specific Permissions for **non-commercial use** apply to the other materials that are included in this edition of *The Synoptic Gospel*. To obtain permission for any **commercial use** or reproduction of the following materials please visit *synopticgospel.com/copyright/permissions/* and then submit a request using the form at: *synopticgospel.com/copyright/permission-request-form/*

A) **Cover**: With the exception of the painting "*La Ultima Cena*" by Juan De Juanes (c. 1562), no element of the cover design, including the artwork, graphics or logos, may be used in any way without the permission of Smart Publishing Ltd. which can be requested at:
synopticgospel.com/copyright/permission-request-form/
The *Jesus Logo* trademark is owned by Smart Publishing Ltd. © 2007. ® 2012.

B) **Notes**: Beyond the uses defined in Part 3. below (*Fair Dealing*) no part of Notes 1-4 inclusive may be copied, printed, or reproduced for any type of use, without the permission of the publisher and copyright owner, Smart Publishing Ltd., which can be requested at:
synopticgospel.com/copyright/permission-request-form/

C) **Maps**: The Map of Israel and of Jerusalem may be reproduced in whole or in part for **non-commercial use** and display if the acknowledgement reads: *The Synoptic Gospel* © 2009 by Smart Publishing Ltd. For any commercial reproduction or use please request permission.

3. Fair Dealing

Fair Dealing is an exception (*Section 29*) to the Canadian Copyright Act (*R.S.C., 1985, c. C-42*) that allows for the use of small sections of a work (in the case of this work, fewer than five Verses) to be reproduced for non-commercial purposes without the prior written approval of the copyright holder. Common Fair Dealing uses include private study, education, research, review, news reporting, criticism, parody, and satire.
Detailed information is available at: *synopticgospel.com/copyright* & *laws-lois.justice.gc.ca/eng/acts/c-42/page-6.html*
All Verses and material used according to Fair Dealing best practices must be reproduced accurately, and acknowledged as "*The Synoptic Gospel* © 2009 by Smart Publishing Ltd."

* * * * * * *

Updated Copyright Statement & Permissions

In all situations and circumstances, the most current *Copyright Statement With Permissions of Use and To Quote* for this Smart Publishing Ltd. publication as found at: *synopticgospel.com/copyright* are in force, and if different from what is stated in this printed publication then the current online version shall supersede these printed permissions.

synopticgospel.com/copyright/permissions/

TABLE OF BOOK CONTENTS

"The Words That I have Spoken To You Are Spirit, and They Are Life."

~ Jesus Christ
TSG 519.4 (John 6:63)

This Gospel Is Dedicated To Humanity's Savior,

Our Lord, Jesus Christ.

Thank You!

TABLE OF GOSPEL CONTENTS

S͞YNOPTIC GOSPEL

SYNOPTIC GOSPEL

The SYNOPTIC GOSPEL

Sʜᴇ Sʏɴᴏᴘᴛɪᴄ Gᴏsᴘᴇʟ

FOREWORD

It is important that every person hear about the life and teachings of Jesus Christ. Few disagree that this story is found within the four Gospel accounts that open the New Testament of the Christian *Bible*, namely *Matthew, Mark, Luke* and *John*.

Within these four Gospel narratives there are many places where two, three, and even all four of them, mention the same saying, or describe the same event. In these many sets of parallel and overlapping verses there are almost always also differences within the specific details that each account records.

Over the centuries, many types of *harmonies* (which align the verses of the Gospels in parallel columns) and *mergers* (which combine or unify the individual words of the Gospels) have been created in an attempt to reconcile the differing chronologies of the four Gospel accounts, and to include or unify all of their words. In order to harmonize all of the details from the sections of parallel verses and produce one single and complete Gospel story of the life and teachings of Jesus Christ, a Four Gospel Harmony and word-for-word Merger called *FIVE COLUMN: The Synoptic Gospel* was created. This book reprints the unified *fifth column* text of that Harmony as **The Synoptic Gospel**: *The Story of The Life of Jesus*.

About the *STANDARD Edition*

This *Standard Edition* is a reduced size printed version of *The Synoptic Gospel,* which does not include all of the features of the *Complete Edition,* including:

1. 340+ references to the Old Testament Scriptures and historical figures,
2. The Chapter Maps of Israel and of Jerusalem (see *Note 4.3* on page *xi*),
3. The *Table of Chapter Contents* found at the start of each Chapter,
4. *Note 5: An Overview of The Four Gospels* + *The Four Gospels Comparison Chart* (*synopticgospel.com/notes/four-gospels-comparison),*
5. Seven *Articles* about why the Four Gospel Harmony *FIVE COLUMN,* and the merger of their texts as *The Synoptic Gospel,* was created,
6. The *Gospel Verse Cross-Reference* (*Appendix*) which shows if a verse from the four original Gospels is part of a synoptic set, and where that verse is located within *FIVE COLUMN* and *The Synoptic Gospel* (online at: *synopticgospel.com/cross-reference);*

These additional features are included in the *Complete Edition* printed book and the PDF version of *The Synoptic Gospel,* and also within the *FIVE COLUMN* Four Gospel Harmony and Word-for-word Merger, which are available at: *synopticgospel.com/purchase*

INTRODUCTION

To **FIVE COLUMN**: *The Synoptic Gospel*

The New Testament Greek word *euangelion* (evangel) means *good message*, which became *gospel* in Old English meaning *god term* or *god-spell*, and is most commonly referred to today as *good news*.

Since at least the Latin *Vulgate Bible* of 405 CE the canon of the Christian New Testament has opened with the four Gospel accounts of *Matthew, Mark, Luke* and *John*, each of which records a version of the good news of the life and teachings of Jesus Christ. Each Gospel account was written by a different man, and told to a different audience, from a different point of view; and each narrative has a slightly different emphasis, focus and reason why it was written.

While the four Gospel accounts are generally united in their overall theme and storyline, they each also contain unique sayings and stories which when taken together provide a more complete, composite picture of the teachings and personality of Jesus Christ.

Within the four Gospels there are many instances where the same saying, teaching or story is recorded in two or three of the accounts, while some sayings and events from the life of Jesus are mentioned within all four. In the many places where more than one Gospel account is describing the same event, those verses are thought of as "parallel", in that their content is the same or similar, occasionally even using identical wording.

Because there is so much material shared between the four Gospels accounts, particularly *Mark, Matthew* and *Luke*, they are often referred to as "synoptic" which is a Greek compound word that means "seeing together" or "seeing as one". In this case, synoptic means seeing the four Gospel narratives of the New Testament as one single record of the things that Jesus Christ said and did and taught.

In the many places where the Gospel stories closely parallel each other, there are almost always also differences in the wording and specific details that each account records. While these differences are usually minor and inconsequential, they sometimes produce contradictions, and occasionally even apparent conflicts.

Despite their differences, because there is so much similarity and overlap shared between the four New Testament Gospels, they have long been used together, both as a **harmony** which displays the Gospels in columns side-by-side, and as a **merger** (also known as a *synopsis*) which eliminates the duplication between the sections of parallel verses, and combines the remaining words to produce one single, complete version of each saying and event.

The *FIVE COLUMN* Four Gospel Harmony was compiled to provide a complete, chronological record of all of the sayings and events that are contained within the four Gospel accounts of the New Testament. With all of the events arranged in order, the parallel and overlapping sections of verses were reconciled, and merged into the *fifth column* on a word-for-word basis using a system of precise notation which was part of a harmonization and unification process that involved sixteen steps. The unified text that is produced in the *fifth column* of *FIVE COLUMN* is known as *The Synoptic Gospel*.

The main consideration of this work ensures that every detail from each of the four Gospel texts is included or accounted for, and that not one single word is unnecessarily omitted. The process of removing the duplication between the parallel sections of words and verses reduced the word count from the 83,680 words of the *New American Standard Bible* (NASB) version of the four Gospel accounts, to the 65,776 words of *The Synoptic Gospel* unified text, which is almost 22% shorter compared to reading each of the four individual Gospel accounts back-to-back.

While eliminating both the confusion caused by the differing chronologies of the four Gospels, and resolving the wording differences within their many sections of overlapping and parallel verses, this work produces an easy to follow narrative that preserves the full detail of every word, teaching, and miracle of Jesus Christ, as found within the four Gospel accounts of the New Testament.

May God continue to Bless and Inspire all who seek to know and understand the teaching Life and healing Ministry of Jesus Christ, The Son of God.

Daniel John

December, 2014

NOTES ON READING THIS BOOK

The following is an abridged section of Notes that details the features of this book. The full set of Notes for this work, including all of *Note 1 (The Sixteen Steps of The Merging Process)* and *Note 5 (An Overview of The Four Gospels),* can be viewed in the *Complete* and *Study* editions of the PDF and printed books of the *Complete Edition* of *The Synoptic Gospel*, and also in *FIVE COLUMN: The Synoptic Gospel,* and also online at: *synopticgospel.com/booknotes*

NOTE 1

HOW THIS BOOK WAS COMPILED

The text that is provided within this book is reprinted directly from the *fifth column* of the Four Gospel Harmony and Merger *FIVE COLUMN: The Synoptic Gospel*, which was compiled from the complete texts of the *New American Standard Bible* (NASB) edition of the four New Testament Gospels of *Matthew*, *Mark*, *Luke* and *John*.

The 83,680 words that are contained within the four Gospel accounts (NASB Edition) were chronologically aligned to form a single, complete narrative (a harmony) and then the texts of the four Gospels were combined on a word-for-word basis (a merger/synopsis) according to a compiling and editing process that involved sixteen steps, which unified the texts of the overlapping and parallel sections of verses to produce a single, complete Gospel text.

For more information about how the text of this book was produced, including the sixteen steps of the harmonization and merging process, see the first Note (*Note 1 - How This Book Was Compiled*) in *Notes On Reading This Book* in *FIVE COLUMN: The Synoptic Gospel*, or visit:

synopticgospel.com/notes/note-1

The facing page is a half-scale sample taken from *FIVE COLUMN: The Synoptic Gospel.* It shows the four columns of Gospel text aligned (harmony) and combined (merger) to produce the *fifth column* narrative (on the left) which is reproduced as the text of this book.

For more information about *FIVE COLUMN* visit:

synopticgospel.com/fivecolumn

8 - TRIALS ≡ CRUCIFIXION

Act 2: Jesus is Accused
by The High Priest

Scene 4: **Peter's Second Denial**

Palace of Caiaphas, Jerusalem, *Judea*   early Friday morning, April 3rd / 33 CE

The Full Gospel Story

	Matthew	Mark	Luke	John
1				
When	26:71~ When		22:58~ A little later,	
[Peter] had gone out [through] the gateway <and onto the porch>,	26:71⁻¹ [he] had gone out [to] the gateway,			
another	26:71⁻² another		22:58⁻¹ another	18:26~ One of the
servant-girl	26:71⁻³ servant-girl	14:69~ The servant-girl		18:26⁻¹ slaves
of the High Priest, being a relative of the one whose ear <had> cut off,				18:26⁻² of the high priest, being a relative of the one whose ear Peter cut off,
saw him, and	26:71⁻⁴ saw him and	14:69⁻¹ saw him, and	22:58⁻² saw him and	
said,		14:69⁻² began once more to say	22:58⁻³ said,	18:26⁻³ said,
"You are one of them		14:69~ "This is one of them!"	22:58⁻⁴ "You are one of them	
too!			22:58⁻⁵ too!	
Did I not see you in the garden with Him?"				18:-26 "Did I not see you in the garden with Him?"
2 <And she> said	26:71⁻⁵ said			
to the bystanders	26:71⁻⁶ to those	14:69⁻³ to the bystanders,		
who were there, "This man was with Jesus of Nazareth!"	26:71~ who were there, "This man was with Jesus of Nazareth!"			
3 And again	26:72~ And again	14:70~ But again		
Peter	26:72⁻¹ he	14:70⁻¹ he	22:58⁻⁶ But Peter	18:25⁻³ He
denied it	26:72⁻² denied it	14:70⁻² denied it.		18:25⁻⁴ denied it,
with and oath,	26:72⁻³ with an oath,			18:25⁻⁵ and
and				
said, "I am not!"			22:-58 said, "Man, I am not!"	18:-25 said, "I am not."
I do not know the man."	26:72~ "I do not know the man."			

NOTE 2 - GOSPEL STORYLINE DIVISIONS

For ease of reading and referencing, the entire text of *The Synoptic Gospel* is divided into three major types of divisions, based on the location of the events, and the duration of time that they cover.

2.1 - STORYLINE DIVISIONS

1. **Chapter** - This largest division segments the entire Gospel storyline into ten pieces. The length of time covered by a *Chapter* can range from a single day, to a week, or a year, or even cover indefinite periods of time, such as the introduction and *Genealogies* of *Chapter 0 - Prologue*.

2. **Act** - Each *Chapter* is divided into as many as nine *Acts* of related events that all happened during the same shorter period of time, and usually also in the same approximate geographical location. Generally, the period of time covered by an *Act* might take place during an afternoon, or over a few days, weeks, or months.

3. **Scene** - Each *Act* is divided into as many as nine *Scenes of action*, each of which describe a single parable or event, or a few related events, if they all happened in the same place, and during the same short period of time. A *Scene* may relate the conversation of a few minutes, as a single teaching or parable, or cover a longer span of time, such as the two days that Jesus spent in Samaria. The *Prologue* and *Epilogue* Scenes of this book cover long, indefinite intervals of time. In terms of length, a Scene may consist of just one sentence, or more than thirty *Verses*. The entire Gospel text of this book is divided into 360 Scenes of action.

These three major storyline divisions are specified in:

1. the *Table of Gospel Contents* found at the beginning of this book
2. the *title block* that begins each *Scene*, as this example for *Scene 121*:

```
┌─────────────────────────────────────────────────────────────┐
│  Chapter 1 - The Birth of Jesus                               │
│                                                               │
│       Act 2 - The Annunciation To Mary                        │
│                                                               │
│    Scene 1 - Gabriel Tells Mary That She Will Birth A Son     │
└─────────────────────────────────────────────────────────────┘
```

4. **Verse** - For ease of reference, the groups of words and sentences that comprise each *Scene* are numbered as *Verses*, which generally consist of a single important detail, or a few closely related pieces of information. A *Verse* can range in length from a few words to a full sentence, or three.

For more information on Verses and the reference system used to arrange the text of this book, see the following two pages.

2.2 - TSG VERSE REFERENCE SYSTEM

For ease of reading and referencing, as with any long book or play, the text of *The Synoptic Gospel* is divided into *Chapters*, *Acts* and *Scenes*, based on the chronological time of the occurrence in relation to all of the other events in the combined Gospel story, along with the location and the duration of the event.

Scene Reference Number

The entire storyline of *The Synoptic Gospel* is divided into ten *Chapters* (0-9), each of which may consist of up to nine *Acts* (1-9), which are further sub-divided into as many as nine *Scenes of action* (1-9). Using this system, each of the 360 Scenes within *The Synoptic Gospel* is designated by a three digit *scene reference number* (123).

From the *scene reference number* it can be roughly determined when in time the action of the *Scene* took place, in relation to all of the other events of the Gospel storyline. For example, a *scene reference number* of "111" indicates, beginning with the first digit on the left - the first *Chapter* (although there is a *Chapter 0 - Prologue*), while the second (or middle) digit indicates the first *Act*, and the final digit is the *Scene* number. Knowing that the title of *Chapter 1* is *The Birth of Jesus* gives an indication of when in time this Scene of action may have occurred, in relation to the sequence of the other events that are mentioned within the combined Gospel story.

To avoid confusion when quoting *Synoptic Gospel* Scene references, each number in the sequence should be read or said so that the number for the *Chapter*, *Act* and *Scene* is distinct, as in, "Scene one, one, one", and not "Scene one hundred and eleven".

Verse Reference Number

The text of each *Scene* of *The Synoptic Gospel* is subdivided into *Verses* which consist of from one to three full sentences. The Verses of each Scene are consecutively numbered, and the assigned *verse reference number* is listed after the *scene reference number*, and following a period. Verses are designated by either a single digit *verse reference number*, as 111.1 (Verse 1), or by two digits, as 111.23 (Verse 23).

To avoid confusion when quoting *Synoptic Gospel* Verse references, each number in the sequence should be read or said so that the number for each *Chapter*, *Act*, *Scene*, and *Verse* is distinct; as in, "Scene one, one, one, Verse one".

2.3 - TSG VERSE NOTATIONS

As each Scene of *The Synoptic Gospel* is referenced by a three digit *scene reference number*, each *Verse reference* is a four or five digit number.

Following are examples of the notation system that references the Verses of *The Synoptic Gospel*.

Single Verse Reference

	notation	Chapter	Act	Scene	Verse	digits
single-digit verse	111.1	1	1	1	1	4
double-digit verse	111.12	1	1	1	12	5

Multiple Verse Reference

Multiple Verses can be simultaneously referenced using the following system of notation:

	notation	Chapter	Act	Scene	Verses
verses 1 to 3	111.1-3	1	1	1	1-3
verses 1 to 12	111.1-12	1	1	1	1-12
verses 1 and 5	111.1, 5	1	1	1	1 & 5
verses 1 to 3, and 5	111.1-3, 5	1	1	1	1-3 & 5

Multiple Verse References from Multiple Scenes

Verses from multiple Scenes can be noted by separating each reference with a semicolon ";" as:

232.1; 234.6-8; 443.5; 845.1-3, 5, 8-12; 932.6, 9

NOTE 3 - DATES LISTED IN THIS BOOK

3.1 - DATE NOTATIONS USED IN THIS BOOK

The Gregorian calendar, as used today throughout much of the world, is divided into two distinct eras of time that are derived from the traditional year which had been calculated as the one in which Jesus Christ was born. This division produces a date in time that occurred either before the birth of Jesus, or one that happened after He was born; or as **BCE** for *Before the Common Era* (or *Current Era* or *Christian Era*), and **CE** for the *Common Era, Current Era* or *Christian Era*.

3.2 - ASSIGN A DATE TO EACH SCENE

So that the four differing timelines of the events that are mentioned within the texts of the four Gospel accounts could be unified, each Scene of *The Synoptic Gospel* was assigned a date in time for when the recorded action in the Scene may have taken place. Dates are assigned to each Scene according to a chronological timeline which was constructed around the significant dates of the birth of Jesus, His baptism (as the *Messiah* - the *Christ*) and the beginning of His public ministry, as well as His arrest, death, resurrection, and ascension into Heaven. Other dates that help focus the timeline include the three Passovers and the other Feasts that Jesus attended in Jerusalem, which are mentioned only within *The Gospel of John*.

Details provided within the text of some Scenes allow the season, the month, and occasionally even the day of the week to be determined; and for those Scenes that narrate the arrest, trials and crucifixion of Jesus, sometimes even the hour of the day is mentioned, or can be determined, or estimated. As it was a major source of conflict with the Pharisees, another timing detail that is noted are those events that took place on a Sabbath. Where no date or timing info is provided within the text of the Scene itself, only the year and the season or month is assigned, usually based on the date of the Scene that precedes it.

As it is not always possible to know with precision or certainty when in time the hundreds of individual sayings and events from the life of Jesus Christ may have occurred, it is unlikely that the dates assigned to each and every Scene in this book are always accurate, but they are reasonable given the available Scriptural and historical sources of information, and our current understanding of them. While every effort has been made to be accurate in the dating of each Scene, beyond the important dates which establish the timeline, and the Feasts and Festivals that Jesus observed in Jerusalem, along with the Sabbaths, it generally does not matter very much if He healed someone in the year 31 or 32 CE, or whether it was during the spring or the summer, because in the end the Gospel story is about the things that Jesus Christ said and did, and not usually about when He may have said or did them, some 2,000 years ago. The date and other timing details associated with each Scene is listed in the *title block* that begins the Scene, unless they are the same as the previous Scene.

3.3 - THE SYNOPTIC GOSPEL TIMELINE

In order to chronologically sequence all of the many sayings of Jesus Christ, and to arrange all of the events that make up the full Gospel account of His life and ministry, it is necessary to establish a timeline, based in part on the dates of a few important events: including the **Birth** of Jesus, His **Baptism** (as the *Messiah/Christ*) and the beginning of His Ministry, His **Death**, and His **Ascension** into Heaven.

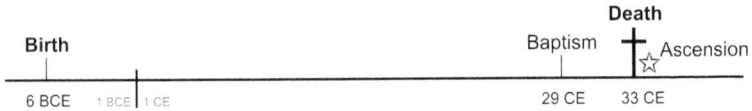

```
                                                          Death
  Birth                                        Baptism    †  Ascension
                                                            ☆
  ├──────────────────────────────────────────────┼────────┤
  6 BCE    1 BCE | 1 CE                          29 CE    33 CE
```

Against this basic timeline each *Scene of action* in this book is assigned a date, based on how the text of those verses fit within the overall combined timeline that was established for the four Gospels. The assignment of dates to the Scenes of this book is done to be as accurate as possible, given the limited information provided within each of the Gospel accounts themselves, and the scarcity of supporting historical information about the life of Jesus. It should be kept in mind that the importance of the Gospel story of the life and teachings of Jesus Christ is found in what the Son and Word of God said and did, and excepting the major events of His life, it is not usually important when during His life and ministry any specific event may have occurred.

The full details behind the selection of the dates used in *FIVE COLUMN* and *The Synoptic Gospel* will be made available in *The Timeline of The Life of Jesus Christ*, which will be published as a future work.

NOTE 4 - OTHER NOTES

4.1 - Locations

Excepting the *Prologue* and *Epilogue*, each Scene of *The Synoptic Gospel* is assigned a geographical location for where the action likely occurred. When it can be determined from the Gospel account, the name of the town or location where the action took place is mentioned, along with the territory name which is *italicized*, as in, "Jerusalem, *Judea*". When it is possible other location and geographical features are also included, as in, "Sea of Galilee, *Galilee*", or "Garden of Gethsemane, Mount of Olives, Jerusalem, *Judea*". In those many places where a geographical location cannot be determined from the text of the Gospels or other sources of information, the assigned location is usually the same location as that of the previous Scene. In those places where an outright guess had to be made, the listed location is usually only of the regional territory, as in *Judea* or *Galilee*.

The location of each Scene is listed before the date in each Scene's title block, or in the title block of the Scene that proceeds it if the location is the same.

4.2 - Quotations and References

This *Standard* edition of *The Synoptic Gospel* does not contain the references to the quotations from the Old Testament, or to the people and places, that are found within *FIVE COLUMN,* and also within the PDF, ePub and printed *Complete Editions* of *The Synoptic Gospel.*

4.3 - Maps

This *Standard* printed edition does not contain the nine *Chapter Maps* that show where Jesus went on His travels. The *Chapter Maps* are included in the *Complete* PDF and printed editions of this work, and also in *FIVE COLUMN.* Following is a sample of the Map of Jerusalem, and of Israel. The Maps are © 2009 by Smart Publishing Ltd.

Map of Jerusalem

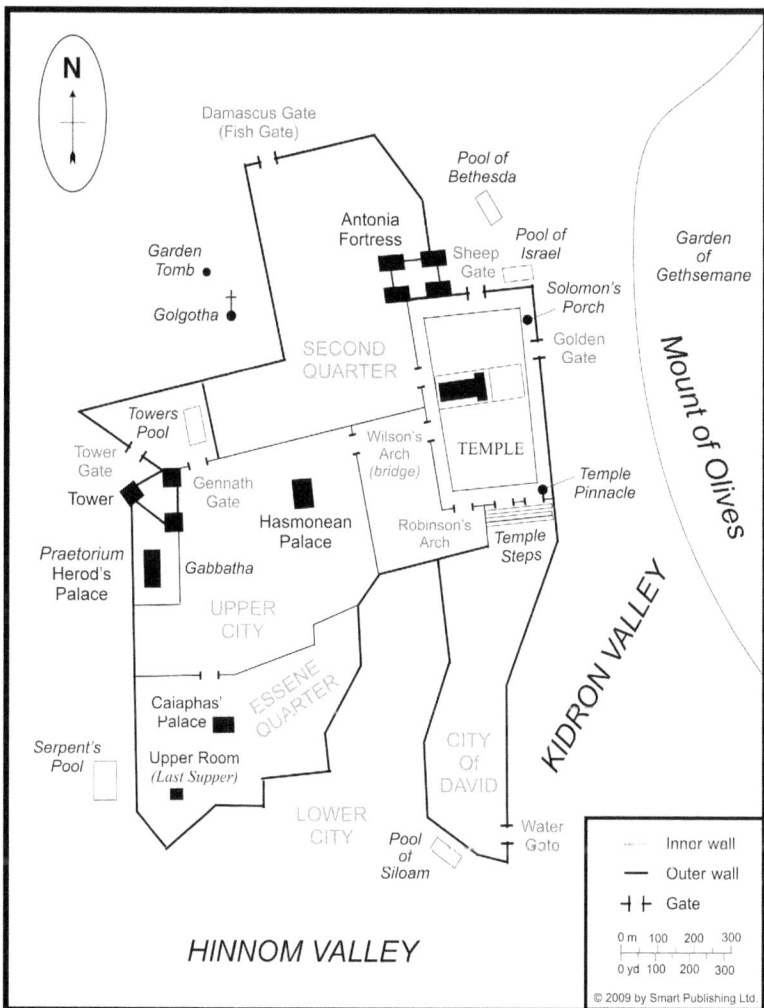

Map of Israel

THE TEXT OF

S̽The YNOPTIC GOSPEL™

The Story of The Life of Jesus

In 360 Scenes of Action

CHAPTER 0 - PROLOGUE

Act 1 - Foreword

Scene 011   **Prologue**
Luke 1:1-4

1 Inasmuch as many have undertaken to compile an account of the things accomplished among us, just as they were handed down to us by those who from the beginning were eyewitnesses and servants of the Word, 2 it seemed fitting for me as well, having investigated everything carefully from the beginning, to write it out for you in consecutive order, most excellent Theophilus, so that you may know the exact truth about the things you have been taught.

Scene 012   **The Word of God**
John 1:1-5, 9-10, 14

1 In the beginning was the *Word*,[1.] and the Word was with *God*,[2.] and the Word was *God*.[3.]

2 He was in the beginning with God.

3 All things came into being through Him, and apart from Him nothing came into being that has come into being.

4 In Him was life, and the life was the Light of men.

5 And the Word became flesh, and dwelt among us. 6 There was the true Light, which coming into the world, enlightens every man.

7 The Light shines in the darkness, and the darkness did not comprehend it.

8 He was in the world, and the world was made through Him, and the world did not know Him - 9 but we saw His glory, glory as of the only begotten from The Father, full of grace and truth.

1. Greek: Λόγος / logos = word, something spoken, discourse (reason, wisdom)

2. Greek: Θεόν / Theon = a God or Deity; The Supreme Deity; God The Father

3. Greek: Θεὸς / Theos = a God or Deity, Divine, Godly, God-like

---

Act 2 - The Genealogy of Jesus

Scene 021   **The Genealogy of The Messiah**
Matthew 1:1-17

---

1 The record of the genealogy of Jesus the Messiah, the son of David, the son of Abraham:

2 Abraham was the father of Isaac, 3 Isaac the father of Jacob, 4 and Jacob the father of Judah and his brothers.

5 Judah was the father of Perez and Zerah by Tamar, 6 Perez was the father of Hezron, 7 and Hezron the father of Ram.

8 Ram was the father of Amminadab, 9 Amminadab the father of Nahshon, 10 and Nahshon the father of Salmon.

11 Salmon was the father of Boaz by Rahab, 12 Boaz was the father of Obed by Ruth, 13 and Obed the father of Jesse.

14 Jesse was the father of David the King. 15 David was the father of Solomon by Bathsheba, who had been the wife of Uriah.

16 Solomon was the father of Rehoboam, 17 Rehoboam the father of Abijah, 18 and Abijah the father of Asa.

19 Asa was the father of Jehoshaphat, 20 Jehoshaphat the father of Joram, 21 and Joram the father of Uzziah.

22 Uzziah was the father of Jotham, 23 Jotham the father of Ahaz, 24 and Ahaz the father of Hezekiah.

25 Hezekiah was the father of Manasseh, 26 Manasseh the father of Amon, 27 and Amon the father of Josiah.

28 Josiah became the father of Jeconiah and his brothers, at the time of the deportation to Babylon.

29 After the deportation to Babylon: Jeconiah became the father of Shealtiel, 30 and Shealtiel the father of Zerubbabel.

31 Zerubbabel was the father of Abihud, 32 Abihud the father of Eliakim, 33 and Eliakim the father of Azor.

34 Azor was the father of Zadok, 35 Zadok the father of Achim, 36 and Achim the father of Eliud.

37 Eliud was the father of Eleazar, 38 Eleazar the father of Matthan, 39 and Matthan the father of Jacob.

40 Jacob was the father of Joseph the husband of Mary, by whom Jesus was born, who is called the Messiah.

41 So all of the generations from Abraham to David are fourteen generations;

42 and from David to the deportation to Babylon, fourteen generations;

43 and from the deportation to Babylon to the Messiah, are fourteen generations.

Scene 022   **The Genealogy of The Son of God**
Luke 3:~23-38

1 Jesus was, as supposed, the son of Joseph, 2 the son of Eli,
  3 the son of Matthat, 4 the son of Levi, 5 the son of Melchi,
  6 the son of Jannai, 7 the son of Joseph, 8 the son of Mattathias,
  9 the son of Amos, 10 the son of Nahum, 11 the son of Hesli,
  12 the son of Naggai, 13 the son of Maath, 14 the son of Mattathias,
  15 the son of Semein, 16 the son of Josech, 17 the son of Joda,
  18 the son of Joanan, 19 the son of Rhesa, 20 the son of Zerubbabel,
  21 the son of Shealtiel, 22 the son of Neri, 23 the son of Melchi,
  24 the son of Addi, 25 the son of Cosam, 26 the son of Elmadam,
  27 the son of Er, 28 the son of Joshua, 29 the son of Eliezer,
  30 the son of Jorim, 31 the son of Matthat, 32 the son of Levi,
  33 the son of Simeon, 34 the son of Judah, 35 the son of Joseph,
  36 the son of Jonam, 37 the son of Eliakim, 38 the son of Melea,
  39 the son of Menna, 40 the son of Mattatha, 41 the son of Nathan,
  42 the son of David, 43 the son of Jesse,
  44 the son of Obed, 45 the son of Boaz, 46 the son of Salmon,
  47 the son of Nahshon, 48 the son of Amminadab, 49 the son of Admin,
  50 the son of Ram, 51 the son of Hezron, 52 the son of Perez,
  53 the son of Judah, 54 the son of Jacob, 55 the son of Isaac,
  56 the son of Abraham, 57 the son of Terah,
  58 the son of Nahor, 59 the son of Serug, 60 the son of Reu,
  61 the son of Peleg, 62 the son of Heber, 63 the son of Shelah,
  64 the son of Cainan, 65 the son of Arphaxad, 66 the son of Shem,
  67 the son of Noah, 68 the son of Lamech, 69 the son of Methuselah,
  70 the son of Enoch, 71 the son of Jared, 72 the son of Mahalaleel,
  73 the son of Cainan, 74 the son of Enosh, 75 the son of Seth,
  76 the son of Adam, 77 the son of God.

CHAPTER 1 - THE BIRTH OF JESUS

Act 1 - The Prophecy About John

Scene 111 **The Birth of John Is Foretold To Zacharias**
The Temple, Jerusalem, *Judea*   mid June / 7 BCE   *Mark 1:1 / Luke 1:5-23*

1 The beginning of the gospel of Jesus Christ, the Son of God.

2 In the days of Herod the Great, King of Judea, there was a priest of the division of Abijah named Zacharias, who had a wife from the daughters of Aaron named Elizabeth. 3 They were both righteous in the sight of God, walking blamelessly in all of the commandments and requirements of the Lord; 4 but they had no child, because Elizabeth was barren, and they were both advanced in years.

5 Now it happened that while Zacharias was performing his priestly service before God, in the appointed order of his division according to the custom of the priestly office, he was chosen by lot to enter the Temple of the Lord and burn incense.

6 While the whole multitude of people were in prayer outside at the hour of the incense offering, an angel of the Lord appeared to him, standing to the right of the altar of incense. 7 Zacharias was troubled when he saw the angel, and fear gripped him.

8 But the angel said to him, "Do not be afraid, Zacharias, for your petition has been heard, and your wife Elizabeth will bear you a son; and you will give him the name John.

9 "You will have joy and gladness, and many will rejoice at his birth, for he will be great in the sight of the Lord. 10 He will drink no wine or liquor; and he will be filled with the Holy Spirit while yet in his mother's womb; and He will turn many of the sons of Israel back to the Lord their God.

11 "It is he who will go as a forerunner before Him in the Spirit and power of Elijah, to turn the hearts of the fathers back to the children, and the disobedient to the attitude of the righteous, so as to make ready a people prepared for the Lord."

12 Zacharias said to the angel, "How will I know this for certain? For I am an old man, and my wife is advanced in years."

13 The angel answered, and said to him, "I am Gabriel, who stands in the presence of God; and I have been sent to speak to you, and to bring you this good news. 14 And behold, you shall be silent and unable to speak until the day when these things take place, because you did not believe my words, which will be fulfilled in their proper time."

15 The people were waiting for Zacharias, and were wondering at his delay in the Temple. 16 When he came out, he was unable to speak to them, and they realized that he had seen a vision in the Temple, because he kept making signs to them, and remained mute.

17 When the days of his priestly service were ended, he went back home.

Scene 112   **Elizabeth Becomes Pregnant With John**

Judean hill country, *Judea*   summer / 7 BCE   *Luke 1:24-25*

1 After these days Zacharias' wife Elizabeth became pregnant; 2 and she kept herself in seclusion for five months, saying, "This is the way that the Lord has dealt with me in the days when He looked with favor upon me, to take away my disgrace from among men."

Act 2 - The Annunciation To Mary

Scene 121   **Gabriel Tells Mary That She Will Birth A Son**

Nazareth, *Galilee*   late December / 7 BCE   *Luke 1:26-38*

1 Now in the sixth month, the angel Gabriel was sent from God to a city in Galilee called Nazareth, 2 to a virgin engaged to a man of the house of David whose name was Joseph; and the virgin's name was Mary.

3 Coming in, Gabriel said to her, "Greetings, favored one! The Lord is with you." 4 But Mary was very perplexed at this statement, and pondered what kind of salutation this was.

5 The angel said to her, "Do not be afraid, Mary; for you have found favor with God! 6 And behold, you will conceive in your womb and bear a son; and you shall name Him Jesus.

7 "He will be great; and will be called the Son of the Most High! 8 And the Lord God will give Him the throne of His father David, and He will reign over the house of Jacob forever, and His Kingdom will have no end."

9 Mary said to the angel, "How can this be, since I am a virgin?"

10 The angel answered, and said to her, "The Holy Spirit will come upon you, and the power of the Most High will overshadow you; and for that reason the Holy Child shall be called the Son of God.

11 "And behold, even your relative Elizabeth has also conceived a son in her old age, and she who was called barren is now in her sixth month; for nothing is impossible with God."

12 Mary said, "Behold, the bondslave of the Lord! May it be done to me according to your word." 13 And Gabriel departed from her.

Scene 122   **Mary Visits Elizabeth**

Judean hill country, *Judea*   late December / 7 BCE   *Luke 1:39-56*

1 Then Mary arose, and went in a hurry to a city in the hill country of Judea; and she entered the house of Zacharias, and greeted Elizabeth.

2 When Elizabeth heard Mary's greeting, the baby leaped in her womb; and Elizabeth was filled with the Holy Spirit,

3 And she cried out with a loud voice, and said, "Blessed are you among women, and blessed is the fruit of your womb! 4 How has it happened to me, that the mother of my Lord would come to me? For behold, when the sound of your greeting reached my ears, the baby leaped in my womb for joy.

continued >

Scene 122 - *continued*

5 "Blessed is she who believed that there would be a fulfillment of what had been spoken to her by the Lord!"

6 Mary said: "My soul exalts the Lord, and my spirit has rejoiced in God my Savior, for He has had regard for the humble state of His bondslave.

7 "And behold, from this time on, all generations will count me blessed, for the Mighty One has done great things for me; and Holy is His Name!

8 "His mercy is upon generation after generation, toward those who fear Him. 9 He has done mighty deeds with His arm; He has scattered those who were proud in the thoughts of their heart. 10 He has brought down rulers from their thrones, and has exalted those who were humble. 11 He has filled the hungry with good things, and sent away the rich empty-handed. 12 He has given help to Israel His servant, in remembrance of His mercy, as He spoke to our fathers, to Abraham and his descendants, forever."

13 Mary stayed with Elizabeth about three months, and then she returned to her home.

Act 3 - The Birth of John

Scene 131   **The Birth and Naming of John**

Judean hill country, *Judea*   late March / 6 BCE   *Luke 1:57-66*

---

1 Now when the time came for Elizabeth to give birth, she gave birth to a son. 2 Her neighbors and her relatives heard that the Lord had displayed His great mercy toward her, and they were rejoicing with her.

3 And it happened that on the eighth day they came to circumcise the child, and they were going to name him Zacharias, after his father, but his mother answered and said, "No indeed, but he shall be called John."

4 They said to her, "There is no one among your relatives who is called by that name." 5 And they made signs to his father, as to what he wanted him to be called.

6 Zacharias asked for a tablet, and he wrote as follows: "His name is John." And they were all astonished.

7 And immediately the mouth of Zacharias was opened, and his tongue began to speak in praise of God.

Scene 132   **The Prophecy of Zacharias About John**

Judean hill country, *Judea*   late March / 6 BCE   *Luke 1:67-80*

1 John's father Zacharias was filled with the Holy Spirit, and he prophesied, saying: "Blessed be the Lord God of Israel, for He has visited us, and accomplished redemption for His people!

2 "He has raised up a horn of salvation for us in the house of David, His servant, as He spoke by the mouth of His Holy Prophets from of old; 3 Salvation from our enemies, and from the hand of all who hate us, to show mercy toward our fathers; 4 and to remember His holy covenant, the oath which He swore to Abraham our father; 5 to grant that we, being rescued from the hand of our enemies, might serve Him without fear, in holiness and righteousness before Him, all our days.

6 "And you, child, will be called the Prophet of the Most High; for you will go on before the Lord to prepare His way; 7 to give to His people the knowledge of salvation by the forgiveness of their sins, because of the tender mercy of our God, with which the Sunrise from on high will visit us; 8 to shine upon those who sit in darkness and the shadow of death, and to guide our feet into the way of peace."

9 Fear came upon all those living around them, and all these matters were being talked about in all the hill country of Judea. 10 All who heard them kept them in mind, saying, "What will this child turn out to be?" for the hand of the Lord was certainly with him.

11 The child continued to grow and to become strong in Spirit; and he lived in the deserts until the day of his public appearance to Israel.

Act 4 - The Birth of Jesus

Scene 141   **An Angel Solves Joseph's Dilemma**

Nazareth, *Galilee*   spring / 6 BCE   *Matthew 1:18-25~*

1 Now the birth of Jesus Christ was as follows: When His mother Mary had been betrothed to Joseph, before they came together, she was found to be with Child by the Holy Spirit. 2 And Joseph her husband, being a righteous man, and not wanting to disgrace her, planned to send her away secretly.

3 But when he had considered this, behold, an angel of the Lord appeared to him in a dream, saying, "Joseph, son of David, do not be afraid to take Mary as your wife; for the Child who has been conceived in her is of the Holy Spirit. 4 She will bear a Son; and you shall call His name Jesus, for He will save His people from their sins."

5 Now all this took place to fulfill what was spoken by the Lord through the prophet Isaiah: "Behold, the young maiden shall be with child, and shall bear a Son; and they shall call His name Immanuel," which translated means, "God with us."

6 Joseph awoke from his sleep, and did as the angel of the Lord commanded him, and took Mary as his wife; 7 but he kept her a virgin until she gave birth to a son.

Scene 142	**Joseph and Mary Journey To Bethlehem**	
	Bethlehem, *Judea* late September / 6 BCE	*Luke 2:1-5*

1 In those days, a decree went out from Caesar Augustus, that a census be taken of all the inhabited earth. 2 This was the first census taken while Quinctilius was Governor of Syria, and everyone was on his way to register for the census, each to his own city.

3 In order to register, Joseph went up from the city of Nazareth in Galilee, to the city of David (which is called Bethlehem) in Judea, because he was of the house and family of David; 4 along with Mary, who was engaged to him, and was with child.

Scene 143	**The Birth of Jesus**	
	Bethlehem, Judea late September / 6 BCE	*Luke 2:6-7*

1 While they were there, the days were completed for Mary to give birth; and she gave birth to her firstborn son. 2 She wrapped Him in swaddling cloths, and laid Him in a manger, because there was no room for them in the inn.

Scene 144	**Angelic Announcement To The Shepherds**	*Luke 2:8-20*

1 In the same region there were some shepherds staying out in the fields, and keeping watch over their flock at night. 2 And an angel of the Lord suddenly stood before them, and the glory of the Lord shone around them.

3 They were terribly frightened, but the angel said to them, "Do not be afraid; for behold, I bring you good news of great joy, which will be for all people! 4 For today in the city of David, there has been born for you a Savior, who is Christ, the Lord. 5 This will be a sign for you: you will find a baby wrapped in swaddling cloths, and lying in a manger."

6 And suddenly there appeared with the angel a multitude of the Heavenly host, who were praising God, and saying, "Glory to God in the Highest! 7 And on earth, peace among men with whom He is pleased."

8 When the angels had gone away into heaven, the shepherds began saying to one another, "Let us go straight to Bethlehem, and see this thing that has happened, which the Lord has made known to us!" 9 So they went quickly, and found their way to Mary and Joseph, and the baby, as He lay in the manger.

10 When the shepherds saw this, they made known the statement which had been told to them about this Child. 11 All who heard it wondered at the things which were told to them by the shepherds, but Mary pondered all these things, treasuring them in her heart.

12 The shepherds went back, glorifying and praising God for all that they had heard and seen, just as they had been told.

Scene 145	**The Naming of Jesus**	
	Judea early October / 6 BCE	*Matthew 1:~25 / Luke 2:21*

1 When eight days had passed, before His circumcision, His name was called Jesus, the name given by the angel, before He was conceived in the womb.

Act 5 - Jesus Is Presented In The Temple

Scene 151   **Righteous Simeon Prophesies About Jesus**

The Temple, Jerusalem, *Judea*   early November / 6 BCE   *Luke 2:22-35*

---

1 When the days for their purification according to the law of Moses were completed, they brought Jesus up to Jerusalem, to present Him to the Lord 2 (as it is written in the Law of the Lord, "Every firstborn male that opens the womb shall be called holy to the Lord"), 3 and to offer a sacrifice according to what was said in the Law, "A pair of turtledoves, or two young pigeons."

4 There was a man in Jerusalem whose name was Simeon, who was righteous and devout. He was looking for the consolation of Israel, and the Holy Spirit was upon him. 5 It had been revealed to him by the Holy Spirit that he would not see death before he had seen the Lord's Christ.

6 He came in the Spirit into the Temple; and when the parents brought in the child Jesus to carry out for Him the custom of the Law, Simeon took Him into his arms, and he blessed God, and said, 7 "Now Lord, You are releasing Your bond-servant to depart in peace, according to Your word; for my eyes have seen Your salvation, which You have prepared in the presence of all peoples; a Light of revelation to the Gentiles, and the glory of Your people Israel!"

8 And Simeon blessed them, and said to Mary His mother, "Behold, this Child is appointed for the fall and rise of many in Israel, and for a sign to be opposed, to the end that the thoughts from many hearts may be revealed. 9 And a sword will pierce even your own soul."

10 His father and mother were amazed at the things which were being said about Jesus.

Scene 152   **Anna The Prophetess**

The Temple, Jerusalem, *Judea*   early November / 6 BCE   *Luke 2:36-38*

---

1 There was a prophetess, Anna, the daughter of Phanuel, of the tribe of Asher. 2 She was advanced in years, and had lived with her husband for seven years after her marriage, and then as a widow to the age of eighty-four. 3 She never left the Temple, serving night and day with fastings and prayers.

4 At that very moment, she came up and began giving thanks to God, and continued to speak of Jesus to all those who were looking for the redemption of Jerusalem.

Scene 153   **Return To Nazareth**

Nazareth, *Galilee*   early November / 6 BCE   *Luke 2:39-40*

---

1 When they had performed everything according to the Law of the Lord, they returned to Galilee, to their own city of Nazareth.

2 The Child continued to grow and become strong, increasing in wisdom; and the grace of God was upon Him.

Act 6 - To Egypt and Back

Scene 161   **King Herod and The Magi From The East**
          Jerusalem, *Judea*   late autumn / 6 BCE   *Matthew 2:1-12*

1 After Jesus was born in Bethlehem of Judea, in the days of Herod the King, Magi from the east arrived in Jerusalem, saying, "Where is He who has been born the King of the Jews? For we saw His star in the east, and have come to worship Him."

2 When King Herod heard this, he was troubled, and all of Jerusalem with him. 3 Gathering together all the chief priests and scribes of the people, he inquired of them where the Messiah was to be born.

4 They said to him, "In Bethlehem of Judea; for this is what has been written by the prophet: 5 'And you, Bethlehem, land of Judah, are by no means least among the leaders of Judah; for out of you shall come forth a Ruler who will shepherd My people Israel.' "

6 Then Herod secretly called the Magi, and determined from them the exact time that the star had appeared. 7 And he sent them to Bethlehem, saying, "Go and search carefully for the Child; 8 and when you have found Him, report to me, so that I too may come and worship Him."

9 After hearing the King, the Magi went on their way; and the star, which they had seen in the east, went on before them, until it came and stood over the place where the Child was. 10 When they saw the star, they rejoiced with exceeding great joy.

11 After coming into the house, they saw the Child, with Mary His mother; and they fell to the ground and worshiped Him. 12 Then, opening their treasures, they presented to Him gifts of gold, frankincense, and myrrh.

13 Having been warned by God in a dream not to return to Herod, the Magi left for their own country by another way.

Scene 162   **Joseph Is Warned To Flee To Egypt**
          Nazareth, *Galilee to Egypt*   late autumn / 6 BCE   *Matthew 2:13-15~*

1 Now when the Magi had gone, behold, an angel of the Lord appeared to Joseph in a dream, and said, "Get up! Take the Child and His mother, and flee to Egypt, and remain there until I tell you; for Herod is going to search for the Child to destroy Him." 2 So Joseph got up, and took the Child and His mother while it was still night, and left for Egypt; 3 and they remained there until the death of Herod.

Scene 163   **Herod Orders The Death of The Male Babies**
          Jerusalem, *Judea*   winter / 5 BCE   *Matthew 2:16-18*

1 When Herod saw that he had been tricked by the Magi, he became very enraged, and he sent men to slay all the male children who were in Bethlehem, and all its vicinity; from two years old and under, according to the time which he had determined from the Magi. 2 Then, what had been spoken through Jeremiah the prophet was fulfilled: "A voice was heard in Ramah, weeping and great mourning; Rachel weeping for her children, and she refused to be comforted, because they were no more."

Scene 164   **Joseph, Mary and Jesus Return From Egypt**
Egypt to Nazareth, *Galilee*   spring / 4 BCE   *Matthew 2:~15, 19-23*

1 When Herod died, behold, an angel of the Lord appeared to Joseph in a dream in Egypt, and said, "Get up! Take the Child and His mother, and go into the land of Israel; for those who sought the Child's life are dead." 2 This was to fulfill what had been spoken by the Lord through the prophet: "Out of Egypt I called My Son."

3 So Joseph got up, took the Child and His mother, and came into the land of Israel. 4 But when he heard that Archelaus was reigning over Judea in place of his father Herod, he was afraid to go there.

5 Then, after being warned by God in a dream, Joseph left for the region of Galilee, and they came and lived in a city called Nazareth. 6 This was to fulfill what was spoken through the prophets: He shall be called a Nazarene.

```
Act 7 - Young Jesus In The Temple
```

Scene 171   **I Had To Be In My Father's House**
The Temple, Jerusalem, *Judea*   Passover - March / 7 CE   *Luke 2:41-52*

1 Now His parents went to Jerusalem every year at the Feast of the Passover, and when Jesus became twelve they went up there according to the custom of the Feast.

2 As they were returning, after spending the full number of days, the boy Jesus stayed behind in Jerusalem. 3 But His parents were unaware of it, and supposed Him to be in the caravan, and they went a day's journey.

4 When they began looking for Him among their relatives and acquaintances, and did not find Him, they returned to Jerusalem looking for Him.

5 After three days they found Jesus in the Temple, sitting in the midst of the teachers, both listening to them and asking them questions. 6 All who heard Him were amazed at His understanding, and His answers.

7 When His parents saw Him, they were astonished; and His mother said to Him, "Son, why have You treated us this way? Behold, Your father and I have been anxiously looking for You!"

8 Jesus said to them, "Why were you looking for Me? Did you not know that I had to be in My Father's house?" 9 But they did not understand this statement which He made to them.

10 Jesus returned to Nazareth with them, and He obeyed them; and His mother treasured all these things in her heart.

11 And Jesus kept increasing in wisdom and stature, and in favor with God and men.

CHAPTER 2 - THE MESSIAH IS ANOINTED

Act 1 - John Becomes The Baptist

Scene 211   **John Begins His Ministry of Baptism**
Jordan River, Judea   spring / 29 CE
Matthew 3:1-6 / Mark 1:2-6 / Luke 3:1-6 / John 1:6-8

1 In the fifteenth year of the reign of Tiberius Caesar, when Pontius Pilate was the Governor of Judea, and Herod Antipater was Tetrarch of Galilee, 2 and his brother Philip was Tetrarch of the region of Ituraea and Trachonitis, and Lysanias was Tetrarch of Abilene, 3 in the High Priesthood of Annas and Caiaphas, 4 the Word of God came to John, the son of Zacharias, in the wilderness of Judea.

5 John was a man sent from God, and he came as a witness to testify about the Light, so that all might believe through him. 6 He was not the Light, but he came to testify about the Light.

7 And John the Baptist came into all the districts around the Jordan, preaching a baptism of repentance for the forgiveness of sins, saying, "Repent, for the Kingdom of Heaven is at hand!"

8 For this is the one referred to, "Behold, I send My messenger ahead of You, who will prepare Your way", 9 as it is written in the words of the book of Isaiah the prophet, when he said, "The voice of one crying in the wilderness: 'Make ready the way of the Lord; Make His paths straight! 10 Every ravine will be filled, and every mountain and hill will be brought low; the crooked will become straight, and the rough roads smooth; and all flesh will see the salvation of God.' "

11 Now John was clothed with a garment of camel's hair, and wore a leather belt around his waist; and his diet was locusts and wild honey.

12 Then all the people of Jerusalem, and all the country of Judea, and all the district around the Jordan, were going out to him; 13 and they were being bapt-- ized by him in the Jordan River, as they confessed their sins.

Scene 212   **John Warns The Pharisees**
Matthew 3:7-10 / Luke 3:7-9

1 When John saw the many Pharisees and Sadducees coming out to be baptized by him, he began saying to them, "You brood of vipers! Who warned you to flee from the wrath to come?

2 "Therefore bear fruit in keeping with repentance; 3 and do not suppose that you can begin to say to yourselves, 'We have Abraham for our father'; for I say to you, that from these stones God is able to raise up children to Abraham. 4 Indeed, the axe is already laid at the root of the trees, and every tree that does not bear good fruit is cut down, and thrown into the fire!"

Scene 213   **The Teachings of John The Baptist**

Jordan River, *Judea*   spring / 29 CE   *Luke 3:10-14*

1 The crowds were questioning John, saying, "What shall we do?" 2 And he would answer, and say to them, "The man who has two tunics is to share with him who has none; and he who has food is to do likewise."

3 Some tax collectors also came to be baptized, and they asked him, "Teacher, what shall we do?"

4 He said to them, "Collect no more than what you have been ordered to."

5 And some soldiers were questioning John, saying, "And what about us, what shall we do?"

6 He said to them, "Do not take money from anyone by force, or accuse anyone falsely; and be content with your wages."

Scene 214   **John Preaches About The Coming Messiah**

Jordan River, near Bethabara, *Perea*   summer / 29 CE

Matthew 3:11-12 / Mark 1:7-8 / Luke 3:15-18

1 Now while all the people were in a state of expectation, and wondering in their hearts about whether John was the Christ, he answered as he was preaching, and said to them, "As for me, I baptize you with water for repentance; 2 but One is coming after me who is mightier than I, and I am not fit to stoop down and untie the thong of His sandals. 3 He will baptize you with the Holy Spirit, and fire!

4 "His winnowing fork is in His hand, and He will thoroughly clear His threshing floor, and will gather the wheat into His barn, 5 but He will burn up the chaff with unquenchable fire."

6 And with many other exhortations John preached the gospel to the people.

Scene 215   **John Denies That He Is The Christ or Elijah**   *John 1:19-28*

1 This is the testimony of John, when the Jews sent to him priests and Levites from Jerusalem, to ask him, "Who are you?"

2 John confessed, and he did not deny, but confessed, "I am not the Christ."

3 They asked him, "What then? Are you Elijah?" And he said, "I am not."

4 "Are you the Prophet?" And he answered, "No."

5 Then they said to him, "Who are you, so that we may give an answer to those who sent us? What do you say about yourself?"

6 John said, "I am a voice of one crying in the wilderness, 'Make straight the way of the Lord,' as Isaiah the prophet said."

7 Then, those who had been sent from the Pharisees asked him, "Why then are you baptizing, if you are not the Christ, nor Elijah, nor the Prophet?"

8 He answered them, saying, "I baptize in water, but among you stands One whom you do not know. It is He who comes after me, the thong of whose sandal I am not worthy to untie."

9 These things took place in Bethabara beyond the Jordan, where John was baptizing.

Act 2 - The Baptism of Jesus

Scene 221   **John Is At First Unwilling To Baptize Jesus**

Jordan River, near Bethabara, *Perea*   late summer / 29 CE

Matthew 3:13-15 / Mark 1:9~ / John 1:29-31

---

1 In those days, Jesus arrived from Nazareth in Galilee, coming to John at the Jordan to be baptized by him.

2 When John saw Jesus coming to him, he said, "Behold, the Lamb of God who takes away the sin of the world!

3 "This is He on behalf of whom I said, 'After me comes a Man who has a higher rank than I, for He existed before me.' 4 I did not recognize Him, but so that He might be manifested to Israel, I came baptizing in water."

5 John tried to prevent Jesus, saying, "I have need to be baptized by You, and You come to me?"

6 But Jesus said to him, "Permit it at this time; for in this way it is fitting for us to fulfill all righteousness." 7 Then John permitted Him.

Scene 222   **Jesus Is Baptized By John In The Jordan River**

Matthew 3:16-17 / Mark 1:~9-11 / Luke 3:21-22

---

1 When all the people were baptized, Jesus was also baptized by John in the Jordan river.

2 After being baptized, Jesus immediately came up out of the water; and while He was praying, behold, the heavens were opened, 3 and John saw the Holy Spirit of God, descending in bodily form like a dove, and lighting upon Jesus.

4 And behold, a voice came out of the heavens, and said, "You are My beloved Son, in You I am well-pleased!"

Scene 223   **John Testifies That Jesus Is The Son of God**

John 1:15, 32-34

---

1 John testified, and cried out, saying, "I have seen the Spirit descending as a dove out of heaven, and He remained upon Jesus.

2 "I did not recognize Him, but He who sent me to baptize in water said to me, 'He upon whom you see the Spirit descending and remaining upon Him, this is the One who baptizes in the Holy Spirit.'

3 "I myself have seen, and have testified, that this is the Son of God!

4 "This is He of whom I said, 'He who comes after me has a rank higher than I, for He existed before me.' "

Act 3 - The Messiah Is Tempted

Scene 231   **Jesus Fasts In The Wilderness For Forty Days**

Judean wilderness, *Judea*   late summer / 29 CE

Matthew 4:1-2 / Mark 1:12-13~ / Luke 4:1-2

---

1 When Jesus, full of the Holy Spirit, returned from the Jordan, He was immediately impelled to go out into the wilderness, where He was led around by the Spirit. 2 And He was in the wilderness with the wild beasts for forty days, being tempted by Satan, the Devil.

3 Jesus ate nothing during those days; and after He had fasted for forty days and forty nights He became hungry.

Scene 232   **Satan Tries To Tempt Jesus**

Matthew 4:3-11 / Mark 1:~13 / Luke 4:3-13

---

1 Then the Devil came, and said to Jesus, "If You are the Son of God, command these stones to become bread."

2 But Jesus answered, and said to him, "It is written; 'Man shall not live on bread alone, but on every Word that proceeds out of the mouth of God.' "

3 Then the Devil took Jesus into the holy city, Jerusalem, and had Him stand on the pinnacle of the Temple. 4 And the Devil said to Him, "If You are the Son of God, throw Yourself down from here, for it is written, 'He will command His angels concerning You, to guard You'; 5 and 'On their hands they will bear You up, so that You will not strike Your foot against a stone.' "

6 Jesus answered, and said to him, "On the other hand, it is also written, 'You shall not put the Lord your God to the test.' "

7 Again, the Devil took Jesus up on a very high mountain, and showed Him all the kingdoms of the world and their glory, in a moment of time. 8 And the Devil said to Him, "I will give you all this domain and its glory, for it has been handed over to me, and I give it to whomever I wish. 9 Therefore, if You fall down and worship me, it shall all be Yours."

10 Then Jesus answered, and said to him, "Go, Satan! For it is written; 'You shall worship the Lord your God, and serve Him only.' "

11 When the Devil had finished every temptation he left Him, until an opportune time. 12 And behold, angels came and began to minister to Jesus.

CHAPTER 3 - THE FIRST YEAR of His Ministry

Act 1 - Jesus Begins His Ministry

Scene 311   **Jesus Meets Andrew and Simon**

Jordan River, *Judea*   early autumn / 29 CE   *Luke 3:23~ / John 1:35-42*

1 Jesus began His ministry when He was about thirty years of age.

2 One day, John the Baptist was standing with two of his disciples; and he looked at Jesus as He walked, and said, "Behold, the Lamb of God!"

3 The two disciples heard John speak, and they followed Jesus.

4 Jesus turned, and saw them following, and He said to them, "What do you seek?"

5 They said to Him, "Rabbi (which translated means "Teacher"), where are You staying?"

6 He said to them, "Come, and you will see." 7 So they came and saw where Jesus was staying; and they stayed with Him that day, for it was about the tenth hour.

8 One of the two who heard John speak, and followed Jesus, was named Andrew. 9 Andrew found his brother Simon, and said to him, "We have found the Messiah!" (which translates as "Christ"); and he brought him to Jesus.

10 Jesus looked at him, and said, "You are Simon, the son of John. You shall be called Cephas" (which is translated "Peter").

Scene 312   **Jesus Meets Philip and Nathanael**   *John 1:43-51*

1 The next day Jesus purposed to go into Galilee; and He found Philip, and said to him, "Follow Me." 2 Now Philip was from Bethsaida, the city of Andrew and Peter.

3 Philip found Nathanael, and said to him, "We have found Him of whom Moses in the Law and also the Prophets wrote - Jesus of Nazareth, the son of Joseph."

4 Nathanael said to him, "Can anything good come out of Nazareth?"

5 Philip said to him, "Come and see!"

6 When Jesus saw Nathanael coming to Him, He said, "Behold, an Israelite indeed, in whom there is no deceit."

7 Nathanael said to Him, "How do You know me?"

8 Jesus answered him, "Before Philip called you, when you were under the fig tree, I saw you."

9 Nathanael answered Him, "Rabbi, You are the Son of God! You are the King of Israel!"

10 Jesus said to him, "You believe because I said to you that I saw you under the fig tree; you will see greater things than these. 11 Truly, truly, I say to you, that you will see the heavens opened, and the angels of God ascending and descending upon the Son of Man!"

Scene 313   **Jesus Turns Water Into Wine At A Wedding**

Cana, *Galilee*   autumn / 29 CE   *John 2:1-12*

1 On the third day there was a wedding in Cana of Galilee. 2 Mary, the mother of Jesus was there, and Jesus and His disciples were invited to the wedding.

3 When the wine ran out, His mother said to Jesus, "They have no wine."

4 He said to her, "Woman, what does that have to do with us? My hour has not yet come."

5 Mary said to the servants, "Whatever He says to you, do it."

6 Now there were six stone waterpots set there for the Jewish custom of purification, each able to hold twenty or thirty gallons. 7 Jesus said to them, "Fill the pots with water." So they filled them up to the brim.

8 Then He said to them, "Now draw some out, and take it to the headwaiter." So they took it to him.

9 When the headwaiter tasted the water which had become wine, and did not know where it came from - but the servants who had drawn the water knew - he called the bridegroom, and said to him, 10 "Every man serves the good wine first, and when the people have drunk freely then he serves the poorer wine; but you have kept the good wine until now!"

11 This first sign which Jesus did in Cana of Galilee manifested His glory; and His disciples believed in Him.

12 After this, Jesus went down to Capernaum with His mother and His brothers, and His disciples, and they stayed there a few days.

> ## Act 2 - The First Passover

Scene 321   **Jesus Expels The Merchants From The Temple**

The Temple, Jerusalem, *Judea*   Passover - April / 30 CE   *John 2:13-25*

1 The Passover of the Jews was near, and Jesus went up to Jerusalem.

2 In the Temple He found those who were selling the oxen, sheep and doves; and the money changers seated at their tables.

3 Then Jesus made a scourge of cords, and He drove them all out of the Temple, with the sheep and the oxen; 4 and He poured out the coins of the money changers, and overturned their tables.

5 And He said to those who were selling the doves, "Take these things away! Stop making My Father's house a place of business!"

6 His disciples remembered that it was written, "Zeal for Your house will consume me."

7 Then the Jews said to Him, "What sign do You show us as your authority for doing these things?"

8 Jesus answered them, "Destroy this temple, and in three days I will raise it up."

9 The Jews said, "It took forty-six years to build this Temple, and will You raise it up in three days?" 10 But He was speaking of the temple of His body.

11 So when Jesus was raised from the dead, His disciples remembered that He had said this; and they believed the Scripture, and the Word which He had spoken.   *continued >*

Scene 321 - *continued*

12 Now while He was in Jerusalem, many believed in His Name, observing the signs which He was doing during the Passover Feast. 13 But Jesus, on His part, was not entrusting Himself to them, for He knew all men, 14 and because He did not need anyone to testify concerning man, because He Himself knew what was in man.

Scene 322   **A Pharisee Named Nicodemus**

Jerusalem, *Judea*   Passover - April / 30 CE   *John 3:1-21*

1 Now there was a Pharisee named Nicodemus, a ruler of the Jews; 2 he came to Jesus at night, and said to Him, "Rabbi, we know that You have come from God as a Teacher, for no one can do these signs that You do unless God is with him."

3 Jesus answered, and said to him, "Truly, truly, I say to you, unless one is born again, he cannot see the Kingdom of God."

4 Nicodemus said to Him, "How can a man be born when he is old? He cannot enter a second time into his mother's womb and be born, can he?"

5 Jesus answered, "Truly, truly, I say to you, unless one is born of water and the Spirit, he cannot enter into the Kingdom of God. 6 That which is born of the flesh is flesh, and that which is born of the Spirit is Spirit.

7 "Do not be amazed that I said to you, 'You must be born again.' 8 The wind blows where it wishes, and you hear the sound of it, but do not know where it comes from, or where it is going; so is everyone who is born of the Spirit."

9 Nicodemus said, "How can these things be?"

10 Jesus answered him, "Are you the teacher of Israel, and do not understand these things? 11 Truly, truly, I say to you, we speak of what we know, and testify of what we have seen, and you do not accept our testimony. 12 If I told you earthly things and you do not believe, how will you believe if I tell you Heavenly things?

13 "No one has ascended into Heaven but He who descended from Heaven: the Son of Man. 14 As Moses lifted up the serpent in the wilderness, even so must the Son of Man be lifted up, so that everyone who believes in Him will have eternal life.

15 "For God so loved the world, that He gave His only begotten Son, that whoever believes in Him shall not perish, but have eternal life. 16 For God did not send the Son into the world to judge the world, but that the world might be saved through Him.

17 "He who believes in Him is not judged; 18 but he who does not believe has been judged already, because he has not believed in the Name of the only begotten Son of God.

19 "This is the judgment: that the Light has come into the world, and men loved the darkness rather than the Light, for their deeds were evil. 20 For everyone who does evil hates the Light, and does not come to the Light, for fear that his deeds will be exposed.

21 "But he who practices the truth comes to the Light, so that his deeds may be manifested, as having been wrought in God."

Scene 323   **The Disciples of Jesus Begin Baptizing**

Jordan River, Aenon, *Judea*   late spring / 30 CE   *John 3:22-30; 4:1-2*

1 After these things, Jesus and His disciples came into the Judean countryside, and He was spending time with them there and baptizing; although Jesus Himself was not baptizing, but His disciples were.

2 John was also baptizing in Aenon near Salim, because there was much water there; and the people were coming and being baptized, for John had not yet been thrown into prison.

3 The Lord knew that the Pharisees had heard that He was making and baptizing more disciples than John.

4 When a discussion arose on the part of John's disciples with a Jew about purification, they came to John, and said to him, "Rabbi, He who was with you beyond the Jordan, to whom you have testified, behold, He is baptizing, and all are coming to Him."

5 John answered, and said to them, "A man can receive nothing unless it has been given to him from Heaven. 6 You yourselves are my witnesses that I said, 'I am not the Christ,' but 'I have been sent ahead of Him.'

7 "He who has the bride is the bridegroom; but the friend of the bridegroom, who stands and hears him, rejoices greatly because of the bridegroom's voice. 8 So this joy of mine has been made full!

9 "He must increase, but I must decrease."

Scene 324   **Believe In The Son and Have Eternal Life**   *John 3:31-36*

1 John said, "He who comes from above is above all; 2 he who is of the earth is from the earth, and speaks of the earth.

3 "He who comes from Heaven is above all. 4 What He has seen and heard, of that He testifies; and no one receives His testimony.

5 "He who has received His testimony has set his seal to this; that God is true. 6 For He whom God has sent speaks the words of God, for He gives the Spirit without measure.

7 "The Father loves the Son, and has given all things into His hand.

8 "He who believes in the Son has eternal life; 9 but he who does not obey the Son will not see life, and the wrath of God will abide on him."

Act 3 - A Journey Through Samaria

Scene 331   **King Herod Imprisons John The Baptist**

Judea   late spring / 30 CE

Matthew 4:12; 14:3-5 / Mark 1:14~, 6:17-20 / Luke 3:19-20 / John 4:3-4

1 Of all the wicked things which Herod the Tetrarch had done, he added this to them all: he sent and had John arrested; and he bound him, and locked him up in prison. 2 For John had reprimanded Herod because he had married Herodias, the wife of his brother Philip; and he had been saying to Herod, "It is not lawful for you to have your brother's wife."

3 Herodias had a grudge against John, and wanted to put him to death, but Herod could not do so, for he was afraid of John, knowing that he was a righteous and holy man; 4 and Herod feared the crowd because they regarded John as a prophet; and so he kept him safe. 5 When Herod heard John he was very perplexed, but he enjoyed listening to him.

6 When Jesus heard that John had been taken into custody, He withdrew from Judea and went into Galilee, and He had to pass through Samaria.

Scene 332   **The Woman At Jacob's Well**

Sychar, *Samaria*   late spring / 30 CE   *John 4:5-12*

1 Jesus came to a city of Samaria called Sychar, near the parcel of ground that Jacob gave to his son Joseph. 2 Jacob's well was there, and being wearied from His journey, Jesus was sitting by the well.

3 At about the sixth hour, a woman of Samaria came there to draw water.

4 Jesus said to her, "Give Me a drink," for His disciples had gone away into the city to buy food.

5 The Samaritan woman said to Him, "How is it that You, being a Jew, ask me for a drink, since I am a Samaritan woman?" 6 (For Jews have no dealings with Samaritans.)

7 Jesus answered, and said to her, "If you knew the gift of God, and who it is who says to you, 'Give Me a drink,' you would have asked Him, and He would have given you living water."

8 She said to Him, "Sir, You have nothing to draw with, and the well is deep; how will You get the living water? 9 You are not greater than our father Jacob, are You, who gave us this well, and drank from it himself, and his sons, and his cattle?"

Scene 333   **I Am The Living Water**

Sychar, *Samaria*   late spring / 30 CE   *John 4:13-30*

---

1 Jesus answered, and said to her, "Everyone who drinks of this water will thirst again; but whoever drinks of the water that I will give him shall never thirst, 2 because the water that I will give him will become in him a well of water, springing up to eternal life!"

3 The woman said to Him, "Sir, give me this water, so that I will not be thirsty, nor come all the way here to draw."

4 Jesus said to her, "Go, and call your husband to come here."

5 The woman answered, and said, "I have no husband."

6 He said to her, "You have correctly said, 'I have no husband'; for you have had five husbands, and the one whom you are with now is not your husband; this you have said truly."

7 The woman said to Jesus, "Sir, I perceive that You are a Prophet. 8 Our fathers worshiped on this mountain, and you people say that in Jerusalem is the place where men ought to worship."

9 Jesus said to her, "Woman, believe Me, an hour is coming when neither on this mountain, nor in Jerusalem, will you worship The Father. 10 You worship what you do not know; we worship what we know, for salvation is from the Jews.

11 "But an hour is coming, and now is, when the true worshipers will worship The Father in Spirit and in truth; for such people The Father seeks to be His worshipers. 12 God is Spirit; and those who worship Him must worship in Spirit, and truth."

13 The woman said to Him, "I know that the Messiah is coming (He who is called Christ); when that One comes, He will declare all things to us."

14 Jesus said to her, "I who speak to you am He."

15 At this point, His disciples came, and they were amazed that He had been speaking with a woman; yet no one said, "What do You seek?" or, "Why do You speak with her?"

16 So the woman left her waterpot and went into the city, and said to the men, "Come and see a man who told me all the things that I have done! 17 Could this be the Messiah?"

18 So the people went out of the city, and were coming to Jesus.

Scene 334   **Many Samaritans Believe In Jesus**   *John 4:31-44*

---

1 Meanwhile, His disciples were urging Jesus, saying, "Rabbi, eat." But He said to them, "I have food to eat that you do not know about." 2 So the disciples were saying to one another, "No one brought Him anything to eat, did he?"

3 Jesus said to them, "My food is to do the will of Him who sent Me, and to aooomplioh I lio work.

4 "Do you not say, 'There are yet four months, and then comes the harvest'? 5 Behold, I say to you, lift up your eyes and look on the fields, that they are white for harvest! 6 Already he who reaps is receiving wages, and is gathering fruit for life eternal, so that he who sows and he who reaps may rejoice together.

continued >

Scene 334 - *continued*

7 "For in this case the saying is true, 'One sows, and another reaps.'

8 "I sent you to reap that for which you have not labored; others have labored, and you have entered into their labor."

9 From that city many of the Samaritans believed in Him, because of the word of the woman who testified, "He told me all the things that I have done."

10 The Samaritans asked Jesus to stay with them, and He stayed there for two days.

11 Many more believed because of His words; 12 and they were saying to the woman, "It is no longer because of what you said that we believe, for we have heard for ourselves, and know that this One is indeed the Savior of the world!"

13 After two days, Jesus went forth from there into Galilee, for He Himself testified that a prophet has no honor in his own country.

> ## Act 4 - Jesus Settles In Capernaum

Scene 341   **Through Nazareth and Cana**
Nazareth & Cana, *Galilee*   late spring / 30 CE
Matthew 4:13~ / Luke 4:14 / John 4:45-46~

1 Jesus returned to Galilee in the power of the Spirit, and the Galileans received Him, having seen all the things that He did in Jerusalem at the Passover, for they themselves also went to the Feast; 2 and news about Him spread through all the surrounding district.

3 Leaving Nazareth, Jesus came again to Cana in Galilee, where He had turned the water into wine.

Scene 342   **Healing The Son of A Royal Official**
Capernaum, *Galilee*   *John 4:~46-54*

1 There was a royal official whose son was sick at Capernaum. 2 When he heard that Jesus had come out of Judea and into Galilee, he went to Him; and he implored Jesus to come and heal his son, who was at the point of death.

3 Jesus said to him, "Unless you people see signs and wonders, you simply will not believe."

4 The royal official said to Him, "Sir, come down before my child dies."

5 Jesus said to him, "Go; your son lives!"

6 The man believed the word that Jesus spoke to him, and headed home.

7 As he was going, his slaves met him, saying that his son was living.

8 When he asked them the hour at which he began to get better, they said to him, "The fever left him yesterday, at the seventh hour." 9 So the father knew that it was the hour in which Jesus had said to him, "Your son lives"; and he himself believed, and his entire household.

10 This is the second sign that Jesus performed after He had come out of Judea and into Galilee.

Scene 343   **Jesus Resides In Capernaum**

Capernaum, *Galilee*   late spring / 30 CE   *Matthew 4:~13-17 / Mark 1:~14-15 / Luke 4:15*

1 Jesus came and settled in Capernaum, which is by the sea in the region of Zebulun and Naphtali. 2 This was to fulfill what was spoken through Isaiah the prophet: "The land of Zebulun and the land of Naphtali, by the way of the sea beyond the Jordan, Galilee of the Gentiles - 3 The people who were sitting in darkness saw a great Light, and those who were sitting in the land of the shadow of death, upon them a Light dawned."

4 From that time, Jesus began to preach the gospel of God, and say, "The time is fulfilled, and the Kingdom of Heaven is at hand; repent, and believe in the gospel!"

5 And He began teaching in their synagogues, and was being praised by all.

Scene 344   **Jesus Calls Peter and Andrew, and Others**

Sea of Galilee, near Capernaum, *Galilee*   *Matthew 4:18-20 / Mark 1:16-18 / Luke 5:1-9, ~10*

1 As Jesus was walking by the Sea of Galilee He saw the two brothers, Simon who was called Peter, and Andrew his brother, casting a net into the sea, for they were fishermen.

2 Later, Jesus was standing by the sea, and the crowd was pressing around Him, and listening to the Word of God. 3 And He saw two boats lying at the shore, but the fishermen had gotten out of them, and were washing their nets.

4 Jesus got into Simon's boat, and asked him to move out a little way from the land; then He sat down and began teaching the people from the boat.

5 When He had finished speaking, Jesus said to Simon, "Put out into the deep water, and let down your nets for a catch."

6 Simon answered, and said, "Master, we have worked hard all night and caught nothing; but I will do as You say, and let down the nets."

7 When they had done this, they enclosed a great quantity of fish, and their nets began to break. 8 So they signaled their partners in the other boat for them to come and help; and they came and filled both of the boats, so that they began to sink.

9 When Simon Peter saw this, he fell down at Jesus' feet, saying, "Go away from me Lord, for I am a sinful man," 10 for amazement had seized him and all of his companions, because of the amount of fish which they had caught.

11 Jesus said to them, "Follow Me, and do not fear; from now on I will make you become fishers of men!"

12 Immediately they left their nets, and followed Him.

Scene 345   **Jesus Calls James and John**

Matthew 4:21-22 / Mark 1:19-20 / Luke 5:10~, 11

1 Going on a little farther from there, Jesus saw two other brothers; James, the son of Zebedee, and John his brother, who were partners with Simon. 2 They were in the boat with their father Zebedee, mending the nets.

3 Jesus called them, and when they had brought their boats to land, immediately they left everything, and their father in the boat with the hired servants, and they went away and followed Him.

Act 5 - Jesus Heals Many

Scene 351   **Healing A Demoniac On The Sabbath**
Capernaum, *Galilee*   a Sabbath, summer / 30 CE   *Mark 1:21-28 / Luke 4:31-38~*

1 They went into Capernaum, and on the Sabbath Jesus entered the synagogue, and began to teach them. 2 They were amazed at His teaching, for He was teaching them as one having authority, and not as the scribes.

3 Just then, there was a man in the synagogue possessed by the unclean spirit of a demon. 4 And he cried out with a loud voice, saying, "Let us alone! 5 What business do we have with each other, Jesus of Nazareth? Have You come to destroy us? 6 I know who You are - the Holy One of God!"

7 But Jesus rebuked him, saying, "Be quiet, and come out of him."

8 When the demon had thrown the man down and into convulsions in the midst of the people, the unclean spirit cried out with a loud voice, and came out of him without hurting him.

9 And they were all amazed, and began talking among themselves, and saying, "What is this message? 10 A new teaching with authority! For with authority and power He commands even the unclean spirits, and they obey Him, and come out!" 11 Then Jesus got up, and left the synagogue.

12 And immediately the news about Him spread everywhere into every locality in all the districts surrounding Galilee.

Scene 352   **Jesus Heals Simon Peter's Mother-in-Law**
Matthew 8:14-15 / Mark 1:29-31 / Luke 4:~38-39

1 After they came out of the synagogue, they entered the house of Simon and Andrew, with James and John.

2 When Jesus came into Peter's home, He saw his mother-in-law lying sick in bed, and suffering from a high fever. 3 Immediately they spoke to Jesus, and asked Him to help her.

4 He came to her, and standing over her, He took her by the hand, and raised her up. 5 Then He rebuked the fever, and it left her; and she immediately got up and waited on them.

Scene 353   **Many Come To Be Healed**
Saturday evening, summer / 30 CE   *Matthew 8:16-17 / Mark 1:32-34 / Luke 4:40-41*

1 When evening came, after the sun had set, they began bringing to Him all who were ill with various diseases, and many who were demon-possessed; and the whole city was gathered at the door.

2 Laying His hands on each one of them, Jesus healed all who were ill, and He cast out the spirits with a word. 3 This was to fulfill what was spoken through Isaiah the prophet: "He Himself took our infirmities, and carried away our diseases."

4 Demons were also coming out of many, shouting, "You are the Son of God!" 5 But rebuking them, Jesus would not allow the demons to speak, because they knew that He was the Christ.

Scene 354　　**Preaching and Healing Throughout Galilee**

Galilee　a Sunday, summer / 30 CE　　*Matthew 4:23-25 / Mark 1:35-39 / Luke 4:42-44*

1 Early the next morning, while it was still dark, Jesus got up, left the house, and went away to a secluded place, and was praying there.

2 The crowds were searching for Him, and when Simon and his companions found Him, they said to Him, "Everyone is looking for You."

3 The crowds came and tried to keep Him from going away from them, but He said to them, "I must go to the other cities and towns nearby, so that I may preach the Kingdom of God there also; for I was sent for this purpose."

4 So Jesus was going throughout all of Galilee, teaching in their synagogues, and proclaiming the gospel of the Kingdom; 5 and casting out the demons, and healing every kind of disease and every kind of sickness among the people.

6 The news about Jesus spread throughout all of Syria, and they brought to Him all who were ill, and those suffering with various diseases and pains, demoniacs, epileptics, and paralytics, and He healed them. 7 Large crowds followed Him from Galilee and the Decapolis, and from Jerusalem and Judea, and beyond the Jordan.

Scene 355　　**Cleansing A Leper**

Galilee　　*Matthew 8:2-4 / Mark 1:40-45 / Luke 5:12-16*

1 While He was in one of the cities, there was a man covered with leprosy; and when he saw Jesus, he came and bowed down on his knees before Him, and implored Him, saying, "Lord, if You are willing, You can make me clean!"

2 Moved with compassion, Jesus stretched out His hand and touched him, and said, "I am willing; be cleansed." 3 Immediately the leprosy left the man, and he was cleansed.

4 Jesus sent Him away, and sternly ordered him, saying, "See that you tell no one, but go, and show yourself to the priest, and present the offering for your cleansing that Moses commanded, as a testimony to them."

5 But the man went out and began to proclaim it freely, and the news about Jesus was spreading around even farther. 6 And large crowds were gathering to Him from everywhere, to hear Him, and to be healed of their sicknesses; 7 to such an extent that Jesus could no longer publicly enter a city, but stayed out in the unpopulated areas, where He would often slip away into the wilderness and pray.

Scene 356　　**Resurrecting The Son of A Widow**

Nain, *Galilee*　　*Luke 7:11-18*

1 Soon afterwards Jesus went to a city called Nain; and His disciples were going along with Him, accompanied by a large crowd.

2 As He approached the gate of the city, a dead man was being carried out, the only son of his mother. 3 She was a widow, and a sizeable crowd from the city was with her.

4 When the Lord saw her, He felt compassion for her, and said to her, "Do not weep." 5 Then He came up and touched the coffin, and the bearers came to a halt.　　*continued >*

Scene 356 - *continued*

6 Jesus said, "Young man, I say to you, arise!" and the dead man sat up, and began to speak.

7 Jesus gave him back to his mother, and fear gripped them all. 8 And they began glorifying God, saying, "A great prophet has arisen among us!" and, "God has visited His people!" 9 This report concerning Jesus went out all over Judea, and into all of the surrounding district.

10 Then the disciples of John the Baptist reported to him about all these things.

Act 6 - John Enquires About Jesus

Scene 361   **John Asks Jesus, "Are You The Expected One?"**
Capernaum, *Galilee*   summer / 30 CE   *Matthew 11:2-6 / Luke 7:19-23*

---

1 When John, while imprisoned, heard of the works of Christ, he summoned two of his disciples, and sent them to the Lord, saying, "Are You the Expected One, or do we look for someone else?"

2 When the men came to Jesus, they said to Him, "John the Baptist has sent us to ask You, 'Are you the Expected One, or shall we look for someone else?' "

3 At that very time Jesus cured many people of diseases and afflictions, and evil spirits; and He gave sight to many who were blind.

4 He answered, and said to them, "Go and report to John what you see and hear: the blind receive sight and the lame walk, the lepers are cleansed and the deaf hear, the dead are raised up, and the poor have the gospel preached to them. 5 And blessed is he who does not take offense at Me."

Scene 362   **John Is Elijah Who Was To Come**
Matthew 11:7-15 / Luke 7:24-30

---

1 When the messengers of John had left, Jesus began to speak to the crowds about John. 2 He asked them, "What did you go out into the wilderness to see? A reed shaken by the wind?

3 "But what did you go out to see? A man dressed in soft clothing? 4 Those who are splendidly dressed in soft clothing, and live in luxury, are found in royal palaces.

5 "But what did you go out to see? A prophet? Yes, I tell you, and one who is more than a Prophet. 6 This is the One about whom it is written, 'Behold, I send My messenger ahead of You, who will prepare Your way before You.'

7 "Truly I say to you, among those born of women there has not arisen anyone greater than John the Baptist! 8 Yet the one who is least in the Kingdom of Heaven is greater than he.

9 "From the days of John the Baptist until now, the Kingdom of Heaven suffers violence, and violent men take it by force; 10 for all the prophets, and the Law, prophesied until John. 11 And if you are willing to accept it, John himself is Elijah who was to come. 12 He who has ears to hear, let him hear!"   *continued >*

13 When all the people and the tax collectors heard this, they acknowledged God's justice, having been baptized with the baptism of John. 14 But the Pharisees and the lawyers rejected God's purpose for themselves, not having been baptized by John.

Scene 363   **To What Shall I Compare This Generation?**

Capernaum, *Galilee*   summer / 30 CE   *Matthew 11:16-19 / Luke 7:31-35*

1 Then Jesus said, "To what shall I compare the men of this generation, and what are they like?

2 "They are like children sitting in the market place, who call out to one another, and say, 'We played the flute for you, and you did not dance; we sang a dirge, and you did not weep.' 3 For John the Baptist has come neither eating bread nor drinking wine, and they say, 'He has a demon!'

4 "The Son of Man has come eating and drinking, and you say, 'Behold, a gluttonous man and a drunkard, a friend of tax collectors and sinners.'

5 "Yet wisdom is vindicated by all of her deeds."

Act 7 - Jesus Attends A Feast

Scene 371   **Jesus Heals A Man at The Bethesda Pool**

Bethesda Pool, Jerusalem, *Judea*   a Sabbath, summer / 30 CE   *John 5:1-14*

1 After this, there was a feast of the Jews, and Jesus went up to Jerusalem.

2 Now there is in Jerusalem by the sheep gate a pool, which in Hebrew is called Bethesda, having five porticoes. 3 In these lay a multitude of those who were sick, blind, lame, and withered. 4 They were waiting for the movement of the waters, for an angel of the Lord went down at certain seasons into the pool, and stirred up the water, and whoever then first stepped in after the stirring up of the water was made well from whatever disease with which he was afflicted.

5 A man was there who had been ill for thirty-eight years. 6 When Jesus saw him lying there, and knew that he had been in that condition for a long time, He said to him, "Do you wish to get well?"

7 The sick man answered, "Sir, I have no one to put me into the pool when the water is stirred up, but while I am coming, another steps down before me."

8 Jesus said to him, "Get up, pick up your pallet, and walk." 9 Immediately the man became well, and he picked up his pallet, and began to walk.

10 Now it was the Sabbath on that day, so the Jews were saying to the man who was cured, "It is the Sabbath, and it is not permissible for you to carry your pallet." 11 But he answered them, "He who made me well was the one who said to me, 'Pick up your pallet, and walk.' "

12 They asked him, "Who is the man who said to you, 'Pick up your pallet and walk'?" But the man who was healed did not know who it was, for Jesus had slipped away into the crowd.

13 Afterward, Jesus found him in the Temple, and said to him, "Behold, you have become well. Do not sin anymore, so that nothing worse happens to you."

Scene 372   The Father and The Son

Jerusalem, *Judea*   a Sabbath, summer / 30 CE   *John 5:15-23*

1 The man went away and told the Jews that it was Jesus who had made him well. 2 So the Jews were persecuting Jesus, because He was doing these things on the Sabbath.

3 But Jesus answered them, "My Father is working until now, and I Myself am working."

4 So the Jews were seeking all the more to kill Jesus, because not only was He breaking the Sabbath, but He was also calling God His own Father, thus making Himself equal with God.

5 But Jesus answered, and said to them, "Truly, truly, I say to you, the Son can do nothing of Himself, unless it is something that He sees The Father is doing; 6 for whatever The Father does, these things the Son also does, in the same way.

7 "For The Father loves the Son, and shows Him all of the things that He Himself is doing; 8 and The Father will show Him greater works than these, so that you will marvel! 9 For just as The Father raises the dead, and gives them life, even so the Son also gives life to whom He wishes.

10 "For The Father does not judge anyone, but He has given all judgment to the Son, so that all will honor the Son, even as they honor The Father.

11 "He who does not honor the Son does not honor The Father who sent Him."

Scene 373   Those Who Believe My Words Will Live   *John 5:24-30*

1 "Truly, truly, I say to you, he who hears My words, and believes Him who sent Me, has eternal life, and does not come into judgment, but has passed out of death and into life.

2 "Truly, truly, I say to you, that an hour is coming, and now is, when the dead will hear the voice of the Son of God, and those who hear will live. 3 For just as The Father has life in Himself, even so He gave the Son to also have life in Himself; 4 and because He is the Son of Man, He gave Him authority to execute judgment.

5 "Do not marvel at this, for an hour is coming in which all who are in the tombs will hear His voice, and will come forth; 6 those who did good deeds to a resurrection of life, 7 and those who committed evil deeds, to a resurrection of judgment.

8 "I can do nothing on My own initiative. As I hear, I judge; and My judgment is just, because I do not seek My own will, but the will of Him who sent Me."

Scene 374   **My Testimony About Myself**
          Jerusalem, *Judea*   a Sabbath, summer / 30 CE   *John 5:31-47*

1 "If I alone testify about Myself, My testimony is not true. 2 There is another who testifies of Me, and I know that the testimony which He gives about Me is true. 3 You have sent to John, and he has testified to the truth.

4 "But the testimony which I receive is not from man, but I say these things so that you may be saved.

5 "John was the lamp that was burning and shining, and you were willing to rejoice for a while in his Light. 6 But the testimony which I have is greater than the testimony of John; 7 for the works which The Father has given Me to accomplish - the very works that I do - testify about Me, that The Father has sent Me. 8 And The Father who sent Me, He has testified of Me.

9 "You have neither heard His voice at any time, nor seen His form. 10 You do not have His Word abiding in you, for you do not believe Him whom He has sent.

11 "You search the Scriptures because you think that in them you have eternal life; it is these that testify about Me; 12 and yet you are unwilling to come to Me, so that you may have life. 13 I do not receive glory from men; 14 but I know you, that you do not have the love of God in yourselves.

15 "I have come in My Father's Name, and you do not receive Me; 16 but if another comes in his own name, you will receive him. 17 How can you believe, when you receive glory from one another, and you do not seek the glory that is from The One and only God?

18 "Do not think that I will accuse you before The Father; the One who accuses you is Moses, in whom you have set your hope. 19 For if you believed Moses, you would believe Me, for he wrote about Me.

20 "But if you do not believe his writings, how will you believe My words?"

Scene 375   **The Parable of The Good Samaritan**   *Luke 10:25-37*

1 A lawyer stood up, and put Jesus to the test, saying, "Teacher, what shall I do to inherit eternal life?"

2 Jesus said to him, "What is written in the Law? How does it read to you?"

3 He answered, "You shall love the Lord your God with all your heart, and with all your soul, and with all your strength, and with all your mind; 4 and your neighbor as yourself."

5 Jesus said to him, "You have answered correctly. Do this and you will live."

6 But wishing to justify himself, the lawyer said to Him, "And who is my neighbor?"

7 Jesus replied, and said, "A man was going down from Jerusalem to Jericho, and he fell among robbers; and they stripped him and beat him, and went away leaving him half dead.

8 "By chance a priest was traveling on that road, and when he saw the wounded man, he passed by on the other side.   *continued >*

Scene 375 - *continued*

9 "Likewise a Levite, when he came to the place and saw him, he also passed by on the other side. 10 But a Samaritan who was on a journey came upon him; and when he saw him he felt compassion, and he came to him, and bandaged up his wounds, pouring oil and wine on them. 11 Then he put him on his own beast, and brought him to the inn, and took care of him.

12 "On the next day, he took out two denarii and gave them to the innkeeper, and said, 'Take care of him; and whatever more you spend, I will repay you when I return.' 13 Which of these three do you think proved to be a neighbor to the man who fell into the robbers' hands?"

14 The lawyer said, "The one who showed mercy toward him."

15 Then Jesus said to him, "Go, and do the same."

Scene 376	**Jesus Visits Martha and Mary**	
	Bethany, *Judea* summer / 30 BCE *Luke 10:38-42*	

1 As they were traveling Jesus entered a village, and a woman named Martha welcomed Him into her home.

2 She had a sister named Mary, who was seated at the Lord's feet, and listening to His words. 3 But Martha was distracted with all of her preparations; and she came to Jesus, and said, "Lord, do You not care that my sister has left me to do all of the serving alone? Tell her to help me!"

4 But the Lord answered, and said to her, "Martha, Martha, you are worried and bothered about so many things, but only one thing is necessary; 5 for Mary has chosen the good part, which shall not be taken away from her."

Act 8 - Events In Capernaum

Scene 381	**The Man Paralyzed In A Bed**	
Capernaum, *Galilee*	summer / 30 CE *Matthew 9:2 / Mark 2:1-5 / Luke 5:17-20*	

1 When Jesus returned to Capernaum several days later, it was heard that He was at home, and so many had gathered together that there was no longer any room, not even near the door.

2 He was speaking the Word to them, and there were some Pharisees and teachers of the law sitting there who had come from every village of Galilee and Judea, and from Jerusalem.

3 The power of the Lord was present for Him to perform healing, and they brought to Him a man who was paralyzed, lying on a bed carried by four men. 4 They were trying to bring him in and to set him down in front of Jesus, but being unable to find any way to bring him in because of the crowd, they went up on to the roof, and removed the tiles above Him.

5 When they had dug an opening, they let the paralytic down through the tiles with the stretcher on which he was lying, into the middle of the crowd, in front of Jesus.

6 Seeing their faith, Jesus said to the paralytic, "Take courage, son; your sins are forgiven."

Scene 382   **Jesus Is Accused of Blasphemy**

Capernaum, *Galilee*   summer / 30 CE   *Matthew 9:3-8 / Mark 2:6-13 / Luke 5:21-26*

1 Some of the scribes and Pharisees who were sitting there began to reason in their hearts, and say to themselves, "Why does this man speak that way? This fellow is blaspheming! 2 Who is this man who speaks blasphemies? Who can forgive sins, but God alone?"

3 Immediately Jesus was aware in His Spirit that they were reasoning this way within themselves; and He answered, and said to them, "Why are you thinking evil about these things in your hearts? 4 Which is easier to say? 'Your sins are forgiven', or to say, 'Get up, and pick up your pallet, and walk'?

5 "But so that you may know that the Son of Man has authority on earth to forgive sins," He then said to the paralytic, "I say to you, get up, and pick up your pallet, and go home."

6 And immediately the man got up before them, and picked up what he had been lying on, and went home, glorifying God in the sight of everyone.

7 When the crowds saw this, they were all struck with astonishment, and they began glorifying God, who had given such authority to men. 8 And they were filled with awe, saying, "We have seen remarkable things today. We have never seen anything like this!"

9 Jesus went out by the seashore; and all the people were coming to Him, and He was teaching them.

Scene 383   **Jesus Calls Matthew Levi**

Capernaum, *Galilee*   summer / 30 CE   *Matthew 9:9 / Mark 2:14 / Luke 5:27-28*

1 After that, Jesus went on from there, and as He passed by He noticed a tax collector named Matthew Levi sitting in the tax collector's booth; and He said to him, "Follow Me."

2 Matthew got up, left everything behind, and began to follow Jesus.

Scene 384   **Matthew Gives A Reception For Jesus**

Matthew 9:10-13 / Mark 2:15-17 / Luke 5:29-32

1 Then Matthew gave a large reception for Jesus in his house. 2 And as Jesus was reclining at the table, behold, a great crowd of many tax collectors and sinners came, and were dining with Jesus and His disciples; for there were many of them, and they were following Him.

3 When the Pharisees and their scribes saw that Jesus was eating with the tax collectors and sinners, they began grumbling, and said to His disciples, "Why is your Teacher eating and drinking with the tax collectors and sinners?"

4 When Jesus heard this, He answered and said to them, "It is not those who are healthy who need a physician, but those who are sick.

5 "But go and learn what this means: 'I desire compassion, and not sacrifice,' 6 for I have not come to call the righteous, but sinners to repentance."

Scene 385   **Why Do You Not Fast?**

Capernaum, *Galilee*   summer / 30 CE   *Matthew 9:14-15 / Mark 2:18-20 / Luke 5:33-35*

---

1 The disciples of John the Baptist and the Pharisees were fasting, and John's disciples came to Jesus, and said to Him, "We often fast and offer prayers, and the disciples of the Pharisees also do the same. 2 Why do we and the disciples of the Pharisees fast, but your disciples eat and drink, and do not fast?"

3 Jesus said to them, "While the bridegroom is with them, the attendants of the bridegroom cannot fast, can they? 4 So long as they have the bridegroom with them, they cannot fast; but the days will come when the bridegroom is taken away from them, and then they will fast in those days."

Scene 386   **New Cloth and Wineskins**

Matthew 9:16-17 / Mark 2:21-22 / Luke 5:36-39

---

1 Jesus also told them a parable: "No one tears a piece of unshrunk cloth from a new garment and sews it on an old garment, otherwise the new piece will not match the old; and when the new patch pulls away from the old garment a worse tear results.

2 "Nor do people put new wine into old wineskins, otherwise the new wine will burst the wineskins, and it will be spilled out and lost; and the skins are ruined as well. 3 But new wine must be put into fresh wineskins, and then both are preserved.

4 "And no one after drinking old wine wishes for new, for he says, 'The old is better.' "

Scene 387   **Picking Grain On The Sabbath**

Galilee   a Sabbath, late summer / 30 CE   *Matthew 12:1-8 / Mark 2:23-28 / Luke 6:1-5*

---

1 It happened that Jesus was passing through some grainfields on the Sabbath; and as His disciples began to make their way along they became hungry, and they began to pick the heads of grain, rubbing them in their hands, and eating the grain.

2 When some of the Pharisees saw this, they said to Jesus, "Look, why are your disciples doing what is not lawful to do on the Sabbath?"

3 Jesus answering them, said, "Have you never read what David did when he was in need, and he and his companions who were with him became hungry; 4 how he entered the house of God in the time of Abiathar the High Priest, and took and ate the consecrated bread, and he also gave it to his companions, 5 which was not lawful for him to eat, nor for those with him, or anyone except for the priests alone?

6 "Or have you not read in the Law, that on the Sabbath the priests in the Temple break the Sabbath, and are innocent? 7 But I say to you that something greater than the Temple is here.

8 "And if you had known what this means, 'I desire mercy, and not sacrifice,' you would not have condemned the innocent."

9 And Jesus said to them, "The Sabbath was made for man, and not man for the Sabbath. 10 Therefore, the Son of Man is Lord, even of the Sabbath."

Scene 388   **Healing A Withered Hand On The Sabbath**
Galilee   a Sabbath, late summer / 30 CE
Matthew 12:9-15~ / Mark 3:1-7~, 9 / Luke 6:6-11

1 Departing from there, Jesus entered into their synagogue, and was teaching; and a man was there whose right hand was withered.

2 The scribes and the Pharisees were watching Jesus closely, to see if He would heal him on the Sabbath, so that they might find reason to accuse Him.

3 And they questioned Jesus, asking, "Is it lawful to heal on the Sabbath?"

4 But Jesus knew what they were thinking, and He said to the man with the withered hand, "Get up, and come forward." And the man got up, and came forward.

5 And Jesus said to them, "I ask you, is it lawful to do good or to do harm on the Sabbath, to save a life or to destroy it?" But they kept silent.

6 And Jesus said to them, "What man is there among you who has a sheep, and if it falls into a pit on the Sabbath, will he not take hold of it, and lift it out? 7 How much more valuable is a man than a sheep! 8 So then, it is lawful to do good on the Sabbath."

9 Then looking around at them all with anger, grieved at their hardness of heart, Jesus said to the man, "Stretch out your hand." 10 He stretched it out, and his hand was restored to normal, like the other.

11 But the Pharisees were filled with rage, and they discussed together what they might do to Jesus.

12 They went out and immediately began conspiring with the Herodians against Him, as to how they might destroy Him.

13 Jesus, aware of this, withdrew from there to the sea, with His disciples.

14 A great multitude followed Him; and He told His disciples that a boat should stand ready, in case the people should crowd Him.

Scene 389   **Lord, Teach Us to Pray**
Galilee   late summer / 30 BCE   *Luke 11:1-4*

1 It happened that while Jesus was praying in a certain place, after He had finished, one of His disciples said to Him, "Lord, teach us to pray, just as John taught his disciples."

2 Jesus said to them, "When you pray, say: 'Father, Holy is Your Name! Your Kingdom come. 3 Give us each day our daily bread; 4 and forgive us our sins, as we forgive everyone who is indebted to us.

5 "And lead us not into temptation.' "

Act 9 - The Death of John The Baptist

Scene 391   **The Demand of Herodias**

Jerusalem, *Judea*   late summer / 30 CE   *Matthew 14:6-9 / Mark 6:21-26*

1 The day came for John the Baptist when King Herod on his birthday gave a banquet for his lords and military commanders, and the leading men of Galilee.

2 When the daughter of Herodias came in and danced before them, she pleased Herod and his dinner guests so much, that he said to her, "Ask me for whatever you want, and I will give it to you!"

3 And the King swore an oath to her; "Whatever you ask of me, I will give to you, up to half of my kingdom."

4 The girl went out, and said to her mother, "What shall I ask for?" And Herodias said, "The head of John the Baptist!"

5 Having been prompted by her mother, the girl immediately came in a hurry to the King, and said, "I want you to give me here at once the head of John the Baptist, on a platter."

6 And although Herod was very grieved, yet because of his oaths, and because of his dinner guests, the king was unwilling to refuse her, and he commanded it to be given.

Scene 392   **King Herod Has John Beheaded**

Matthew 14:10-13~ / Mark 6:27-29 / John 6:1

1 Immediately King Herod sent an executioner to behead John in the prison; and he commanded him to bring back his head.

2 The executioner went, and brought John's head on a platter, and gave it to the girl, and she gave it to her mother.

3 When John's disciples heard about this, they came and took his body away, and laid it in a tomb; then they went and reported this to Jesus.

4 When Jesus heard about John, He withdrew from there in a boat to a secluded place by Himself, on the other side of the Sea of Galilee, near Tiberias.

CHAPTER 4 - THE SECOND YEAR of His Ministry

> ## Act 1 - Jesus Chooses Twelve Apostles

Scene 411   **Miracles of Healing**
Capernaum, *Galilee*   spring / 31 CE
Matthew 12:~15-21 / Mark 3:~8, 10-12 / Luke 18~, 19

1 A great number of people heard of all that Jesus was doing, and came to Him. 2 All those who had afflictions pressed around Him, in order to touch Him, for power was coming from Him and healing them all; and those who were troubled with unclean spirits were being cured.

3 Whenever the unclean spirits saw Jesus, they would fall down before Him, and shout, "You are the Son of God!" and He would earnestly warn them not to tell who He was.

4 This was to fulfill what was spoken through Isaiah the prophet: "Behold, My Servant whom I have chosen; My Beloved in whom My Soul is well-pleased! 5 I will put My Spirit upon Him, and He shall proclaim justice to the Gentiles. 6 He will not quarrel, nor cry out; nor will anyone hear His voice in the streets. 7 A battered reed He will not break off, and a smoldering wick He will not put out, until He leads justice to victory.

8 "And in His Name the Gentiles will hope."

Scene 412   **Jesus Appoints Twelve Apostles**
Mount Eremos, near Capernaum, *Galilee*
Matthew 5:1; 10:2-4 / Mark 3:13-19 / Luke 6:12-16 / John 11:~16~

1 When Jesus saw the crowds, He went up on the mountain to pray; and He spent the whole night in prayer to God. 2 When day came, He called His disciples, and summoned to Himself those whom He wanted.

3 After He sat down, they came to Him; and He appointed twelve of them, whom He called apostles, 4 so that they would be with Him, and that He could send them out to preach, and to have authority to cast out the demons.

5 Now the names of the twelve apostles are these: The first is Simon, the son of John, to whom Jesus also gave the name Peter (Cephas); 6 and Andrew his brother;

7 and James, the son of Zebedee; 8 and John his brother (to them He gave the name Boanerges, which means, "Sons of Thunder");

9 and Philip, who was from Bethsaida in Galilee;

10 and Bartholomew from Cana in Galilee;

11 and Matthew Levi, the tax collector from Capernaum;

12 and Thomas, who is called Didymus (which means "twin");

13 and James, the son of Alphaeus;

14 and Judas Thaddaeus, the son of James;

15 and Simon Iscariot, who was called the Zealot;

16 and Judas Iscariot, the son of Simon, the one who would betray Him.

1. may also be Nathanael: John 1:45-49; 21:2 / Acts 1:13

Act 2 - The Sermon On The Mount

Scene 421   **The Beatitudes**
                Mount Eremos, near Capernaum, *Galilee*   spring / 31 CE
                Matthew 5:2-12 / Mark 3:~7-8~ / Luke 6:17, ~18, 20-26

1 Jesus came down with the apostles, and stood on a level place where there was a large crowd of His disciples. 2 And a great throng of people was there from Galilee, and from Jerusalem and all of Judea, and from Idumea, and beyond the Jordan, and the coastal regions of Tyre and Sidon, who had come to hear Jesus, and to be healed of their diseases.

3 Turning His gaze toward His disciples, Jesus opened His mouth, and began to teach them, saying, 4 "Blessed are you who are poor, for yours is the Kingdom of God.

5 "Blessed are the poor in spirit, for theirs is the Kingdom of Heaven.

6 "Blessed are those who mourn, for they shall be comforted.

7 "Blessed are the gentle, for they shall inherit the earth.

8 "Blessed are you who hunger and thirst for righteousness now, for you shall be satisfied.

9 "Blessed are you who weep now, for you shall laugh.

10 "Blessed are the merciful, for they shall receive mercy.

11 "Blessed are the pure in heart, for they shall see God.

12 "Blessed are the peacemakers, for they shall be called sons of God.

13 "Blessed are those who have been persecuted for the sake of righteousness, for theirs is the Kingdom of Heaven.

14 "Blessed are you when people insult you, and men hate you, and persecute you, and scorn your name, and falsely say all kinds of evil things against you, because of Me, the Son of Man. 15 Rejoice and be glad in that day, and leap for joy; for behold, your reward in Heaven is great; for in the same way their fathers persecuted the prophets who were before you.

16 "But woe to you who are rich now, for you are receiving your comfort in full.

17 "Woe to you who are well-fed now, for you shall be hungry.

18 "Woe to you who laugh now, for you shall mourn and weep.

19 "Woe to you when all men speak well of you, for their fathers used to treat the false prophets in the same way."

Scene 422   **You Are The Salt of The Earth**
              Matthew 5:13 / Mark 4:23; 9:50 / Luke 14:34-35

1 "You are the salt of the earth, and salt is good; 2 but if the salt has become unsalty and tasteless, with what will it be seasoned? How can it be made salty again? 3 It is useless for either the soil or the manure pile, and is no longer good for anything except to be thrown out, and trampled under foot by men.

4 "Have salt in yourselves, and be at peace with one another.

5 "If anyone has ears to hear, let them hear."

Scene 423   **You Are The Light of The World**
Matthew 5:14-16 / Mark 4:21-22 / Luke 8:16-17; 11:33

1 And Jesus said to them, "You are the light of the world! 2 A city set on a hill cannot be hidden, 3 and no one after lighting a lamp covers it over with a basket, or puts it under a bed or away in a cellar, 4 but it is put on a lampstand, and it gives light to all who are in the house, so that those who enter may see the light. 5 Therefore, let your light shine before men in such a way that they may see your good works, and glorify your Father who is in Heaven.

6 "For nothing is hidden except to be revealed and become evident; nor has anything been secret that will not come to light and be known."

Scene 424   **The Eye Is The Lamp of The Body**
Matthew 6:22-23 / Luke 11:34-36

1 "The eye is the lamp of the body, so if your eye is clear then your whole body will also be full of light; 2 but if your eye is bad, then your whole body will also be full of darkness. 3 If the light that is in you is darkness, great is that darkness! 4 Watch out then, that the light in you is not darkness.

5 "Therefore, if your whole body is full of light, with no dark part in it, it will be wholly illumined, as when the lamp illumines you with its rays."

Scene 425   **I Have Come To Fulfill The Law**   *Matthew 5:17-20*

1 "Do not think that I came to abolish the Law, or the Prophets; I did not come to abolish, but to fulfill. 2 For truly I say to you, until heaven and earth pass away, not the smallest letter or stroke shall pass from the Law, until everything is fulfilled.

3 "Whoever then annuls one of the least of these commandments, and teaches others to do the same, shall be called least in the Kingdom of Heaven; 4 but whoever keeps them, and teaches them, they shall be called great in the Kingdom of Heaven.

5 "For I say to you, that unless your righteousness surpasses that of the scribes and the Pharisees, you will not enter the Kingdom of Heaven."

Scene 426   **Forgive Your Brother**   *Matthew 5:21-24*

1 "You have heard that the ancients were told, 'You shall not commit murder' 2 and 'Whoever commits murder shall be liable to the court.' 3 But I say to you that everyone who is angry with his brother shall be guilty before the court; 4 and whoever says to his brother, 'You good-for-nothing,' shall be guilty before the supreme court; 5 and whoever says, 'You fool,' shall be guilty enough to go into the fiery hell!

6 "Therefore, if you are presenting your offering at the altar, and there remember that your brother has something against you, leave your offering there before the altar, and go; 7 first be reconciled to your brother, and then come and present your offering."

Scene 427   **Settle With Your Opponent**

Mount Eremos, near Capernaum, *Galilee*   spring / 31 CE
Matthew 5:5:25-26 / Luke 12:57-59

1 "Why do you not on your own initiative judge what is right? 2 For while you are going with your opponent at law to appear before the magistrate, make an effort to settle quickly with him on the way there, so that he may not drag you before the judge, 3 and the judge turn you over to the officer, and the officer throw you into prison.

4 "Truly I say to you, that you will not get out of there until you have paid the very last cent."

Scene 428   **On Adultery and Divorce**   *Matthew 5:27-32*

1 "You have heard that it was said, 'You shall not commit adultery'; 2 but I say to you, that everyone who looks at a woman with lust for her, has already committed adultery with her in his heart.

3 "If your right eye makes you stumble, tear it out and throw it from you, for it is better for you to lose one of the parts of your body, than for your whole body to be thrown into hell.

4 "If your right hand makes you stumble, cut it off and throw it from you, for it is better for you to lose one of the parts of your body, than for your whole body to go into hell.

5 "It was said, 'Whoever sends his wife away, let him give her a certificate of divorce'; 6 but I say to you, that everyone who divorces his wife, except for the reason of unchastity, makes her commit adultery; 7 and whoever marries a divorced woman commits adultery."

Scene 429   **Make No Oath By Heaven or Earth**   *Matthew 5:33-37*

1 "Again, you have heard that the ancients were told, 'You shall not make false vows, but shall fulfill your vows to the Lord.' 2 But I say to you, make no oath at all; either by Heaven, for it is the throne of God, or by the earth, for it is the footstool of His feet, 3 or by Jerusalem, for it is the city of the great King. 4 Nor shall you make an oath by your head, for you cannot make one hair white or black.

5 "But let your statement be 'Yes' or 'No', because anything more than these leads to evil."

Act 3 - The Sermon on True Wealth

Scene 431   **Give to Everyone Who Asks of You**
Mount Eremos, near Capernaum, *Galilee*   *Matthew 5:38-42 / Luke 6:29-30, 34, 38*

1 "You have heard that it was said, 'An eye for an eye, and a tooth for a tooth;' but I say to you, do not resist an evil person; 2 and whoever slaps you on your right cheek, turn and offer the other to him also. 3 If anyone wants to sue you, and take away your shirt, do not withhold your shirt from him - and let him have your coat also! 4 Whoever forces you to go one mile, go with him two.

5 "Give to everyone who asks of you, and do not turn away from the one who wants to borrow from you; 6 and whoever takes away what is yours, do not demand it back. 7 If you lend to those from whom you expect to receive, what credit is that to you? Even sinners lend to sinners in order to receive back the same amount.

8 "Give, and it will be given to you. They will pour into your lap a good measure - pressed down, shaken together, and running over. 9 For by your standard of measure, it will be measured to you in return."

Scene 432   **Love Your Enemy**   *Matthew 5:43-48 / Luke 6:27-28, 32-33, 35-36*

1 "You have heard that it was said, 'You shall love your neighbor and hate your enemy.' 2 But I say to you who hear; love your enemies, and do good to those who hate you; 3 bless those who curse you, and pray for those who mistreat you.

4 "If you greet only your brothers, what more are you doing than others? Do not even the Gentiles do the same? 5 And if you only do good to those who do good to you, what credit is that to you? For even sinners do the same.

6 "But love your enemies, and do good; 7 and lend, expecting nothing in return, and your reward will be great, for you will be sons of the Most High, your Father who is in Heaven; 8 for He Himself is kind to ungrateful and evil men, and He causes His sun to rise on the good and the evil, and He sends rain on the righteous and the unrighteous. 9 Therefore, be merciful, just as your Father is merciful.

10 "If you love those who love you, what credit is that to you? What reward do you have? Do not even the tax collectors do the same? 11 For even sinners love those who love them.

12 "Therefore you are to be perfect, as your Heavenly Father is perfect."

Scene 433   **When You Give To The Poor**   *Matthew 6:1-4*

1 "Beware of practicing your righteousness to be noticed by men, otherwise you will have no reward from your Father who is in Heaven. 2 So when you give to the poor, do not sound a trumpet before you, as the hypocrites do in the synagogues and in the streets, so that they may be honored by men. Truly I say to you, they have their reward in full.

3 "But when you give to the poor, do not let your left hand know what your right hand is doing, so that your giving will be in secret; 4 and your Father, who sees what is done in secret, will reward you."

Scene 434 — When You Pray
Mount Eremos, near Capernaum, *Galilee*   spring / 31 CE   *Matthew 6:5-8*

1 "When you pray, you are not to be like the hypocrites, for they love to stand and pray in the synagogues and on the street corners, so that they may be seen by men. Truly I say to you, they have their reward in full.

2 "But when you pray, go into your room and close the door, and pray to your Father who is in secret; and your Father, who sees what is done in secret, will reward you.

3 "And when you are praying, do not use meaningless repetition as the Gentiles do, for they suppose that they will be heard for their many words, so do not be like them; 4 for your Father knows what you need before you ask Him."

Scene 435 — The Lord's Prayer
Matthew 6:9-15 / Mark 11:25-26

1 "Pray, then, in this way: Our Father who is in Heaven, Holy is Your Name. 2 Your Kingdom come, and Your will be done, on earth as it is in Heaven.

3 "Give us this day our daily bread, 4 and forgive us our debts, as we also have forgiven our debtors.

5 "And do not lead us into temptation, but deliver us from evil, 6 for Yours is the Kingdom, and the power, and the glory, forever. Amen.

7 "Whenever you stand praying, if you have anything against anyone, forgive others for their transgressions, so that your Father who is in Heaven will also forgive you your transgressions.

8 "But if you do not forgive others, then neither will your Father who is in Heaven forgive your transgressions."

Scene 436 — When You Fast
Matthew 6:16-18

1 "Whenever you fast, do not put on a gloomy face as the hypocrites do, for they neglect their appearance so that they will be noticed by men when they are fasting. Truly I say to you, they have their reward in full.

2 "But you, when you fast, anoint your head and wash your face, so that your fasting will not be noticed by men, but by your Father who is in secret; 3 and your Father, who sees what is done in secret, will reward you."

Scene 437 — Life Is Not About Possessions
Luke 12:13-21

1 Someone in the crowd said to Jesus, "Teacher, tell my brother to divide the family inheritance with me."

2 Jesus said to him, "Man, who appointed Me a judge or arbitrator over you?" 3 Then He said to them, "Beware, and be on your guard against every form of greed; for not even when one has an abundance does his life consist of his possessions."

4 And He told them a parable, saying, "The land of a rich man was very productive, and he began reasoning to himself, saying, 'What shall I do, since I have no place to store my crops?'   *continued >*

5 "Then he said, 'This is what I will do: I will tear down my barns, and build larger ones, and there I will store all my grain and my goods. 6 And I will say to my soul, "Soul, you have many goods laid up for many years to come; eat, drink, and be merry!" '

7 "But God said to him, 'You fool! This very night your soul is required of you; and now who will own what you have prepared?'

8 "So is the man who stores up treasure for himself, and is not rich toward God."

Scene 438   **Store Up Treasure In Heaven**
                    Matthew 6:19-21 / Luke 12:33-34

1 "Do not store up for yourselves treasures on earth, where moth and rust destroy, and where thieves break in and steal. 2 But sell your possessions, and give to charity; make yourselves money belts which do not wear out.

3 "Store up for yourselves an unfailing treasure in Heaven, where neither moth nor rust destroys, and where thieves do not break in or steal; 4 for where your treasure is, there your heart will be also."

Scene 439   **Do Not Worry About Food or Clothing**
                    Matthew 6:25-34 / Luke 12:22-32

1 And Jesus said, "For this reason I say to you, do not worry about your life, as to what you will eat, or what you will drink, nor for your body, as to what you will put on; for life is more than food, and the body is more than clothing.

2 "Consider the birds of the air, for they do not sow nor reap; they have no storeroom, and nor do they gather into barns; and yet God, your Heavenly Father, feeds them. 3 You are much more valuable than the birds!

4 "And which of you by worrying can add a single hour to your life's span? 5 If then, you cannot do even a very little thing, why do you worry about other matters?

6 "And why are you worried about clothing? Observe the lilies of the field, and consider how they grow; 7 they do not toil, nor do they spin, yet I say to you, that not even Solomon, in all his glory, clothed himself like one of these. 8 But if God so clothes the grass in the field, which is alive today and tomorrow is thrown into the furnace, how much more will He clothe you, you men of little faith!

9 "So then, do not say, 'What will we eat?' and 'What will we drink?' or 'What will we wear for clothing?' and do not be anxious; 10 for the nations of the world eagerly seek all these things, and your Heavenly Father knows that you need them. 11 But seek first His Kingdom, and His righteousness, and all these things will be added to you.

12 "Do not be afraid, little flock, for your Father has gladly chosen to give you the Kingdom! 13 So do not worry about tomorrow, for tomorrow will care for itself, 14 because each day has enough trouble of its own."

Act 4 - The Sermon on Spiritual Fruit

Scene 441   **On Judging Another Person**
Mount Eremos, near Capernaum, *Galilee*   spring / 31 CE
Matthew 7:1-5 / Luke 6:37, 39, 41-42

1 "Do not judge, and you will not be judged; do not condemn, and you will not be condemned; pardon, and you will be pardoned. 2 For in the way that you judge, you will be judged, and by your standard of measure, it will be measured to you.

3 "Why do you look at the speck that is in your brother's eye, but do not notice the log that is in your own eye? 4 Or how can you say to your brother, 'Brother, let me take out the speck that is in your eye,' when behold, you yourself do not see the log that is in your own eye? 5 You hypocrite! First take the log out of your own eye, and then you will see clearly to take out the speck that is in your brother's eye."

6 And He also spoke a parable to them: "A blind man cannot guide a blind man, can he? Will they not both fall into a pit?"

Scene 442   **Ask, and It Will Be Given To You**
Matthew 7:7-14 / Luke 6:31; 11:5-13

1 Then Jesus said to them, "Suppose that one of you goes to a friend at midnight, and says to him, 'Friend, lend me three loaves, for a friend of mine has come to me on a journey, and I have nothing to give him'; 2 but from inside he answers, and says, 'Do not bother me; the door is shut, and my children and I are in bed; I cannot get up and give you anything.' 3 I tell you, even though he will not get up and give him anything because he is his friend, yet because of his persistence he will get up and give him as much as he needs.

4 "So I say to you: Ask, and it will be given to you; seek, and you will find; knock, and it will be opened to you! 5 For everyone who asks, receives; and he who seeks finds; and to him who knocks, it will be opened.

6 "Now suppose one of you fathers is asked by his son for a fish; he will not give him a snake instead of a fish, will he? 7 Or what man when asked for a loaf, will give him a stone? 8 If you then, being evil, know how to give good gifts to your children, how much more will your Heavenly Father give the Holy Spirit and what is good to those who ask Him.

9 "In everything therefore, treat other people the same way that you want them to treat you; for this is the Law, and the Prophets.

10 "Enter through the narrow gate; for the gate is wide, and the way is broad, that leads to destruction, and there are many who enter through it.

11 "But the gate is small, and the way is narrow that leads to life, and there are few who find it."

Scene 443   **The Fruit of False Prophets**

Matthew 7:6, 15-20 / Luke 6:43-44

1 "Do not give what is holy to dogs, and do not throw your pearls before swine, because they will trample them under their feet, and then turn and tear you to pieces.

2 "Beware of the false prophets who come to you in sheep's clothing, but inwardly are ravenous wolves! 3 You will know them by their fruits, for each tree is known by its fruit. 4 For men do not gather figs from thorns, nor do they pick grapes from a briar bush.

5 "So every good tree bears good fruit, but the bad tree bears bad fruit. 6 For there is no good tree which produces bad fruit, and nor on the other hand can a bad tree produce good fruit. 7 So then, you will know them by their fruits.

8 "Every tree that does not bear good fruit is cut down, and thrown into the fire."

Scene 444   **Build On The Solid Foundation of The Word**

Matthew 7:21-27 / Luke 6:46-49

1 "Not everyone who says to Me, 'Lord, Lord,' will enter the Kingdom of Heaven, but the one who does the will of My Father who is in Heaven will enter.

2 "Many will say to Me on that day, 'Lord, Lord, did we not prophesy in Your Name, and in Your Name cast out demons, and in Your Name perform many miracles?'

3 "Then I will declare to them, 'Why do you call Me, "Lord, Lord," and do not do what I say? 4 I never knew you. Depart from Me, you who practice lawlessness!'

5 "Therefore, everyone who comes to Me, and hears these words of Mine, and acts on them, I will show you whom he may be compared to: He is like a wise man building a house, who dug deep, and laid a foundation on the rock. 6 And when the rains fell and the floods came, the winds blew, and the torrent burst and slammed against that house; and yet the storm could not shake it, and it did not fall, because it had been founded on the rock.

7 "But the one who hears these words of Mine, and does not act on them accordingly, is like a foolish man who built his house on the sand, without any foundation. 8 The rains fell, and the floods came, and the winds blew, and the torrent burst and slammed against that house, and immediately it collapsed - and great was the ruin of that house."

Scene 445   **Jesus Finishes His Sermon**

Matthew 7:28 - 8:1 / Luke 7:1

1 When Jesus had finished all of His discourse in the hearing of the people, the crowds were amazed at His teaching, for He was teaching them as one having authority, and not as their scribes.

2 When Jesus came down from the mountain large crowds followed Him, and He went to Capernaum.

Act 5 - Events In Galilee

Scene 451 **Healing A Centurion's Servant**
Capernaum, *Galilee*   spring / 31 CE   *Matthew 8:5-13 / Luke 7:2-10*

1 When Jesus entered Capernaum, a centurion, whose highly regarded slave was sick and about to die, heard about Him. 2 And he sent some Jewish elders to ask Jesus to come and save the life of his slave, who was lying at home paralyzed, and terribly tormented.

3 When the elders came to Jesus, they earnestly implored Him, saying, "He is worthy for You to grant this to him, for he loves our nation, and it was he who built our synagogue."

4 Jesus said, "I will come and heal him," and He started on His way with them.

5 When Jesus was not far from the house, the centurion said to Him, "Lord, do not trouble yourself further, for I am not worthy for You to come under my roof, and for this reason I did not even consider myself worthy to come to You; but just say the word, and my servant will be healed; 6 for I also am a man placed under authority, with soldiers under me; and I say to this one, 'Go!' and he goes, and to another, 'Come here!' and he comes, and to my slave, 'Do this,' and he does it."

7 When Jesus heard this, He marveled at him; and He turned and said to the crowd that was following, "Truly I say to you, I have not found even in Israel, anyone with such great faith!

8 "I say to you, that many will come from the east and the west, and recline at the table with Abraham, Isaac, and Jacob, in the Kingdom of Heaven; 9 but the sons of the Kingdom will be cast out into the outer darkness; in that place there will be weeping, and gnashing of teeth."

10 Then Jesus said to the centurion, "Go; it shall be done for you as you have believed." 11 And the servant was healed at that very moment.

12 When those who had been sent returned to the house, they found the slave in good health.

Scene 452 **Perfumed Feet In The Home of A Pharisee**
Capernaum, *Galilee*   summer / 31 CE   *Luke 7:36-50*

1 Now one of the Pharisees invited Jesus to dine with him, and He entered the Pharisee's house, and reclined at the table.

2 There was a woman in the city who was a sinner, and when she learned that Jesus was reclining at the table in the Pharisee's house, she brought an alabaster vial of perfume, 3 and standing behind Jesus, weeping at His feet, she began to wet His feet with her tears, and wiping them with the hair of her head, and kissing His feet, and anointing them with the perfume.

4 When the Pharisee who had invited Jesus saw this, he said to himself, "If this man were a prophet, He would know who and what sort of person this woman is who is touching Him; that she is a sinner." *continued >*

5 Jesus said to him, "Simon, I have something to say to you." He replied, "Say it, Teacher."

6 "A moneylender had two debtors: one owed five hundred denarii, and the other fifty. 7 When they were unable to repay, he graciously forgave them both. So which of them will love him more?"

8 Simon answered, and said, "I suppose the one whom he forgave more."

9 Jesus said to him, "You have judged correctly."

10 Turning toward the woman, Jesus said to Simon, "Do you see this woman? 11 When I entered your house, you gave Me no water for My feet; but she has wet My feet with her tears, and wiped them with her hair. 12 You gave Me no kiss; but she, since the time that I came in, has not ceased to kiss My feet. 13 You did not anoint My head with oil, but she has anointed My feet with perfume! 14 For this reason, I say to you, that her sins, which are many, have been forgiven, for she loved much; 15 but he who is forgiven little, loves little."

16 Then Jesus said to the woman, "Your sins have been forgiven."

17 Those who were reclining at the table with Him began to say to themselves, "Who is this man who forgives sins?"

18 And Jesus said to her, "Your faith has saved you. Go in peace."

Scene 453	**Preaching The Kingdom of God**	
	Galilee　　summer / 31 CE　　*Luke 8:1-3*	

1 Soon afterwards, Jesus began going around from one city and village to another, proclaiming and preaching the Kingdom of God.

2 The twelve apostles were with Him, and also some women who had been healed of evil spirits and sicknesses: Mary who was called Magdalene, from whom seven demons had gone out; and Joanna the wife of Chuza, Herod's steward; and Susanna; 3 and many others who were contributing to their support out of their private means.

Scene 454	**Jesus Denounces The Unrepentant Cities**	
	Galilee　　summer / 31 CE　　*Matthew 11:20-24 / Luke 10:12-15*	

1 Then Jesus began to denounce the cities in which most of His miracles were done, because they did not repent.

2 "Woe to you, Chorazin! Woe to you, Bethsaida! For if the miracles had been performed in Tyre and Sidon which occurred in you, they would have repented long ago, sitting in sackcloth and ashes. 3 Nevertheless, I say to you, that it will be more tolerable for Tyre and Sidon in the day of judgment, than for you!

4 "And you, Capernaum, you will not be exalted to Heaven - you will be brought down to Hades; for if the miracles had occurred in Sodom which occurred in you, it would have remained to this day. 5 Nevertheless, I say to you, that it will be more tolerable for the land of Sodom in the day of judgment, than for you."

Scene 455   **Come to Me - My Burden Is Light**
          Galilee   summer / 31 CE   *Matthew 11:25-30 / Luke 10:21-22*

---

1 At that time, Jesus rejoiced greatly in the Holy Spirit, and said, "I praise You, O Father, Lord of Heaven and earth, that You have hidden these things from the wise and intelligent, and have revealed them to infants. 2 Yes, Father, for this way was well-pleasing in Your sight.

3 "All things have been handed over to Me by My Father; 4 and no one knows who the Son is except The Father, and nor does anyone know who The Father is except the Son, 5 and anyone to whom the Son wills to reveal Him.

6 "Come to Me, all who are heavy-laden and weary, and I will give you rest. 7 Take My yoke upon you, and learn from Me, for I am gentle and humble in heart, and you will find rest for your souls; for My yoke is easy, and My burden is light."

```
Act 6 - On Good and Evil Spirits
```

Scene 461   **You Heal by Beelzebul**
          Capernaum, *Galilee*   summer / 31 CE
          Matthew 12:22-24 / Mark 3:20-22 / Luke 11:14-16

---

1 When Jesus came home, the crowd gathered together again, to such an extent that they could not even eat a meal. 2 When His own people heard this, they went to take custody of Him, for they were saying, "He has lost His senses!"

3 Then a demon-possessed man who was blind and mute was brought to Jesus; and He cast out the demon and healed him, so that the mute man spoke and saw. 4 All the crowds were amazed, and were saying, "This man cannot be the Son of David, can he?"

5 But when the Pharisees and the scribes who had come down from Jerusalem heard this, some of them were saying, "He is possessed by Beelzebul!"; 6 and "This man casts out the demons only by the ruler of the demons."

7 Others tested Jesus by demanding a sign out of Heaven from Him.

Scene 462   **How Can Satan Cast Out Satan?**
          Matthew 12:25-29 / Mark 3:23-27 / Luke 11:17-22

---

1 Knowing their thoughts, Jesus called them to Himself, and began speaking to them in parables.

2 He said to them, "How can Satan cast out Satan? 3 If any kingdom is divided against itself that kingdom cannot stand, and is laid waste. 4 And if any house or city is divided against itself, it will not be able to stand, and falls.

5 "So, if Satan has risen up against himself, and casts out Satan, he also is divided against himself. How then will his kingdom stand? He cannot stand, but is finished!

6 "You say that I cast out demons by Beelzebul; and if I cast out demons by Beelzebul, by whom do your sons cast them out? So for this reason, they will be your judges. *continued >*

7 "But if I cast out demons by the Spirit of God, then the Kingdom of God has come upon you!

8 "When a strong man, fully armed, guards his own house, his possessions are undisturbed. 9 But when someone stronger than he attacks him, and over-powers him, he takes away from him all of his armor on which he had relied, and distributes his plunder.

10 "But no one can enter the strong man's house to plunder and carry off his property unless he first binds the strong man, and then he will plunder his house."

Scene 463 **The Unforgivable Sin**
Matthew 12:30-32 / Mark 3:28-30 / Luke 11:23; 12:10

1 "He who is not with Me is against Me, and he who does not gather with Me scatters. 2 Therefore, truly I say to you, all sins, and whatever blasphemies people utter, shall be forgiven the sons of men; 3 but whoever blasphemes against the Holy Spirit is guilty of an eternal sin, and shall never be forgiven.

4 "Whoever speaks a word against the Son of Man, it shall be forgiven him; 5 but whoever blasphemes against the Holy Spirit, it will not be forgiven him, either in this age, or in the age to come." - 6 because they were saying, "He has an unclean spirit."

Scene 464 **On Good and Evil** *Matthew 12:33-37 / Luke 6:45*

1 "Either make the tree good and its fruit good, or make the tree bad and its fruit bad; for the tree is known by its fruit. 2 You brood of vipers, how can you, being evil, speak what is good?

3 "The good man, out of the good treasure of his heart, brings forth what is good; and the evil man, out of his evil treasure, brings forth what is evil; for the mouth speaks of that which fills the heart.

4 "I tell you that in the day of judgment, people shall give an accounting for every careless word that they speak; 5 for by your words you will be justified, and by your words you will be condemned."

Scene 465 **A Wicked Generation Seeks A Sign**
Matthew 12:38-42 / Luke 11:29-32

1 Then some of the scribes and Pharisees said to Jesus, "Teacher, we want to see a sign from You!"

2 As the crowds were increasing, Jesus answered, and said to them, "This generation is an evil and adulterous generation because it seeks for a sign; and yet no sign will be given to it, but the sign of Jonah the prophet. 3 For just as Jonah was three days and three nights in the belly of the sea monster, and became a sign to the Ninevites, so will the Son of Man be to this generation - three days and three nights in the heart of the earth.

4 "The men of Nineveh will stand up with this generation at the judgment, and they will condemn it, because they repented at the preaching of Jonah; 5 and behold, something greater than Jonah is here! *continued >*

Scene 465 - *continued*

6 "The Queen of the South will rise up with the men of this generation at the judgment, and condemn them, because she came from the ends of the earth to hear the wisdom of Solomon; 7 and behold, something greater than Solomon is here."

Scene 466   **On Unclean Spirits**
                   Matthew 12:43-45 / Luke 11:24-28

1 "Now when the unclean spirit goes out of a man, it passes through waterless places seeking rest, and does not find any. 2 Then it says, 'I will return to my house from which I came'; and when it comes, it finds it unoccupied, swept, and put in order.

3 "Then it goes and takes along with it seven other spirits more evil than itself, and they go in, and live there; and the last state of that man becomes worse than the first. 4 That is the way it will also be with this evil generation."

5 While Jesus was saying these things, one of the women in the crowd raised her voice, and said to Him, "Blessed is the womb that bore You, and the breasts at which You nursed!"

6 But He said, "On the contrary; Blessed are those who hear the Word of God, and observe it!"

Scene 467   **Woe to You Pharisees!**
         Capernaum, *Galilee*   summer / 31 CE   *Luke 11:37-44*

1 When He had spoken, a Pharisee asked Jesus to have lunch with him; and He went in, and reclined at the table. 2 The Pharisee was surprised that Jesus had not first ceremonially washed before the meal.

3 But the Lord said to him, "Now you Pharisees clean the outside of the cup and of the platter, but inside of you, you are full of robbery and wickedness. 4 You foolish ones! Did He who made the outside not also make the inside? 5 So give that which is within as charity, and then all things are clean for you.

6 "But woe to you Pharisees! For you pay tithe of mint and rue, and every kind of garden herb, and yet disregard justice, and the love of God; these are the things that you should have done, without neglecting the others.

7 "Woe to you Pharisees! For you love the chief seats in the synagogues, and the respectful greetings in the market places.

8 "Woe to you! For you are like concealed tombs, and the people who walk over them are unaware of it!"

Scene 468   **Woe to You Lawyers as Well!**
                                Luke 11:45-46, 52 - 12:1

1 One of the lawyers said to Jesus in reply, "Teacher, when You say this, You insult us too."

2 So Jesus said, "Woe to you lawyers as well! For you weigh men down with burdens that are hard to bear, while you yourselves will not touch the burdens with even one of your fingers!

3 "Woe to you lawyers! For you have taken away the key of knowledge; 4 you yourselves did not enter, and you hindered those who were entering."

5 When Jesus left there, the scribes and the Pharisees began to be very hostile, and to question Him closely on many subjects, plotting to catch Him in something that He might say.

6 Under these circumstances, after so many thousands of people had gathered together that they were stepping on one another, Jesus began saying to His disciples, "Beware of the leaven of the Pharisees, which is hypocrisy."

Scene 469   **Who Are My Mother and My Brothers?**
                    Matthew 12:46-50 / Mark 3:31-35 / Luke 8:19-21

1 While Jesus was still speaking to the crowds, behold, His mother and brothers arrived, and were standing outside, unable to get to Him because of the crowd. 2 Seeking to speak to Him, they sent word, and called Him.

3 A crowd was sitting around Jesus, and someone reported to Him, "Behold, Your mother and Your brothers are standing outside, wishing to speak to you."

4 But Jesus answered the one who was telling Him, and said, "Who is My mother, and who are My brothers?"

5 Looking about at those who were sitting around Him, Jesus stretched out His hand toward His disciples, and said, "Behold My mother, and My brothers! 6 My mother and My brothers are these who hear the Word of God, and do it. 7 For whoever does the will of God, My Father who is in Heaven, he is My brother, and sister, and mother."

> ## Act 7 - Parables About The Kingdom

Scene 471   **The Parable of The Sower a)**
Sea of Galilee, Capernaum, *Galilee*   *Matthew 13:1-9 / Mark 4:1-9 / Luke 8:4-8*

1 That day Jesus went out of the house, and was sitting by the sea.

2 He began to teach again, and such a very large crowd was journeying from the various cities and gathering to Him, that He got into a boat in the sea, and sat down. 3 The whole crowd was standing on the beach by the sea, and He was teaching them many things in parables.

4 In His teaching He was saying to them, "Listen to this! Behold, the sower went out to sow his seed; 5 and as he sowed, some seeds fell beside the road, and they were trampled under foot, and the birds of the air came and ate them up.

6 "Other seeds fell on rocky ground, where they did not have much soil; and immediately they sprang up because they had no depth of soil. 7 But as soon as they grew up, after the sun had risen, they were scorched, and because they had no root they withered away. 8 Other seed fell among the thorns, and the thorns grew up with them, and choked them out, and they yielded no crop.

9 "Other seeds fell on the good soil, and as they grew up and increased they yielded a crop; and some produced thirty, some sixty, and some a hundred times as much."

10 As Jesus was saying these things, He would call out, "He who has ears to hear, let him hear!"

Scene 472   **Why Do You Speak To Them In Parables?**
Capernaum, *Galilee*   *Matthew 13:10-11, 13-17 / Mark 4:10-13 / Luke 8:9-10; 10:23-24*

1 As soon as Jesus was alone, His disciples, along with the twelve, came and asked Him, "Why do You speak to them in parables?" and they began questioning Him as to what this parable meant.

2 Turning to the disciples, Jesus answered them privately, and said, "To you it has been granted to know the mysteries of the Kingdom of Heaven, but to the rest who are outside, it has not been granted. 3 Therefore, I speak everything to them in parables, so that while seeing they may see and not perceive, and while hearing they may hear, and not understand.

4 "In their case, the prophecy of Isaiah is being fulfilled, which says, 'You will keep on hearing, but will not understand; you will keep on seeing, but will not perceive; 5 for the heart of this people has become dull; with their ears they scarcely hear, and they have closed their eyes, 6 otherwise they would see with their eyes, hear with their ears, and understand with their heart, and return, and be forgiven, and I would heal them.'

7 "But blessed are your eyes, because they see the things you see; and your ears, because they hear! 8 For truly I say to you, that many prophets, kings, and righteous men, desired to see the things which you see, and they did not see them; and to hear the things which you hear, and they did not hear them." 9 And He said to them, "Do you not understand this parable? How will you understand all the parables?"

Scene 473   **The Parable of The Sower b) Explained**
Matthew 13:12, 18-23 / Mark 4:14-20, 24-25 / Luke 8:11-15, 18

1 "Hear then the parable of the sower: The sower sows the seed, and the seed is the Word of God.

2 "Those who are beside the road where the seed is sown are the ones who have heard; and when they hear the Word of the Kingdom, and do not understand it, then immediately the evil one - Satan, the Devil - comes, and takes away the Word which has been sown in their heart, so that they will not believe, and be saved.

3 "In a similar way are the ones on whom seed was sown on the rocky soil; these are the ones who, when they hear the Word, they immediately receive it with joy; and yet, they have no firm root in themselves, and are only temporary; 4 they believe for a while, and then in time of temptation, or when affliction or persecution arises because of the Word, they immediately fall away.

5 "Others are the ones on whom the seed was sown which fell among the thorns; these are the ones who have heard the Word, but as they go on their way, the worries of the world, and the deceitfulness of wealth and riches, and the desire for the pleasures of this life and other things, enter in and choke the Word, and it becomes unfruitful, and they bring no fruit to maturity.

6 "And the ones on whom the seed was sown in the good soil are the ones who hear the Word in a good and honest heart; and they understand it, and accept it, and hold it fast, and indeed bear fruit with perseverance; and they bring forth, some thirty, some sixty, and some a hundred times as much."

7 And Jesus said to them, "So take care what you listen to, and how you listen. 8 By your standard of measure it will be measured to you, and even more will be given to you.

9 "For whoever has, to him more shall be given; and he will have an abundance; 10 but whoever does not have, even what he thinks he has shall be taken away from him."

Scene 474   **The Parable of The Tares a)**
Matthew 13:24-30 / Mark 4:26-29

1 Jesus said, "The Kingdom of God is like a man who casts seed upon the soil, and he goes to bed at night and gets up by day; and the seed sprouts and grows - how, he himself does not know. 2 The soil produces crops by itself; first the blade, then the head, then the mature grain in the head. 3 And when the crop permits, he immediately uses the sickle, because the harvest has come."

4 He presented another parable to them, saying, "The Kingdom of Heaven may be compared to a man who sowed good seed in his field. 5 But while his men were sleeping, his enemy came and sowed tares among the wheat, and went away. 6 Later, when the wheat sprouted and bore grain, then the tares also became evident.

7 "The slaves of the landowner came to him, and said, 'Sir, did you not sow good seed in your field? How then does it have tares?'

8 "He said to them, 'An enemy has done this.'

9 "His slaves said, 'Do you want us to go and gather them up?'   *continued >*

Scene 474 - *continued*

10 "But he said, 'No; for while you are gathering up the tares, you may also uproot the wheat with them. 11 Allow both to grow together until the harvest, and in the time of the harvest I will say to the reapers, "First gather up the tares, and bind them in bundles to burn them up; but gather the wheat into my barn."''

Scene 475   **The Kingdom of Heaven Is Like A Mustard Seed**
             Capernaum, *Galilee*   *Matthew 13:31-32 / Mark 4:30-32 / Luke 13:18-19*

1 Jesus presented another parable to them, and said, "What is the Kingdom of God like, and to what shall I compare it?

2 "The Kingdom of Heaven is like a mustard seed, which a man took and sowed in his garden. 3 When sown upon the soil, it is smaller than all the other seeds, but when it is full grown it is larger than all the garden plants, and forms large branches and becomes a tree, so that the birds of the air can come and nest in its branches."

Scene 476   **More Parables About The Kingdom of Heaven**
             Matthew 13:33-36~, 44-52 / Mark 4:33-34 / Luke 13:20-21

1 Again Jesus said, "To what shall I compare the Kingdom of God?" and He spoke another parable to them: 2 "The Kingdom of Heaven is like leaven, which a woman took and hid in three measures of flour, until it was all leavened.

3 "The Kingdom of Heaven is like a treasure hidden in the field, which a man found and then hid again; and for the joy of it, he goes and sells all that he has, and buys that field.

4 "Again, the Kingdom of Heaven is like a merchant seeking fine pearls, and upon finding one pearl of great value, he went and sold all that he had, and bought it.

5 "Again, the Kingdom of Heaven is like a dragnet that is cast into the sea, and gathered every kind of fish; and when the net was filled, they drew it up on to the beach. 6 Then they sat down, and they gathered the good fish into containers, but the bad ones they threw away. 7 So it will be at the end of the age; the angels will come forth and take out the wicked from among the righteous, and they will throw them into the furnace of fire; in that place there will be weeping, and gnashing of teeth."

8 Jesus asked them, "Have you understood all these things?" They said to Him, "Yes."

9 Then He said to them, "Therefore every scribe who has become a disciple of the Kingdom of Heaven is like the head of a household, who brings out his treasure of both old things and new."

10 With many such parables Jesus was speaking the Word to the crowds, as much as they were able to hear it; and He did not speak to them without a parable, 11 but He was explaining everything privately to His disciples. 12 This was to fulfill what was spoken through the prophet: "I will open My mouth in parables; I will utter things hidden since the foundation of the world!"

13 Then Jesus left the crowds, and went into the house.

Scene 477   **The Parable of The Tares b) Explained**   *Matthew 13:~36-43, 53*

1 The disciples of Jesus came to Him, and said, "Explain to us the parable of the tares of the field."

2 He said, "The One who sows the good seed is the Son of Man, and the field is the world. 3 As for the good seed, these are the sons of the Kingdom; 4 and the tares are the sons of the evil one, and the enemy who sowed them is the Devil. 5 The harvest is the end of the age, and the reapers are angels.

6 "So just as the tares are gathered up, and burned with fire, so shall it be at the end of the age: 7 The Son of Man will send forth His angels, and they will gather out of His Kingdom all of the stumbling blocks, and those who commit lawlessness, and they will throw them into the furnace of fire; in that place there will be weeping, and gnashing of teeth. 8 Then the righteous will shine forth as the sun in the Kingdom of their Father. 9 He who has ears, let him hear." 10 When Jesus had finished these parables, He departed from there.

Act 8 - Mighty Miracles

Scene 481   **Jesus Calms The Stormy Sea**
                  Sea of Galilee, *Galilee*   summer / 31 CE
                  Matthew 8:18, 23-27 / Mark 4:35-41 / Luke 8:22-25

1 On one of those days, when evening came, a crowd was gathered around Jesus, so He gave orders to depart, and said to His apostles, "Let us go over to the other side of the sea."

2 Leaving the crowd, Jesus got into the boat, and His apostles followed Him.

3 When they launched out other boats were with them, and as they were sailing along, Jesus fell asleep on the cushion in the stern.

4 And behold, a great storm arose, and a fierce gale of wind descended upon the sea, so that the waves were breaking over the boat. 5 The boat was filling up, and they began to be in danger; 6 so they came to Jesus, and woke Him up, and said to Him, "Master, Master! Save us, Lord, we are perishing!"

7 He said to them, "Why are you afraid, you men of little faith?"

8 Then Jesus got up and rebuked the winds, and He said to the sea, "Hush, be still." 9 And the wind died down, and the surging waves stopped, and it became perfectly calm.

10 And He said to them, "Do you still not have faith?"

11 The men were very amazed and fearful, and they said to one another, "What kind of a man is this, that He commands even the winds and the sea, and they obey Him?"

Scene 482   **A Demon-Possessed Man Named Legion**
        Gergesa, *Decapolis*   *Matthew 8:28-30 / Mark 5:1-10 / Luke 8:26-31*

1 They sailed to the country of the Gerasenes, which is opposite Galilee, on the other side of the sea.

2 When Jesus got out of the boat and came onto the land, He was immediately met by a man from the city as he was coming out from the tombs. 3 He was possessed with demons, and had not put on any clothing for a long time.

Scene 482 - *continued*

4 He was not living in a house, but had his dwelling among the tombs; for the demons had seized him many times, and would drive him into the desert.

5 He was kept under guard, yet no one was able to bind him anymore, not even with a chain, because he had often been bound with shackles and chains, but he would tear apart the shackles, and break his chains in pieces; and no one was strong enough to subdue him. 6 Constantly, night and day, he was screaming among the tombs and in the mountains, and gashing himself with stones; and He was so extremely violent that no one could pass by that way.

7 Seeing Jesus from a distance, he ran up and bowed down before Him; and he cried out with a loud voice, saying, "What business do we have with each other, Jesus, Son of the Most High God? 8 Have You come here to torment us before the time? I beg You by God, do not torment me!" 9 for Jesus had commanded the unclean spirit, saying, "Come out of the man!"

10 Jesus asked him, "What is your name?"

11 He said, "My name is Legion, for we are many;" for many demons had entered into him. 12 And they began imploring Jesus earnestly not to send them into the abyss.

Scene 483   **Jesus Sends The Demons Into The Swine**

Gergesa, *Decapolis*   summer / 31 CE   *Matthew 8:30-34 / Mark 5:11-20 / Luke 8:32-39*

1 Now there was a large herd of many swine feeding nearby on the mountain, and the demons began to implore Jesus to permit them to enter into the swine, 2 saying, "If You are going to cast us out, send us into the herd of swine, so that we may enter into them."

3 Jesus gave them permission, and He said to them, "Go!"

4 Then the unclean spirits came out of the man, and entered the swine; 5 and the whole herd, about two thousand of them, rushed down the steep bank and into the sea, and drowned in the waters.

6 When their herdsmen saw what had happened they ran away; and they went and reported everything in the city, and out in the country, including what had happened to the demoniac. 7 And behold, the whole city came out to see what had happened, and to meet Jesus.

8 They came to Jesus, and observed the man from whom the demons had gone out sitting down at the feet of Jesus, clothed, and in his right mind - the very man who had had the "legion" - and they became frightened. 9 Those who had seen it described to them how the demon-possessed man had been made well, and all about the swine.

10 When they saw Jesus, all the people of the country of the Gerasenes and the surrounding district began to ask Him to leave their region, for they were gripped with great fear.

11 As Jesus was getting into the boat to return, the man from whom the demons had gone out was begging Him that he might accompany Him, 12 but Jesus did not let him, and He sent him away, saying, "Go, and return to your home, and report to your people what great things God has done for you, and how He had mercy on you."   *continued >*

13 So the man went away, and began to proclaim throughout the whole city and in Decapolis what great things Jesus had done for him; and everyone was amazed.

Scene 484   **Jairus Implores Jesus To Heal His Daughter a)**
Capernaum, *Galilee*   *Matthew 9:1, 18-19 / Mark 5:21-23, ~42~ / Luke 8:40, ~42~*

1 After getting into the boat, Jesus crossed over to the other side of the sea, and came to His own city.

2 As He returned, the people welcomed Him, and a large crowd gathered around Him, for they had all been waiting for Him, so He stayed by the seashore.

3 While Jesus was speaking to them, a synagogue official named Jairus came, who had an only daughter, about twelve years old, who was dying.

4 Seeing Jesus, Jairus bowed down at His feet, and began to earnestly implore Him to come to his house, saying, "My little daughter is at the point of death; but please, come and lay Your hand on her, so that she will get well, and live!"

5 Jesus got up and began to follow him, and so did His apostles.

Scene 485   **A Woman Is Healed of Her Hemorrhage**
Matthew 9:20-22 / Mark 5:24-34 / Luke 8:~42-48

1 As Jesus went off with Jairus, a large crowd was following Him, and pressing in on Him. 2 And a woman was there who had been suffering from a hemorrhage for twelve years, and could not be healed by anyone. 3 She had endured much at the hands of many physicians, and had spent all that she had, and was not helped at all, but rather had grown worse.

4 After hearing about Jesus, she came up in the crowd behind Him, and touched the fringe of His cloak; for she thought to herself, "If I just touch His garment, I will get well." 5 At once her hemorrhage stopped, and the flow of her blood was dried up; and she felt in her body that she was healed of her affliction.

6 Immediately Jesus, perceiving that power had gone forth from Him, turned around in the crowd, and said, "Who is the one who touched My garments?"

7 While they were all denying it, Peter said to Him, "Master, You see the people are crowding and pressing in on You, and You say 'Who touched Me?'"

8 But Jesus said, "Someone did touch Me, for I am aware that power has gone out of Me." 9 And He turned to see the woman who had done this.

10 When the woman saw that she had not escaped notice, she came in fear and trembling, and fell down before Him. 11 And she told Him the whole truth, and declared in the presence of all the people the reason why she had touched Him, and how she had been immediately healed.

12 Jesus said to her, "Daughter, take courage; your faith has made you well! 13 Go in peace, and be healed of your affliction."

Scene 486   **Jesus Heals The Daughter of Jairus b)**

Capernaum, *Galilee*   summer / 31 CE

Matthew 9:23-26 / Mark 5:35-42~, ~42-43 / Luke 8:49-56

1 While He was still speaking, someone came from the house of the synagogue official, saying, "Your daughter has died; do not trouble the Teacher anymore."

2 When Jesus overheard this, He said to Jairus, "Do not be afraid any longer; only believe, and she will be made well." 3 And He did not allow anyone to accompany Him, except Peter and James, and John, the brother of James.

4 When they came to the synagogue official's house, Jesus saw a commotion with flute-players and the crowd of people in noisy disorder, all loudly weeping and wailing, and lamenting for the girl.

5 Entering in, Jesus said to them, "Why make a commotion and weep? Stop weeping and leave - for the girl has not died, but is asleep." 6 And they began laughing at Him, knowing that she had died.

7 When the crowd had been sent out, Jesus took along the girl's father and mother, and His own companions, and entered the room where the child was.

8 Then He took her by the hand, and called to her, saying, "Talitha kum!" which translated means, "Little girl, arise!" 9 Immediately her spirit returned, and the girl got up, and began to walk.

10 Her parents were completely astounded, but Jesus gave them strict orders to tell no one about what had happened; and that she should be given something to eat.

11 This news spread throughout all that land.

Scene 487   **Two Blind Men and A Mute Demon**   *Matthew 9:27-34*

1 As Jesus went on from there, two blind men followed Him, crying out, "Have mercy on us, son of David!"

2 When He entered the house, the blind men came up to Him, and Jesus said to them, "Do you believe that I am able to do this?"

3 They said to Him, "Yes, Lord."

4 Then Jesus touched their eyes, and said, "It shall be done to you according to your faith." And their eyes were opened.

5 Jesus sternly warned them: "See that no one knows about this." 6 But they went out and spread the news about Him throughout all that land.

7 As they were going, a mute, demon-possessed man was brought to Jesus. 8 After the demon was cast out, the mute man spoke; and the crowds were amazed, and were saying, "Nothing like this has ever been seen in Israel!"

9 But the Pharisees were saying, "He casts out the demons by the ruler of the demons."

Scene 488   **Reading In His Hometown On The Sabbath**

Nazareth, *Galilee*   a Sabbath, late summer / 31 CE

Matthew 13:54~ / Mark 6:1-2~ / Luke 4:16-21

1 Jesus came to Nazareth, His hometown where He had been brought up, and His disciples followed Him.

2 When the Sabbath came, as was His custom, He entered the synagogue, and began to teach. 3 He stood up to read, and the book of the prophet Isaiah was handed to Him.

4 He opened the book, and found the place where it is written, "The Spirit of the Lord is upon Me, because He has anointed Me to preach the gospel to the poor. 5 He has sent Me to proclaim release to the captives, and recovery of sight to the blind, to set free those who are oppressed, and to proclaim the favorable year of the Lord."

6 Then Jesus closed the book, gave it back to the attendant, and sat down; and the eyes of everyone in the synagogue were fixed on Him.

7 And He said to them, "Today, this Scripture has been fulfilled in your hearing."

Scene 489   **The Nazarenes Take Offense At Jesus**

Matthew 13:~54-58 / Mark 6:~2-6~ / Luke 4:22-30

1 The many listeners were astonished, and said, "Where did this man get these things, and what is this wisdom given to Him; and such miracles as these performed by His hands?"

2 While all were speaking well of Him, and wondering at the gracious words which were falling from His lips, they were saying, "Is this not the carpenter, Joseph's son? 3 Is not His mother Mary; and His brothers: James and Joseph, and Judas and Simon? 4 And are not all of His sisters here with us? 5 Where then did this man get all these things?" And they took offense at Him.

6 So Jesus said to them, "A prophet is not without honor, except in his hometown, and among his own relatives, and in his own household. 7 Truly I say to you, that no prophet is welcome in his hometown."

8 And He said to them, "No doubt you will quote this proverb to Me, 'Physician, heal yourself! 9 Whatever we heard that was done at Capernaum, do here in your hometown as well.'

10 "But I say to you in truth, that there were many widows in Israel in the days of Elijah, when the sky was shut up for three years and six months, and a great famine came over all the land; 11 and yet Elijah was sent to none of them, but only to Zarephath in the land of Sidon, a woman who was a widow.

12 "And there were many lepers in Israel in the time of Elisha the prophet, and none of them was cleansed, but only Naaman, the Syrian."

13 All the people in the synagogue were filled with rage as they heard these things, 14 and they got up and drove Jesus out of the city, and led Him to the brow of the hill on which their city had been built, in order to throw Him down the cliff; but passing through their midst, He went on His way.

15 And He did not do many miracles there, because of their unbelief, except that He laid His hands on a few sick people, and healed them. 16 And He wondered at their unbelief.

```
┌─────────────────────────────────────────────┐
│       Act 9 - Jesus Sends The Apostles        │
└─────────────────────────────────────────────┘
```

Scene 491　　**Jesus Sends His Twelve Apostles To Preach**

Capernaum, *Galilee*　　late summer / 31 CE

Matthew 9:35 - 10:1 / Mark 6:~6-7 / Luke 9:1-2

1 Jesus was going through all the cities and villages, teaching in their synagogues and proclaiming the gospel of the Kingdom, 2 and healing every kind of disease, and every kind of sickness.

3 Seeing the people, He felt compassion for them, because they were distressed and dispirited, like sheep without a shepherd.

4 And He said to His disciples, "The harvest is plentiful, but the workers are few; therefore beseech the lord of the harvest to send out workers into his harvest."

5 Then Jesus summoned His twelve apostles; and He gave them power and authority over all of the unclean spirits, to cast out the demons, and to heal every kind of disease, and every kind of sickness.

6 And He began to send them out in pairs, to proclaim the Kingdom of God, and to perform healing.

Scene 492　　**Jesus Instructs The Apostles**

Matthew 10:5-10 / Mark 6:8-9 / Luke 9:3

1 Jesus sent the twelve out after instructing them: "Do not go to the Gentiles, and do not enter any city of the Samaritans, but rather go to the lost sheep of the house of Israel. 2 And as you go, preach, saying, 'The Kingdom of Heaven is at hand!'

3 "Heal the sick, raise the dead, cleanse the lepers, and cast out the demons. 4 Freely you received, freely give.

5 "Take nothing for your journey - neither a staff or a bag, nor bread or money. 6 Do not acquire gold or silver, or copper for your belt, but wear sandals, and do not even have two tunics, for the worker is worthy of his support."

Scene 493　　**Peace To Those Who Receive You**

Matthew 10:11-15 / Mark 6:10-11 / Luke 9:4-5

1 Jesus said to them, "Whatever city or village you enter, inquire who is worthy in it, and stay at their house until you leave that city.

2 "As you enter the house, give it your greeting. 3 If the household is worthy, let your peace come upon it; but if it is not worthy, let your peace return to you.

4 "As for those who do not receive you, nor heed your words, as you go out from that house or city shake the dust off the soles of your feet, as a testimony against them.

5 "Truly I say to you, it will be more tolerable for the land of Sodom and Gomorrah in the day of judgment, than for that city!"

Scene 494   **I Send You Out As Sheep Among Wolves**

Capernaum, *Galilee*   late summer / 31 CE   *Matthew 10:16-20 / Luke 12:11-12*

1 "Behold, I send you out as sheep in the midst of wolves; so be as shrewd as serpents, and as innocent as doves. 2 But beware of men, for they will hand you over to the courts, and scourge you in their synagogues.

3 "You will even be brought before governors and kings for My sake, as a testimony to them, and to the Gentiles.

4 "So when they bring you before the synagogues, and hand you over to the authorities and rulers, do not worry about how or what you are to speak in your defense, or what you are to say, for the Holy Spirit will teach you in that very hour what you are to say, 5 for it is not you who speak, but it is the Spirit of your Father who speaks through you."

Scene 495   **You Will Be Persecuted, But Do Not Fear**

Matthew 10:21-31 / Luke 6:40; 12:2-7

1 "Brother will betray brother to death, and a father his child; and children will rise up against parents, and cause them to be put to death.

2 "You will be hated by all because of My Name, but it is the one who has endured to the end who will be saved.

3 "Whenever they persecute you in one city, flee to the next, for truly I say to you that you will not finish going through the cities of Israel until the Son of Man comes.

4 "A disciple is not above his teacher, and nor is a slave above his master; but everyone, after he has been fully trained, will be like his teacher. 5 It is enough for the disciple that he become like his teacher, and the slave like his master.

6 "If they have called the head of the house Beelzebul, how much more will they malign the members of his household! 7 Therefore do not fear them, for there is nothing concealed that will not be revealed, or hidden that will not be known.

8 "Accordingly, whatever I tell you in the darkness, speak in the light; and what you hear whispered in your ear, proclaim upon the housetops!

9 "I say to you, My friends, do not be afraid of those who kill the body, and after that have no more that they can do, because they are unable to kill the soul. 10 But rather I will warn you whom to fear: Fear the One who, after He has killed has authority to cast into hell, and is able to destroy both body and soul. Yes, I tell you, fear Him!

11 "Are not five sparrows sold for a cent? And yet not one of them is forgotten by God, or falls to the ground apart from your Father. 12 But indeed, the very hairs of your head are all numbered; so do not fear, you are more valuable than many sparrows."

Scene 496 — Whoever Confesses The Son of Man

Capernaum, *Galilee*   late summer / 31 CE   *Matthew 10:32-33 / Luke 12:8-9*

1 "Therefore I say to you: Everyone who confesses Me before men, I, the Son of Man, will also confess him before the angels of God, and My Father who is in Heaven.

2 "But whoever denies Me before men, I will also deny him before the angels of God, and My Father who is in Heaven."

Scene 497 — I Have Not Come To Bring Peace

Matthew 10:34-36 / Luke 12:49-53

1 "I have come to cast fire upon the earth, and how I wish that it were already kindled. 2 But I have a baptism to undergo, and I am distressed until it is accomplished.

3 "Do you think that I came to bring peace on the earth? I tell you, no, but rather division, for I did not come to bring peace, but a sword! 4 I have come to set a son against his father, and a father against his son.

5 "From now on, five members in one household will be divided, three against two and two against three. 6 They will be divided mother against daughter, and a daughter against her mother; mother-in-law against daughter-in-law, and a daughter-in-law against her mother-in-law; 7 and a man's enemies will be the members of his own household."

Scene 498 — He Who Is Worthy of Me

Matthew 10:37 - 11:1

1 "He who loves his father or his mother more than Me, is not worthy of Me; and he who loves his son or daughter more than Me, is not worthy of Me. 2 And he who does not take his cross, and follow after Me, is not worthy of Me.

3 "He who has found his life will lose it; and he who has lost his life for My sake, will find it.

4 "He who receives you receives Me; and he who receives Me, receives Him who sent Me.

5 "He who receives a prophet in the name of a prophet, shall receive a prophet's reward; 6 and he who receives a righteous man in the name of a righteous man, shall receive a righteous man's reward. 7 And whoever in the name of a disciple, gives the least of My disciples even a cup of cold water to drink, truly I say to you, he shall not lose his reward."

8 When Jesus had finished giving instructions to His twelve apostles He departed from there, to teach and preach in their cities.

Scene 499 — The Apostles Go Out and Preach The Gospel

Galilee   late summer / 31 CE   *Mark 6:12-13 / Luke 9:6*

1 The twelve apostles departed, and began going throughout the villages, preaching the gospel that men should repent. 2 And they were casting out many demons, and anointing many sick people with oil, and healing them everywhere.

CHAPTER 5 - THE THIRD YEAR of His Ministry

Act 1 - The Bread of Life

Scene 511   **The Apostles Return**
Galilee   early spring / 32 CE
Matthew 14:~13-14 / Mark 6:30-34 / Luke 9:10-11 / John 6:2-3

1 When the apostles returned, Jesus went up on the mountain, and there He sat down with them; and they gave Him an account of all that they had done and taught.

2 Then He said to them, "Come away by yourselves to a secluded place, and rest for a while." For there were many people coming and going, and they did not even have time to eat.

3 Taking Him with them, they went away in the boat, and withdrew to a secluded place by themselves, near a city called Bethsaida. 4 But the crowds were aware of this, because the people saw them going, and many recognized them; and a large crowd followed Him, because they saw the signs which He was performing on those who were sick. 5 So they ran there together on foot from all of the cities, and arrived before them.

6 When Jesus went ashore, He saw the large crowd; and He felt compassion for them, because they were like sheep without a shepherd. 7 He welcomed them, and began speaking to them about the Kingdom of God, and to teach them many things; 8 and He cured those who were sick and had need of healing.

Scene 512   **Jesus Feeds A Crowd of Five Thousand**
near Tiberias, *Galilee*   April / 32 CE
Matthew 14:15-21 / Mark 6:35-44 / Luke 9:12-17 / John 6:4-14

1 When it was evening, and the day was ending, His twelve apostles came to Jesus, and said, "We are here in a desolate place and the hour is already late, so send the crowds away, that they may go into the surrounding countryside and villages, and find lodging, and buy themselves something to eat."

2 But Jesus answered, and said to them, "They do not need to go away - you give them something to eat."

3 Now the Feast of Passover was near, so Jesus, seeing the large crowd, said to Philip, "Where are we to buy bread, so that these may eat?" 4 This He was saying to test Philip, because He Himself knew what He was intending to do.

5 Philip answered Him, "Two hundred denarii worth of bread is not sufficient for everyone to receive even a little."

6 And they said to Jesus, "Shall we go and buy bread for all these people?"

7 He said to them, "How many loaves do you have? Go and look."

8 When they found out, Andrew, Simon Peter's brother, said to Him, "There is a lad here who has five barley loaves and two fish; but what are these for so many people?"   *continued >*

Scene 512 - *continued*

9 Jesus said, "Bring them here to Me."

10 Then He said to His apostles, "Have the people sit down to eat, in groups of about fifty each."

11 Now there was much grass there, so they all sat down on the green grass in groups of hundreds, and of fifties.

12 Then Jesus took the five loaves and the two fish; and looking up to heaven, He gave thanks, blessed the food, and broke the loaves. 13 And He kept giving them to the apostles, and they served them to the crowds of people who were seated.

14 Likewise, He also divided up the two fish among them all, as much as they wanted; and they all ate and were satisfied.

15 When they were filled, Jesus said to His apostles, "Gather up the leftover fragments, so that nothing will be lost."

16 So they picked up the broken pieces which were left over from the five barley loaves and the two fish by those who had eaten, and filled twelve baskets full. 17 There were in number about five thousand men who ate the loaves, besides women and children.

18 When the people saw the sign which Jesus performed, they said, "Truly, this is the Prophet who is to come into the world!"

Scene 513   Jesus Walks On The Sea of Galilee

Sea of Galilee, *Galilee*   spring / 32 CE   *Matthew 14:22-27 / Mark 6:45-50 / John 6:15-20*

1 Jesus, perceiving that the people were intending to come and take Him by force and make Him King, immediately made His apostles go down to the sea, get into the boat, and go ahead of Him to Capernaum, on the other side. 2 So they started to cross the sea, while He Himself was sending the crowds away.

3 After Jesus had bid the crowds farewell, and sent them away, He withdrew and went up on the mountain again, to pray alone by Himself.

4 When evening came, and it had become dark, the boat was already a long distance from the land, in the middle of the sea, and Jesus had not yet come to them, but was still there alone on the land.

5 The sea began to be stirred up, and the boat was being battered by the waves, because a strong wind was blowing against them.

6 Then, when they had rowed about three or four miles, in the fourth watch of the night, Jesus came to them, walking on the sea. 7 Seeing them straining at the oars, He intended to pass by them.

8 When the apostles saw Jesus walking on the sea, and drawing near to the boat, they supposed that it was a ghost and they were terrified; and they cried out in fear, for they all saw Him.

9 Immediately Jesus spoke to them, and said, "Take courage, it is I! Do not be afraid."

Scene 514   **Peter Joins Jesus On The Sea**

Sea of Galilee, *Galilee*   *Matthew 14:28-33 / Mark 6:51-52 / John 6:21*

1 Peter said to Jesus, "Lord, if it is You, command me to come to You on the water." Jesus said to him, "Come."

2 So Peter got out of the boat, and walked on the water, and came toward Jesus. 3 But upon seeing the wind he became frightened, and began to sink: and he cried out, "Lord, save me!"

4 Immediately Jesus stretched out His hand, and took hold of Peter, and said to him, "You of little faith, why did you doubt?" 5 So they were willing to receive Jesus into the boat.

6 When He got into the boat the wind stopped, and immediately the boat was at the land to which they were going. 7 They were utterly astonished, for they had not gained any insight from the incident of the loaves, but their heart was hardened.

8 And those who were in the boat worshiped Jesus, saying, "You are certainly God's Son!"

Scene 515   **Healing In Gennesaret**

Gennesaret, *Galilee*   *Matthew 14:34-36 / Mark 6:53-56*

1 When they had crossed over they came to land at Gennesaret, and moored to the shore.

2 When they got out of the boat, immediately the people of that place recognized Jesus, and they sent word into all the surrounding district; 3 and they began to carry on their pallets all who were sick, to the place they heard that Jesus was. 4 And wherever He went in the villages or the cities or the countryside, they were laying the sick in the market places, and imploring Him that they might just touch the fringe of His cloak; and as many as touched it were cured.

Scene 516   **I Am The Bread of Life**

Capernaum, *Galilee*   *John 6:22-36*

1 The next day, the crowd that stood on the other side of the sea saw that there was only one small boat there, and that the apostles of Jesus had gone away in the boat without Him. 2 Other small boats came there from Tiberias, near the place where they ate the bread, after the Lord had given thanks.

3 When the crowd seeking Jesus saw that He was not there, nor His apostles, they got into their boats, and crossed the sea to Capernaum.

4 When they found Jesus on the other side of the sea, they said to Him, "Rabbi, when did You get here?"

5 Jesus answered, and said, "Truly, truly, I say to you, you seek Me not because you saw signs, but because you ate of the loaves, and were filled. 6 Do not work for the food which perishes, but for the food which endures to eternal life, which the Son of Man will give to you; for on Him The Father, God, has set His seal."

7 Therefore they said to Him, "What shall we do, so that we may work the works of God?"

continued >

Scene 516 - *continued*

8 Jesus answered, and said to them, "This is the work of God; that you believe in Him whom He has sent."

9 So they said to Him, "What do You do for a sign, so that we may see, and believe You? What work do You perform? 10 Our fathers ate manna in the wilderness, as it is written, 'He gave them bread out of heaven to eat.' "

11 Jesus said to them, "Truly, truly, I say to you, it is not Moses who has given you the bread out of heaven, but it is My Father who gives you the true bread out of Heaven. 12 For the bread of God is that which comes down out of Heaven, and gives life to the world."

13 They said to Him, "Lord, always give us this bread!"

14 Jesus said to them, "I am the bread of life; he who comes to Me will not hunger, and he who believes in Me will never thirst.

15 "But I say to you, that you have seen Me, and yet do not believe."

Scene 517   **The Will of The Father**
          Capernaum, *Galilee*   spring / 32 CE   *John 6:37-50*

1 "All that The Father gives to Me will come to Me, and the one who comes to Me I will certainly not cast out; 2 for I have not come down from Heaven to do My own will, but to do the will of Him who sent Me.

3 "This is the will of Him who sent Me, that of all that He has given Me I lose nothing, but raise it up on the last day. 4 For this is the will of My Father, that everyone who beholds the Son, and believes in Him, will have eternal life, 5 and I Myself will raise him up on the last day."

6 Therefore the Jews were grumbling about Jesus, because He said, "I am the bread that came down out of Heaven."

7 And they were saying, "Is this not Jesus, the son of Joseph, whose father and mother we know? How does He now say, 'I have come down out of Heaven'?"

8 Jesus answered, and said to them, "Do not grumble among yourselves. No one can come to Me unless The Father who sent Me draws him; and I will raise him up on the last day.

9 "It is written in the prophets, 'And they shall all be taught of God.' 10 Everyone who has heard, and learned from The Father, comes to Me. 11 Not that anyone has seen The Father, except the One who is from God, He has seen The Father. 12 Truly, truly, I say to you, he who believes has eternal life!

13 "I am the bread of life. 14 Your fathers ate the manna in the wilderness, and they died. 15 This is the bread which comes down out of Heaven, so that one may eat of it, and not die."

Scene 518   **Eat My Flesh, and Drink My Blood**

Capernaum, *Galilee*   *John 6:51-59*

1 Jesus said, "I am the living bread that came down out of Heaven; if anyone eats of this bread, he will live forever; 2 and the bread which I will give for the life of the world is My flesh."

3 Then the Jews began to argue with one another, saying, "How can this man give us His flesh to eat?"

4 So Jesus said to them, "Truly, truly, I say to you, unless you eat the flesh of the Son of Man, and drink His blood, you have no life in yourselves. 5 He who eats My flesh, and drinks My blood, has eternal life, and I will raise him up on the last day. 6 For My flesh is true food, and My blood is true drink.

7 "He who eats My flesh and drinks My blood abides in Me, and I in him. 8 As the living Father has sent Me, and I live because of The Father, so he who eats Me will also live because of Me.

9 "This is the bread which came down out of Heaven, not as the fathers ate and died; he who eats this bread will live forever."

10 Jesus said these things in the synagogue, as He taught in Capernaum.

Scene 519   **Some Disciples Stumble At This**   *John 6:60-71*

1 When they heard this, many of His disciples said, "This is a difficult statement; who is able to hear it?"

2 Jesus, aware that His disciples grumbled at this, said to them, "Does this cause you to stumble? What then, if you see the Son of Man ascending to where He was before? 3 It is the Spirit who gives life, the flesh does not benefit.

4 "The words that I have spoken to you are Spirit, and they are life. 5 But there are some of you who do not believe." For Jesus knew from the beginning the ones who did not believe, and who it was that would betray Him.

6 And He was saying, "For this reason I said to you that no one can come to Me, unless it has been granted to them from The Father."

7 As a result of this, many of His disciples withdrew, and were not walking with Him anymore. 8 So Jesus said to the twelve, "You do not also want to go away, do you?"

9 Simon Peter answered Him, "Lord, to whom shall we go? You have the words of eternal life! 10 We have believed, and have come to know, that You are the Holy One of God."

11 Jesus answered them, "Did I Myself not choose the twelve of you, and yet one of you is a devil?" 12 Now He meant Judas, the son of Simon Iscariot, for he, one of the twelve, was going to betray Him.

Act 2 - In Galilee, and Beyond

Scene 521   **Eating With Unwashed Hands**

Capernaum, *Galilee*   summer / 32 CE   *Matthew 15:1-14 / Mark 7:1-16*

---

1 Then some Pharisees and scribes came from Jerusalem, and gathered around Jesus. 2 And they saw that some of His disciples were eating their bread with impure hands, that is, unwashed.

3 The Pharisees and the scribes asked Jesus, "Why do Your disciples not walk according to the tradition of the elders? 4 For they do not wash their hands when they eat bread, but they eat their bread with impure hands." 5 (For the Pharisees and all the Jews do not eat unless they carefully wash their hands, thus observing the traditions of the elders; 6 and when they come in from the market place they do not eat unless they first cleanse themselves; 7 and there are many other things which they observe, such as the washing of cups and pitchers, copper pots and dining couches.)

8 Jesus answered, and said to them, "Why do you yourselves transgress the commandment of God, to keep the tradition of men? 9 For You are experts at setting aside the commandment of God, in order to keep your tradition.

10 "For through Moses, God said, 'Honor your father and your mother'; and, 'He who speaks evil of his father or his mother is to be put to death.' 11 But you say, 'Whoever says to his father or his mother, "Whatever I have that would help you is Corban," ' (which means it has been given to God) so you no longer permit him to do anything to honor his father or his mother. 12 And by this you invalidate the Word of God for the sake of your tradition, which you have handed down; and you do many things such as that."

13 And He said to them, "You hypocrites! Rightly did Isaiah prophesy of you, as it is written: 'This people honors Me with their lips, but their heart is far away from Me. But in vain do they worship Me, teaching as doctrines the precepts of men!' "

14 After Jesus called the crowd to Himself, He again began saying to them, "Listen to Me, all of you - hear and understand! There is nothing outside the man which can defile him if it goes into him. 15 It is not what enters into the mouth that defiles the man, but the things which proceed out of the mouth are what defile the man. 16 If anyone has ears to hear, let him hear!"

17 Then His apostles came and said to Jesus, "Do You know that the Pharisees were offended when they heard this statement?"

18 But He answered, and said, "Every plant which My Heavenly Father did not plant shall be uprooted. 19 Leave them alone; they are the blind guides of the blind; 20 and if a blind man guides a blind man both will fall into a pit."

Scene 522 **The Things From The Heart Defile The Man**

Capernaum, *Galilee*   summer / 32 CE   *Matthew 15:15-20 / Mark 7:17-23*

1 When Jesus left the crowd and entered the house, His disciples questioned Him, and Peter said, "Explain the parable to us."

2 Jesus said to them, "Are you still so lacking in understanding also? 3 Do you not understand that anything that goes into the mouth from outside cannot defile a man because it does not go into his heart, but it passes into the stomach and is eliminated, thus purifying all foods.

4 "The things which proceed out of the mouth come from the heart, and those are what defile a man. 5 For from within, out of the heart of men, come evil thoughts; pride, envy, false witness, slander, foolishness and wickedness; deeds of coveting, as well as deceit, sensuality, fornications, adulteries, thefts, and murders. 6 All these are the evil things which proceed from within and defile a man; 7 but to eat with unwashed hands does not defile him."

Scene 523 **The Wisdom of A Canaanite Woman**

District of Tyre near Sidon, *Phoenicia*   *Matthew 15:21-28 / Mark 7:24-30*

1 Jesus got up and went away from there, and withdrew to the district of Tyre and Sidon. 2 He entered a house, and wanted no one to know of it, and yet He could not escape notice.

3 After hearing of Jesus, a Canaanite woman of the Syrophoenician race from that region came out, whose little daughter had an unclean spirit.

4 Immediately she came and fell at His feet, and began to cry out, saying, "Have mercy on me, Lord, son of David! My daughter is cruelly demon-possessed." 5 And she kept asking Jesus to cast the demon out of her daughter, but He did not answer her a word.

6 His disciples came and implored Him, saying, "Send her away, because she keeps shouting at us."

7 But Jesus answered, and said, "I was sent only to the lost sheep of the house of Israel."

8 Then she bowed down before Him, saying, "Lord, help me!"

9 He answered her, "Let the children be satisfied first; for it is not good to take the children's bread, and throw it to the dogs."

10 She said to Him, "Yes, Lord, but even the dogs under the table feed on the children's crumbs, which fall from their master's table."

11 Then Jesus said to her, "O woman, your faith is great! Because of this answer it shall be done for you as you wish. Go; the demon has gone out of your daughter." 12 And her daughter was healed at once.

13 Going back to her home, the woman found the child lying on the bed, the demon having left.

Scene 524   **Jesus Restores The Hearing of A Deaf Man**

Decapolis   summer / 32 CE   *Matthew 15:29-31 / Mark 7:31-37*

1 Departing from there, Jesus passed through Sidon; and leaving the district of Tyre He traveled to the Sea of Galilee, within the region of Decapolis.

2 Having gone up on the mountain, Jesus was sitting there; and large crowds came to Him, bringing with them those who were lame, crippled, blind, mute, and many others; and they laid them down at His feet, and He healed them.

3 They brought to Him one who was deaf and spoke with difficulty, and they implored Him to lay His hand on him. 4 Jesus took him by himself, aside from the crowd, and put His fingers into the man's ears.

5 After spitting, Jesus touched his tongue with the saliva; and looking up to heaven with a deep sigh, He said to him, "Ephphatha!" that is, "Be opened!" 6 And immediately his ears were opened, and the impediment of his tongue was removed, and he began to speak clearly.

7 The crowd marveled as they saw the mute speaking, the crippled restored, the lame walking, and the blind seeing. 8 And they were utterly astonished, saying, "He has done all things well. He makes even the deaf to hear, and the mute to speak!" 9 And they glorified the God of Israel.

10 Jesus gave them orders not to tell anyone; but the more He ordered them, the more widely they continued to proclaim it.

Scene 525   **Jesus Feeds Four Thousand People**

Decapolis   *Matthew 15:32-38 / Mark 8:1-9*

1 In those days, there was again a large crowd, and they had nothing to eat.

2 Jesus called His apostles to Him, and said, "I feel compassion for the people, because they have now remained with Me for three days, and have nothing to eat. 3 I do not want to send them away hungry to their homes, for some of them have come from a great distance, and they might faint on the way."

4 His apostles said to Him, "Where will we be able to find enough loaves of bread here in this desolate place, to satisfy such a large crowd of people?"

5 Jesus asked them, "How many loaves do you have?" They said, "Seven."

6 Then Jesus directed the people to sit down on the ground, and taking the seven loaves, He gave thanks, and broke them. 7 Then He started giving them to His apostles to serve, and they served them to the people.

8 They also had a few small fish, and after Jesus had blessed them, He ordered these to be served as well.

9 They all ate and were satisfied; and they picked up seven large baskets full of the broken pieces that were left over. 10 There were about four thousand men who ate, besides women and children; and then Jesus sent them away.

Scene 526　　**The Pharisees and Sadducees Seek A Sign**

Dalmanutha, *Galilee*　　summer / 32 CE

Matthew 15:39 - 16:4~ / Mark 8:10-12 / Luke 12:54-56

1 After sending the crowds away, Jesus got into the boat with His disciples, and came to the district of Dalmanutha, in the region of Magadan.

2 The Pharisees and Sadducees came and began to argue with Jesus; and to test Him, they asked Him to show them a sign from Heaven.

3 Sighing deeply in His spirit, He said to them, "Why does this generation seek for a sign?

4 "When you see a cloud rising in the west, immediately you say, 'A shower is coming,' and so it turns out; 5 and when you see a south wind is blowing, you say, 'It will be hot today,' and it turns out that way. 6 You hypocrites! You know how to analyze the appearance of the earth and the sky, but why can you not discern the signs of this present time?

7 "Truly I say to you, an evil and adulterous generation seeks for a sign; 8 and no sign will be given to this generation, except the sign of Jonah."

Scene 527　　**Beware Of The Leaven of The Pharisees**

Sea of Galilee, *Galilee*　　summer / 32 CE　　*Matthew 16:~4-12 / Mark 8:13-21*

1 Leaving them, Jesus embarked with His apostles, and they crossed to the other side of the sea. 2 They had forgotten to bring any bread, and did not have more than one loaf in the boat with them.

3 Jesus was giving orders to them, saying, "Watch out! Beware of the leaven of the Pharisees and of the Sadducees, and the leaven of Herod!"

4 So they began to discuss with one another the fact that they had no bread, saying, "He said that because we did not bring any bread."

5 But Jesus, aware of this, said to them, "You men of little faith! Why do you discuss the fact that you have no bread? 6 Do you not yet see or understand? Do you have a hardened heart? 7 Having eyes, do you not see? And having ears, do you not hear?

8 "Do you not remember when I broke the five loaves for the five thousand? And how many baskets full of broken pieces did you pick up?" They said to Him, "Twelve."

9 "Or when I broke the seven loaves for the four thousand, and how many large baskets did you pick up?" They said, "Seven."

10 Then He said to them, "So how is it that you do not yet understand, that I did not speak to you concerning bread, but to beware of the leaven of the Pharisees, and of the Sadducees?"

11 Then they understood that He did not say to beware of the leaven of bread, but of the teachings of the Pharisees, and the Sadducees.

Scene 528 **Healing A Blind Man At Bethsaida**

Bethsaida, *Trachonitis*   summer / 32 CE   *Mark 8:22-26*

1 When they came to Bethsaida, they brought a blind man to Jesus, and implored Him to touch him.

2 Taking the blind man by the hand, Jesus brought him out of the village. 3 Then after spitting on his eyes, and laying His hands on him, Jesus asked him, "Do you see anything?"

4 He looked up, and said, "I see men! But I see them like trees, walking around."

5 Again Jesus laid His hands on the man's eyes; and when he looked intently he was restored, and began to see everything clearly.

6 And Jesus sent him to his home, saying, "Do not enter the village."

Scene 529   **Healing A Crippled Woman On The Sabbath**

Bethsaida, *Trachonitis*   a Sabbath, summer / 32 CE   *Luke 13:10-17*

1 Jesus was teaching in one of the synagogues on the Sabbath, and a woman was there who for eighteen years had a sickness caused by a spirit, who was bent over, and could not straighten up at all.

2 When Jesus saw her, He called her over, and said to her, "Woman, you are freed from your sickness." 3 Then He laid His hands on her, and immediately she was made erect again, and began glorifying God.

4 But the synagogue official, indignant because Jesus had healed on the Sabbath, began saying to the crowd, "There are six days in which work should be done, so come during them and get healed, and not on the Sabbath day!"

5 But the Lord answered him, and said, "You hypocrites! Does not each of you on the Sabbath untie his ox or his donkey from the stall, and lead him away to water him? 6 And this woman, a daughter of Abraham as she is, whom Satan has bound for eighteen long years, should she not have been released from this bond on the Sabbath day?"

7 As Jesus said this, all of His opponents were being humiliated; and the entire crowd was rejoicing over all of the glorious things being done by Him.

Act 3 - A Trip To Trachonitis

Scene 531   **Who Do The People Say That I Am?**

Caesarea Philippi, *Trachonitis*   summer / 32 CE
Matthew 16:13-20 / Mark 8:27-30 / Luke 9:18-21

1 Jesus went out with His apostles, and came to the villages in the district of Caesarea Philippi.

2 On the way, it happened that while He was praying alone with His apostles, He questioned them saying, "Who do the people say that I am?"

3 They answered Him, saying, "Some say John the Baptist, and others say Elijah; but still others, that Jeremiah, or one of the prophets of old, has risen again."

4 Jesus continued questioning them, and asked, "But who do you say that I am?"

5 Simon Peter answered, and said to Him, "You are the Christ, the Son of the living God."

6 Jesus said to him, "Blessed are you, Simon Barjona, because flesh and blood did not reveal this to you, but My Father who is in Heaven.

7 "I also say to you that you are Peter, and upon this rock I will build My Church; and the gates of Hades will not overpower it! 8 I will give you the keys of the Kingdom of Heaven; and whatever you bind on earth will be bound in Heaven, and whatever you loose on earth will be loosed in Heaven."

9 Then He warned the apostles, and instructed them that they should not tell anyone that He was the Christ.

Scene 532   **Jesus Rebukes Peter**

Caesarea Philippi, *Trachonitis*   *Matthew 16:21-23 / Mark 8:31-33 / Luke 9:22*

1 From that time, Jesus began to teach His disciples that He must go to Jerusalem, saying, "The Son of Man must suffer many things, and be rejected by the elders, and the chief priests and the scribes, and be killed; and on the third day be raised up again."

2 He was stating the matter plainly, but Peter took Him aside, and began to rebuke Him, saying, "God forbid it, Lord! This shall never happen to You."

3 Jesus turned around, and seeing His apostles He rebuked Peter, and said to him, "Get behind Me, Satan! 4 You are a stumbling block to Me, for you are not setting your mind on God's interests, but on man's."

Scene 533   **If Anyone Wishes To Follow Me**

Matthew 16:24-28 / Mark 8:34 - 9;1 / Luke 9:23-27

1 Then Jesus summoned the crowd with His disciples, and He said to them all, "If anyone wishes to come after Me, he must deny himself, and take up his cross every day, and follow Me.

2 "For whoever wishes to save his life will lose it; but whoever loses his life for My sake, and the gospel's, he is the one who will save it.   *continued >*

Scene 533 - *continued*

3 "For what will it profit a man if he gains the whole world, but loses himself, and forfeits his soul? 4 What will a man give in exchange for his soul?

5 "For whoever is ashamed of Me and My words in this sinful and adulterous generation, the Son of Man will also be ashamed of him when He comes in His glory, and the glory of His Father, with the holy angels.

6 "For the Son of Man is going to come in the glory of His Father with His angels, and then He will repay every man according to his deeds."

7 And Jesus said to them, "Truly I say to you, that some of those who are standing here who will not taste death until they see the Son of Man coming in the Kingdom of God, after it has come with power!"

Scene 534   **Jesus Is Transfigured With Moses and Elijah**
Mount Hermon, *Trachonitis*   summer / 32 CE
Matthew 17:1-9 / Mark 9:2-10 / Luke 9:28-36~

1 Six days later, Jesus took Peter and James, and John his brother, and led them up on a high mountain, to pray by themselves.

2 While Jesus was praying, He was transfigured before them; and the appearance of his face became different, and shone like the sun, 3 and His garments became radiant and exceedingly white, and gleaming as light - as no launderer on earth can whiten them.

4 And behold, two men, Moses along with Elijah, appeared to them, and they were talking with Jesus. 5 Appearing in glory, they were speaking of His departure which He was about to fulfill at Jerusalem.

6 Now Peter and his companions had been overcome with sleep, but when they were fully awake they saw His glory, and the two men standing with Him.

7 As they were leaving, Peter said to Jesus, "Master, it is good for us to be here! If you wish, let us make three tabernacles; one for You, and one for Moses, and one for Elijah" - 8 not realizing what he was saying, for he did not know what to answer, for they were terrified.

9 While Peter was still speaking, a bright cloud formed, and began to overshadow them; and they were afraid as they entered the cloud.

10 And behold, a voice came out of the cloud, and said, "This is My beloved Son, My Chosen One with whom I am well-pleased. Listen to Him."

11 When the apostles heard the voice they fell face down to the ground, and were terrified.

12 Jesus came to them, and touched them, and said, "Get up, and do not be afraid." 13 And lifting up their eyes they looked around, and saw no one with them anymore, except Jesus Himself alone.

14 As they were coming down from the mountain, Jesus commanded them not to relate to anyone what they had seen, saying, "Tell the vision to no one, until the Son of Man has risen from the dead."

15 They seized upon that statement, discussing with one another what "rising from the dead" meant.

Scene 535   **Why Must Elijah Come First?**

Mount Hermon, *Trachonitis*   *Matthew 17:10-13 / Mark 9:11-13 / Luke 9:~36*

---

1 The three apostles asked Jesus, "Why is it that the scribes say that Elijah must come first?"

2 He answered, and said to them, "Elijah does come first, and will restore all things. 3 And yet, how is it written of the Son of Man, that He will suffer many things, and be treated with contempt?

4 "But I say to you that Elijah has indeed already come, and they did not recognize him, but they did to him whatever they wished, just as it is written of him. 5 So also is the Son of Man going to suffer at their hands."

6 Then the apostles understood that He had spoken to them about John the Baptist. 7 And they kept silent, and reported to no one in those days any of the things which they had seen.

Scene 536   **Jesus Cures A Demon-Possessed Boy**

Matthew 17:14-18 / Mark 9:14-27 / Luke 9:37-43~

---

1 The next day, when they had come down from the mountain and back to the apostles, they saw a large crowd around them, and some scribes arguing with them. 2 When the crowd saw Jesus they were amazed, and immediately began running up to greet Him.

3 When Jesus came to the crowd, He asked His apostles, "What are you discussing with them?"

4 A man from the crowd came up to Jesus, and falling on his knees before Him, answered saying, "Teacher, I brought You my son. I beg you to have mercy on him, for he is my only boy. 5 He is a lunatic and is very ill, possessed by a spirit which makes him mute; and it has often thrown him into both the fire and the water, to destroy him. 6 Whenever it seizes him he suddenly screams, and it slams him to the ground, and throws him into a convulsion; and he foams at the mouth and grinds his teeth, and stiffens out; 7 and only with difficulty does it leave him, mauling him as it goes. 8 I brought him to your disciples, and begged them to cast it out, but they could not cure him."

9 Jesus answered, and said, "O you unbelieving and perverted generation! How long shall I be with you, and how long shall I put up with you? 10 Bring your son here to Me."

11 They brought the boy to Him; and while he was approaching, immediately when he saw Jesus the demon slammed the boy to the ground, and threw him into a convulsion; and he began rolling around, and foaming at the mouth.

12 Jesus asked his father, "How long has this been happening to him?"

13 He said, "From childhood. But if You can do anything, take pity on us, and help us."

14 Jesus said to him, "If you can?' All things are possible to the one who believes." 15 Immediately the boy's father cried out, and said, "I do believe! Help my lack of faith."

16 When Jesus saw that a crowd was rapidly gathering, He rebuked the unclean spirit, saying, "You deaf and mute spirit, I command you: Come out of him, and do not enter him again!" *continued >*

Scene 536 - *continued*

17 After crying out, and throwing him into terrible convulsions, the demon came out of him, and the boy was cured at once; but he became so much like a corpse that most of them said, "He is dead." 18 But Jesus took him by the hand, raised him up, and gave him back to his father.

19 And they were all amazed at the greatness of God; and everyone was marveling at all that Jesus was doing.

Scene 537   **Why Could We Not Drive Out The Demon?**

        Trachonitis   *Matthew 17:19-21 / Mark 9:28-29 / Luke 17:5-6*

1 When Jesus entered the house, His apostles began questioning Him privately, and asked, "Why could we not drive out the demon?"

2 He said to them, "Because of the littleness of your faith."

3 The apostles said to the Lord, "Increase our faith!"

4 Jesus replied, "Truly I say to you, if you had faith the size of a mustard seed, you would say to this mountain, 'Be uprooted, and move from here to there' and it would obey you and move; and nothing will be impossible for you." 5 Then He said to them, "But this kind does not go out by anything except prayer and fasting."

Scene 538   **Follow Me**

        Galilee   *Matthew 8:19-22 / Mark 9:30 / Luke 9:57-62*

1 From there they went out and began to go through Galilee, and Jesus did not want anyone to know about it.

2 As they were going along the road a scribe came, and said to Jesus, "Teacher, I will follow You, wherever You go."

3 Jesus said to him, "The foxes have holes, and the birds of the air have nests, but the Son of Man has nowhere to lay His head."

4 Then Jesus said to another of the disciples, "Follow Me." But he said, "Lord, permit me first to go and bury my father."

5 Jesus said to him, "Follow Me, and allow the dead to bury their own dead. 6 But as for you, go and proclaim everywhere the Kingdom of God."

7 Another said, "I will follow You, Lord, but first, permit me to say good-bye to those at home." 8 But Jesus said to him, "No one, after putting his hand to the plow, and looking back, is fit for the Kingdom of God."

> ## Act 4 - Return to Capernaum

Scene 541   **Jesus Foreshadows His Death and Resurrection**

    Galilee   summer / 32 CE   *Matthew 17:22-23 / Mark 9:31-32 / Luke 9:~43-45*

1 While they were traveling through Galilee, Jesus was teaching His disciples; and He said to them, "Let these words sink into your ears; for the Son of Man is going to be delivered into the hands of men, and they will kill Him; 2 and when He has been killed, He will be raised on the third day."

3 But they did not understand this statement, because it was concealed from them so that they would not perceive it; 4 and they were afraid to ask Him about this statement, and were deeply grieved.

Scene 542   **Paying The Poll-Tax**

Capernaum, *Galilee*   summer / 32 CE   *Matthew 17:24-27 / Mark 9:33~*

1 When they came to Capernaum, those who collected the two-drachma tax came to Peter, and said, "Does your Teacher not pay the two-drachma tax?" He said, "Yes."

2 When Peter came into the house, Jesus spoke to him first, saying, "What do you think, Simon? From whom do the kings of the earth collect customs and poll-tax - from their sons, or from strangers?"

3 When Peter said, "From strangers," Jesus said to him, "Then the sons are exempt.

4 "However, so that we do not offend them, go to the sea and throw in a hook, and take the first fish that comes up; and when you open its mouth, you will find a shekel. 5 Take that, and give it to them, for you and Me."

Scene 543   **The Greatest In The Kingdom of Heaven**

Matthew 18:1-5 / Mark 9:~33-37 / Luke 9:46-48

1 When Jesus was in the house, He began to question the apostles, and He asked them, "What were you discussing on the way?"

2 But they kept silent, for on the way they had discussed with one another as to which of them was the greatest, and an argument had started among them.

3 They asked Jesus, "Who then, is the greatest in the Kingdom of Heaven?"

4 Knowing what they were thinking in their hearts, Jesus sat down, called the twelve, and said to them, "If anyone wants to be first, he shall be the last of all, and the servant of all."

5 And He called a child to Himself, and stood him by His side. 6 Taking him in His arms, Jesus said to them, "Truly I say to you, unless you are converted and become like children, you will not enter the Kingdom of Heaven; for the one who is least among all of you, this is the one who is great. 7 Whoever then humbles himself as this child, he is the greatest in the Kingdom of Heaven.

8 "Whoever receives one child like this in My Name receives Me; 9 and whoever receives Me, receives Him who sent Me."

Scene 544   **Do Not Cause The Children To Stumble**

Matthew 18:6, 10, 14 / Mark 9:42 / Luke 17:?

1 "See that you do not despise one of these little ones, for I say to you that their angels in Heaven continually see the face of My Father who is in Heaven.

2 "Whoever causes one of these little ones who believe in Me to stumble, it would be better for him if a heavy millstone were hung around his neck, and he were thrown into the sea, and drowned in its depth.

3 "So it is the will of your Father who is in Heaven that not one of these little ones perish."

Scene 545   On Stumbling Blocks and Hell Fire

Capernaum, *Galilee*   summer / 32 CE   *Matthew 18:7-9 / Mark 9:43-49 / Luke 17:1*

1 Jesus said to His disciples, "Woe to the world because of its stumbling blocks, for it is inevitable that stumbling blocks come, but woe to the person through whom they come.

2 "If your hand causes you to stumble, cut it off and throw it from you; for it is better for you to enter life crippled, than having your two hands to go into hell; into the eternal, unquenchable fire; 3 where their worm does not die, and the fire is not quenched.

4 "Or if your foot causes you to stumble, cut it off! It is better for you to enter life lame, than to have your two feet and be cast into hell.

5 "If your eye causes you to stumble, pluck it out and throw it from you! It is better for you to enter into life in the Kingdom of God with one eye, than to have two eyes and be cast into the fiery hell; 6 where their worm does not die, and the fire is not quenched. 7 For everyone will be salted with fire."

Scene 546   If Your Brother Sins

Matthew 18:15-20 / Luke 17:3-4

1 "Be on your guard! If your brother sins, go and show him his fault, and rebuke him in private. 2 If he listens to you, and repents, forgive him; you have won your brother! 3 And if he sins against you seven times a day, and returns to you seven times, saying, 'I repent', forgive him.

4 "But if he does not listen to you, take one or two more with you, so that by the mouth of two or three witnesses every fact may be confirmed.

5 "If he refuses to listen to them, tell it to the Church; 6 and if he refuses to listen even to the Church let him be to you as a Gentile and a tax collector. 7 For truly I say to you, whatever you bind on earth shall be bound in Heaven, and whatever you loose on earth shall be loosed in Heaven.

8 "Again I say to you, that if two of you on earth agree about anything that they may ask, it shall be done for them by My Father who is in Heaven; 9 for where two or three have gathered together in My Name, I am there in their midst."

Scene 547   On Forgiveness and The Unforgiving Slave   *Matthew 18:21-35*

1 Peter said to Jesus, "Lord, how often shall my brother sin against me, and I forgive him? Up to seven times?"

2 Jesus said to him, "I do not say to you up to seven times, but up to seventy times seven. 3 For this reason the Kingdom of Heaven may be compared to a king who wished to settle accounts with his slaves.

4 "When he began to settle them, one who owed him ten thousand talents was brought to him. 5 But since he did not have the means to repay, his lord commanded him to be sold, along with his wife and children, and all that he had, and repayment to be made.

6 "So the slave fell to the ground, and prostrated himself before him, saying, 'Have patience with me, and I will repay you everything!' 7 And the lord of that slave felt compassion, and he forgave him the debt, and released him.   *cont.* >

8 "But that slave went out and found one of his fellow slaves who owed him a hundred denarii, and he seized him, and began to choke him, saying, 'Pay back what you owe!'

9 "So his fellow slave fell to the ground, and began to plead with him, saying, 'Have patience with me, and I will repay you.' 10 But he was unwilling, and he went and threw him in prison, until he should pay back what he owed.

11 "When the other slaves saw what had happened, they were deeply grieved, and they came and reported it to their lord.

12 "His lord summoned him, and said, 'You wicked slave! I forgave you all that debt because you pleaded with me. 13 Should you not also have had mercy on your fellow slave, in the same way that I had mercy on you?' 14 And his lord, moved with anger, handed him over to the torturers, until he repaid all that he owed.

15 "My Heavenly Father will also do the same to you, if each of you does not forgive his brother from your heart."

Scene 548   **He Who Is Not Against Us Is For Us**
Mark 9:38-41 / Luke 9:49-50

1 The apostle John said to Jesus, "Master, we saw someone casting out demons in Your Name, and we tried to prevent him because he was not following along with us."

2 But Jesus said, "Do not hinder him, for there is no one who will perform a miracle in My Name, and then be able to speak evil of Me. 3 He who is not against us is for us.

4 "And whoever gives you a cup of water to drink, because of your name as a follower of Christ, truly I say to you, he will not lose his reward."

```
Act 5 - Jesus Send Seventy Disciples
```

Scene 551   **The Trials of Discipleship**
Galilee   summer / 32 CE   *Luke 14:25-33*

1 Now large crowds were traveling with Jesus, and He turned to them, and said, "If anyone comes to Me, and does not hate his own father and mother, and wife and children, and brothers and sisters, and even his own life, he cannot be My disciple. 2 Whoever does not carry his own cross, and come after Me, cannot be My disciple.

3 "For which one of you, when he wants to build a tower, does not first sit down and calculate the cost, to see if he has enough to complete it? 4 Otherwise, when he has laid a foundation, and is not able to finish, all who observe it will ridicule him, saying, 'This man began to build, and was not able to finish!'

5 "Or what king, when he sets out to meet another king in battle, will not first sit down and consider whether he is strong enough with ten thousand men to encounter the one coming against him with twenty thousand? 6 Otherwise, while the other is still far away he sends a delegation, and asks for terms of peace. 7 So then, none of you can be My disciple, who does not give up all of his own possessions."

Scene 552   **Jesus Sends Seventy Disciples To Preach**
          Capernaum, *Galilee*   summer / 32 CE   *Luke 10:1-11, 16*

1 After this, the Lord appointed seventy disciples; and He sent them out in pairs ahead of Him, to every city and place where He Himself was going to come.

2 And He said to them, "The harvest is plentiful, but the laborers are few; therefore beseech the Lord of the harvest to send more laborers out into His harvest. 3 Go! Behold, I send you out as lambs in the midst of wolves.

4 "Carry no money belt, no bag, and no shoes; and greet no one on the way.

5 "Whatever house you enter, first say, 'Peace be to this house!' 6 If a man of peace is there, your peace will rest on him; but if not, it will return to you.

7 "Stay in that house, eating and drinking what they give you, for the laborer is worthy of his wages. 8 Do not keep moving from house to house, and whichever city you enter and they receive you, eat what is set before you; 9 and heal those in it who are sick, and say to them, 'The Kingdom of God has come near to you!'

10 "But whichever city you enter and they do not receive you, go out into its streets and say, 'Even the dust of your city, which clings to our feet, we wipe off in protest against you! 11 And be sure of this, that the Kingdom of God has come near.'

12 "The one who listens to you listens to Me, and the one who rejects you rejects Me; 13 and he who rejects Me, rejects the One who sent Me."

Scene 553   **King Herod Is Perplexed About Jesus**
          Jerusalem, *Judea*   summer / 32 CE   *Matthew 14:1-2 / Mark 6:14-16 / Luke 9:7-9*

1 At that time, King Herod, the Tetrarch of Galilee, heard the news about Jesus, for His name had become well known. 2 And he was greatly perplexed, because people were saying, "This is John the Baptist! He has risen from the dead, and that is why these miraculous powers are at work in him."

3 But some were saying, "He is Elijah", and others that He is a prophet, or that one of the prophets of old had risen again.

4 But Herod said, "I myself had John beheaded, so who is this man about whom I hear such things?" 5 And he wanted to see Jesus.

```
                    Act 6 - On Dining Etiquette
```

Scene 561   **A Sabbath Meal With Pharisees**
          Capernaum, *Galilee*   a Sabbath, summer / 32 CE   *Luke 14:1-6*

1 When Jesus went into the house of one of the leaders of the Pharisees on the Sabbath to eat bread, they were watching Him closely.

2 There in front of Jesus was a man suffering from dropsy, and He asked the lawyers and the Pharisees, "Is it lawful to heal on the Sabbath, or not?" But they kept silent.

3 Then Jesus took hold of the man, and healed him, and sent him away.

4 And He said to them, "Which of you will have a son or an ox fall into a well on the Sabbath day, and not immediately pull him out?" 5 And they could make no reply to this.

Scene 562   **Do Not Take The Place of Honor**   *Luke 14:7-11*

1 Then Jesus began speaking a parable to the invited guests, when He noticed how they were picking out the places of honor at the table.

2 He said to them, "When you are invited to a wedding feast, do not take the place of honor, for someone more distinguished than you may have been invited, and the one who invited you will come and say to you, 'Give your place to this man,' and then in disgrace you will proceed to occupy the last place.

3 "But when you are invited, go and recline at the last place, so that when the one who invited you comes, they may say to you, 'Friend, move up higher', and then you will have honor in the sight of all who are at the table with you.

4 "For everyone who exalts himself will be humbled, and he who humbles himself will be exalted."

Scene 563   **Invite The Poor, and Be Blessed**   *Luke 14:12-15*

1 Jesus went on to say to the one who had invited Him, "When you give a luncheon or a dinner do not invite your friends or your brothers, or your relatives or rich neighbors, otherwise they may also invite you in return, and that will be your repayment.

2 "But when you give a reception invite the poor, the crippled, the lame, and the blind, and you will be blessed; 3 for since they do not have the means to repay you, you will be repaid at the resurrection of the righteous."

4 When one of those reclining at the table with Jesus heard this, he said to Him, "Blessed is everyone who will eat bread in the Kingdom of God!"

Scene 564   **The Seventy Disciples Return**

Capernaum, *Galilee*   summer / 32 CE   *Luke 10:17-20*

1 The seventy disciples returned with joy, saying, "Lord, even the demons are subject to us in Your Name!"

2 Jesus said to them, "I saw Satan falling like lightning from Heaven! 3 Behold, I have given you authority to tread on serpents and scorpions, and over all the power of the enemy; and nothing will injure you.

4 "Nevertheless, do not rejoice in this - that the spirits are subject to you - but rejoice that your names are recorded in Heaven."

Act 7 - A Collection of Parables

Scene 571   **The Joy Over One Sinner Who Repents**

Capernaum, *Galilee*   summer / 32 CE   *Matthew 18:11-13 / Luke 15:1-10*

1 Now all the tax collectors and the sinners were coming near Jesus to listen to Him, and both the Pharisees and the scribes began to grumble, saying, "This man receives sinners, and eats with them."

2 So Jesus told them this parable, saying, "What do you think? What man among you, if he has a hundred sheep, and one of them has gone astray, does not leave the ninety-nine in the open pasture, and go and search for the one which is lost, until he finds it? 3 And when he has found it, truly I say to you, he lays it on his shoulders, and rejoices over it more than over the ninety-nine which have not gone astray. 4 And when he comes home, he calls together his friends and his neighbors, saying to them, 'Rejoice with me, for I have found my sheep which was lost!'

5 "I tell you, in the same way there will be more joy in Heaven over one sinner who repents, than over ninety-nine righteous persons who need no repentance.

6 "Or what woman, if she has ten silver coins and loses one coin, does not light a lamp and sweep the house, and search carefully until she finds it? 7 And when she has found it, she calls together her friends and neighbors, saying, 'Rejoice with me, for I have found the coin which I had lost!'

8 "I tell you, in the same way there is joy in the presence of the angels of God over one sinner who repents. 9 For the Son of Man has come to save that which was lost."

Scene 572   **The Prodigal Son**   *Luke 15:11-24*

1 Then Jesus said, "A man had two sons. The younger of them said to his father, 'Father, give me the share of the estate that falls to me.' So the man divided his wealth between them. 2 Not many days later, the younger son gathered everything together, and went on a journey to a distant country, and there he squandered his estate with loose living.

3 "Now when he had spent everything, a severe famine occurred in that country, and he began to be impoverished. 4 So he went and hired himself out to one of the citizens of that country, who sent him into his fields to feed swine. 5 No one was giving anything to him, and he would have gladly filled his stomach with the pods that the swine were eating.

6 "When he came to his senses, he said, 'How many of my father's hired men have more than enough bread, while I am here dying from hunger? 7 I will get up and go to my father, and I will say to him, "Father, I have sinned against Heaven and in your sight. 8 I am no longer worthy to be called your son; make me as one of your hired men." ' 9 So he got up, and went to his father.

10 "While he was still a long way off, his father saw him, and felt compassion for him; and he ran and embraced him, and kissed him.   *continued >*

11 "The son said to him, 'Father, I have sinned against Heaven, and in your sight. I am no longer worthy to be called your son.'

12 "But the father said to his slaves, 'Quickly! Bring out the best robe, and put it on him; and put a ring on his hand, and sandals on his feet. 13 And bring the fattened calf, kill it, and let us eat and celebrate! For this son of mine was dead, and has come to life again; he was lost, and has been found!'

14 "And they began to celebrate."

Scene 573　　**Rejoice! Your Lost Brother Has Been Found**　　*Luke 15:25-32*

1 "Now his older son was in the field, and when he approached the house he heard music and dancing; so he summoned one of the servants, and asked them what was happening.

2 "The servant said to him, 'Your brother has come, and your father has killed the fattened calf, because he has received him back safe and sound.'

3 "Then the son became angry, and he was not willing to go in; so his father came out, and began pleading with him.

4 "But he answered, and said to his father, 'Look! For so many years I have been serving you, and I have never neglected a command of yours, and yet you have never given me even a young goat so that I might celebrate with my friends. 5 But when this son of yours comes, who has devoured your wealth with prostitutes, you kill the fattened calf for him!'

6 "His father said to him, 'Son, you have always been with me, and all that is mine is yours. 7 But we had to celebrate and rejoice, for your brother was dead, and has begun to live; he was lost, and has been found!' "

Scene 574　　　　　**The Shrewd Manager**　　　　*Luke 16:1-9*

1 Jesus also said to His disciples, "There was a rich man who had a manager, and this manager was reported to him as squandering his possessions. 2 So he called the manager, and said to him, 'What is this I hear about you? Give an accounting of your management, for you can no longer be the manager.'

3 "The manager said to himself, 'What shall I do, since my master is taking the management away from me? I am not strong enough to dig, and I am ashamed to beg. 4 I know what I shall do, so that when I am removed from the management people will welcome me into their homes.'

5 "Then He summoned each of his master's debtors; 6 and he said to the first, 'How much do you owe my master?' He said, 'A hundred measures of oil.'

7 The manager said to him, 'Take your bill, sit down, and quickly write fifty.'

8 "Then he said to another, 'How much do you owe?' He said, 'A hundred measures of wheat.' 9 The manager said to him, 'Take your bill, and write eighty.'

10 "And the rich man praised the unrighteous manager, because he had acted shrewdly; 11 for the sons of this age are more shrewd in relation to their each other, than are the sons of light.

12 "So I say to you, make friends for yourselves by means of the wealth of unrighteousness, so that when it fails they will receive you into the eternal abode."

Scene 575   **He Who Is Faithful With Little Things**

Capernaum, *Galilee*   summer / 32 CE   *Matthew 6:24 / Luke 16:10-17*

1 "He who is faithful in a very little thing is faithful also in much; 2 and he who is unrighteous in a very little thing is also unrighteous in much. 3 Therefore, if you have not been faithful in the use of unrighteous wealth, who will entrust you with true riches? 4 And if you have not been faithful with that which is another's, who will give you that which is your own?

5 "No one can serve two masters, for either he will hate the one and love the other, or he will be devoted to one and despise the other. 6 You cannot serve God and wealth."

7 Now the Pharisees, who are lovers of money, were listening to all these things, and scoffing at Him.

8 Jesus said to them, "You are those who justify yourselves in the sight of men, but God knows your hearts; 9 for that which is highly esteemed among men is detestable in the sight of God.

10 "The Law and the Prophets were proclaimed until John, and since that time the gospel of the Kingdom of God has been preached, and everyone is forcing his way into it. 11 But it is easier for the heaven and the earth to pass away, than for one stroke of a letter of the Law to fail."

Scene 576   **Lazarus and The Rich Man**   *Luke 16:19-31*

1 Then Jesus said, "There was a rich man, and he habitually dressed in purple and fine linen, joyously living in splendor every day. 2 And a poor man named Lazarus was laid at his gate, covered with sores, and longing to be fed with the crumbs which were falling from the rich man's table; and even the dogs were coming and licking his sores.

3 "Now the poor man died, and was carried away by the angels to Abraham's bosom; and the rich man also died, and was buried.

4 "In Hades, the rich man lifted up his eyes, and saw Abraham far away, and Lazarus in his bosom. 5 Being in torment, he cried out, and said, 'Father Abraham, have mercy on me, and send Lazarus so that he may dip the tip of his finger in water, and cool off my tongue, for I am in agony in this flame!'

6 "But Abraham said, 'Child, remember that during your life you received your good things, and likewise Lazarus bad things; but now he is being comforted here, and you are in agony. 7 And besides all of this, there is a great chasm between us and you, so that those who wish to go from here to you are not able, and none may cross over from there to us.'

8 "The rich man said, 'Then I beg you, father, that you send Lazarus to my father's house, for I have five brothers, in order that he may warn them, so that they will not also come to this place of torment.'

9 "But Abraham said, 'They have Moses and the Prophets; let them hear them.' 10 He said, 'No, father Abraham, but if someone goes to them from the dead, they will repent!'

11 "But Abraham said to him, 'If they do not listen to Moses and the Prophets then they will not be persuaded, even if someone rises from the dead.' "

Scene 577   **Pray, and Don't Lose Heart**   *Luke 18:1-8*

1 Jesus told them a parable, to show that at all times they should pray, and not lose heart, saying, "In a certain city there was a judge who did not fear God, and he did not respect man.

2 "And there was a widow in that city, who kept coming to him, and saying, 'Give me legal protection from my opponent!' 3 For a while he was unwilling, but later he said to himself, 'Even though I do not fear God nor respect man, yet because this widow bothers me I will give her legal protection, otherwise by continually coming, she will wear me out.' "

4 And Jesus said, "Hear what the unrighteous judge said. 5 Will God not bring about justice for His elect who cry to Him day and night, or will He delay helping them? 6 I tell you that He will bring about justice for them quickly!

7 "However, when the Son of Man comes, will He find faith on the earth?"

Scene 578   **The Pharisee and The Tax Collector**   *Luke 18:9-14*

1 Jesus also told this parable to some people who trusted in themselves that they were righteous, and who viewed others with contempt:

2 "Two men went up into the Temple to pray, one a Pharisee, and the other a tax collector.

3 "The Pharisee stood, and was praying this to himself: 'God, I thank You that I am not like other people: swindlers, unjust, adulterers, or even like this tax collector. 4 I fast twice a week, and I pay tithes of all that I get.'

5 "But the tax collector, standing some distance away, was unwilling even to lift up his eyes to Heaven, but he was beating his breast, and saying, 'God, be merciful to me, the sinner.'

6 "I tell you that this man went to his house justified rather than the other; for everyone who exalts himself will be humbled, but he who humbles himself will be exalted."

CHAPTER 6 - THE FINAL YEAR of His Ministry

Act 1 - The Feast of Tabernacles

Scene 611   **His Brothers Did Not Believe In Him**
                   Galilee   October / 32 CE   *John 7:1-9*

1 Jesus was walking in Galilee, for He was unwilling to walk in Judea, because the Jews were seeking to kill Him.

2 Now the Feast of Tabernacles was near, therefore His brothers said to Jesus, "Leave here and go into Judea, so that Your disciples may see the works which You are doing, for no one does anything in secret when he seeks to be known publicly. 3 If You do these things, show Yourself to the world." 4 For His brothers did not believe in Him.

5 Jesus said to them, "My time is not yet here, but your time is always opportune. 6 The world cannot hate you, but it hates Me, because I testify that its deeds are evil. 7 You go to the feast; I will not go to this feast yet, because My time has not come." 8 Having said these things to them, Jesus stayed in Galilee.

Scene 612   **Why Do You Seek To Kill Me?**
The Temple, Jerusalem, *Judea*   Feast of Tabernacles, October / 32 CE   *John 7:10-24*

1 When His brothers had gone up to the feast, then Jesus Himself also went up, not publicly, but in secret. 2 So the Jews were seeking Him at the feast, and saying, "Where is He?"

3 There was much grumbling among the crowds concerning Him. Some were saying, "He is a good man," but others were saying, "No, on the contrary, He leads the people astray." 4 Yet no one was speaking openly of Him for fear of the Jews.

5 When it was the middle of the Feast, Jesus went up into the Temple, and began to teach. 6 The Jews were astonished, saying, "Having never been educated, how has this man become learned?"

7 So Jesus answered them, and said, "My teaching is not Mine, but His who sent Me. 8 If anyone is willing to do His will, he will know of the teaching, whether it is of God, or whether I speak from Myself.

9 "He who speaks from himself seeks his own glory; 10 but He who is seeking the glory of the One who sent Him is true, and there is no unrighteousness in Him. 11 Did not Moses give you the Law? And yet none of you carries out the Law. 12 Why do you seek to kill Me?"

13 The crowd answered, "You have a demon! Who seeks to kill You?"

14 Jesus answered them, "I did one deed, and you all marvel. 15 Because Moses has given you circumcision - not that it is from Moses, but from the fathers - and on the Sabbath you circumcise a man. 16 If a man receives circumcision on the Sabbath, so that the Law of Moses will not be broken, are you angry with Me because I made an entire man well on the Sabbath?

17 "Do not judge according to appearance, but judge with righteous judgment."

Scene 613   **Where I Am Going You Cannot Come**
The Temple, Jerusalem, *Judea*   Feast of Tabernacles, October / 32 CE   *John 7:25-36*

1 Some of the people from Jerusalem were saying, "Is this not the man whom they are seeking to kill? 2 Look, He is speaking publicly, and they are not saying anything to Him. The rulers do not really know that this is the Christ, do they?

3 "We know where this man is from, but whenever the Christ may come, no one knows where He is from."

4 Therefore, Jesus cried out while teaching in the Temple, and said, "You both know Me, and you know where I am from. 5 And I have not come for Myself, but He who sent Me is true, whom you do not know. 6 But I know Him, because I am from Him, and He sent Me."

7 So they were seeking to seize Jesus, but no man laid his hand on Him, because His hour had not yet come.

8 Many in the crowd believed in Him, and were saying, "When the Christ comes, He will not perform more signs than this man has, will He?"

9 When the Pharisees heard the crowd muttering these things about Jesus, they and the chief priests sent attendants to seize Him.

10 Therefore Jesus said, "For a little while longer I am with you, and then I go to Him who sent Me. 11 You will seek Me, and will not find Me; and where I am you cannot come."

12 The Jews then said to one another, "Where does this man intend to go, that we will not find Him? 13 Is He intending to go into the Dispersion among the Greeks, and teach them? 14 What is this statement that He said; 'You will seek Me and will not find Me; and where I am you cannot come'?"

Scene 614   **Come To Me, and Drink**
The Temple, Jerusalem, *Judea*   Feast of Tabernacles, October / 32 CE   *John 7:37-44*

1 Now on the last day, the great day of the Feast, Jesus stood and cried out, "If anyone is thirsty, let him come to Me and drink! 2 He who believes in Me, as the has Scripture said, 'From his innermost being will flow rivers of living water.' "

3 This Jesus spoke of The Spirit, whom those who believed in Him were to receive; for The Spirit had not yet been given, because He was not yet glorified.

4 Some of the people therefore, when they heard these words, were saying, "This is certainly the Prophet," and others were saying, "This is the Christ."

5 Still others were saying, "Surely the Christ is not going to come from Galilee, is He? Has not the Scripture said that the Christ comes from the descendants of David, and from Bethlehem, the village where David was?

6 So a division occurred in the crowd because of Him. Some of them wanted to seize Jesus, but no one laid hands on Him.

Scene 615   **The Pharisees Are Divided**   *John 7:45 - 8:1*

1 The temple attendants went to the chief priests and the Pharisees, who asked them, "Why did you not bring Him?"

2 The attendants answered, "Never has a man spoken the way that this man speaks."

3 The Pharisees said to them, "You have not also been led astray, have you? No one of the rulers or Pharisees has believed in Him, has he? 4 But this crowd, which does not know the Law, is accursed!"

5 Nicodemus, who had come to Jesus before, being one of them, said, "Our Law does not judge a man unless it first hears from him, and knows what he is doing, does it?"

6 They answered him, "You are not also from Galilee, are you? Search and see, that no prophet arises out of Galilee."

7 Everyone went to his home, but Jesus went to the Mount of Olives.

Act 2 - Discussions In The Temple

Scene 621   **Jesus Forgives An Adulteress**
The Temple, Jerusalem, *Judea*   October / 32 CE   *John 8:2-11*

1 Early in the morning, Jesus came again into the Temple, and all the people were coming to Him, so He sat down, and began to teach them.

2 The scribes and the Pharisees brought a woman who was caught committing adultery; and having set her in the center of the courtyard, they said to Him, "Teacher, this woman has been caught in adultery, in the very act. 3 Now in the Law, Moses commanded us to stone such women; what then, do You say?" 4 They were saying this to test Him, so that they might have grounds to accuse Him. 5 But Jesus stooped down, and wrote on the ground with His finger.

6 When they persisted in asking Him, He straightened up, and said to them, "He who is without sin among you, let him be the first to throw a stone at her." 7 Again He stooped down, and wrote on the ground.

8 When they heard it, being convicted by their conscience, they began to go out one by one, beginning with the older ones; and He was left alone with the woman where she was, in the middle of the courtyard.

9 Straightening up, Jesus said to her, "Woman, where are they? Did no one condemn you?" She said, "No one, Lord."

10 And Jesus said, "I do not condemn you, either. Go, and from now on, sin no more."

Scene 622   **My Testimony and Judgment Is True**
The Temple Treasury, Jerusalem, *Judea*   *John 8:12-20*

---

1 Again Jesus spoke to them, saying, "I am the Light of the world. He who follows Me will not walk in darkness, but will have the Light of life."

2 The Pharisees said to Him, "You are testifying about Yourself; Your testimony is not true."

3 Jesus answered, and said to them, "Even if I testify about Myself, My testimony is true, for I know where I have come from, and where I am going; *cont. >*

4 but you do not know where I come from, or where I am going.

5 "You judge according to the flesh, but I am not judging anyone. 6 But even if I do judge, My judgment is true, for I am not alone in it, but I and The Father who sent Me.

7 "In your law it is written that the testimony of two men is true. 8 I am He who testifies about Myself, and The Father who sent Me testifies about Me."

9 So they said to Him, "Where is Your Father?"

10 Jesus answered, "You know neither Me, nor My Father. If you knew Me, you would know My Father also."

11 These words Jesus spoke in the treasury, as He taught in the Temple; and no one seized Him, because His hour had not yet come.

Scene 623   **You Are From Below, I Am From Above**   *John 8:21-30*

---

1 Then Jesus said to them again, "I go away, and you will seek Me, and you will die in your sins. 2 Where I am going, you cannot come."

3 So the Jews were saying, "Surely He will not kill Himself, will He, since He says, 'Where I am going, you cannot come'?"

4 Then Jesus said to them, "You are from below, I am from above. You are of this world, I am not of this world. 5 Therefore I said to you that you will die in your sins, because if you do not believe that I am He, you will die in your sins."

6 So they said to Him, "Who are You?"

7 Jesus said to them, "What have I been saying to you from the beginning? 8 I have many things to speak and to judge concerning you, but He who sent Me is true, and the things which I heard from Him, these I speak to the world."

9 They did not realize that He was speaking to them about The Father, so Jesus said, "When you lift up the Son of Man, then you will know that I am He; 10 and that I do nothing on My own initiative, but I speak these things as The Father has taught Me.

11 "And He who sent Me is with Me; He has not left Me alone, for I always do the things that are pleasing to Him."

12 As Jesus spoke these things many came to believe in Him.

Scene 624   **Abraham Is Our Father**   *John 8:31-42*

---

1 Jesus said to those Jews who had believed in Him, "If you abide in My Word, then you are truly My disciples; 2 and you will know the truth, and the truth will make you free."

3 They answered Him, "We are Abraham's descendants, and have never been enslaved to anyone. How can You say, 'You will become free'?"

4 Jesus answered them, "Truly, truly, I say to you, everyone who commits sin is the slave of sin. 5 The slave does not remain in the house forever, but the son does remain forever. 6 So if the Son sets you free, you will really be free.

7 "I know that you are Abraham's descendants, yet you seek to kill Me, because My Word has no place in you. 8 I speak the things which I have seen with My Father, and you do the things which you heard from your father."

9 They said to Him, "Abraham is our father."   *continued >*

Scene 624 - *continued*

10 Jesus said to them, "If you are Abraham's children, then do the deeds of Abraham. 11 But as it is, you are seeking to kill Me, a man who has told you the truth which I heard from God; this Abraham did not do. You are doing the deeds of your father."

12 They said to Him, "We have not been born through fornication; we have one Father: God."

13 Jesus said to them, "If God were your Father you would love Me, because I have come from God; 14 and I have not come for Myself, but He sent Me."

Scene 625	**Your Father Is The Devil**	John 8:43-47

1 Jesus said to them, "Why do you not understand what I am saying? It is because you can not hear My Word.

2 "You are of your father the Devil, and you want to do the desires of your father. 3 He was a murderer from the beginning, and he does not stand in the truth, because there is no truth in him. 4 Whenever he speaks a lie, he speaks from his own nature, for he is a liar, and the father of lies. 5 But because I speak the truth, you do not believe Me.

6 "Which one of you convicts Me of sin? 7 If I am speaking the truth, why do you not believe Me? 8 He who is of God hears the Words of God; 9 and for this reason you do not hear them, because you are not of God."

Scene 626	**You Have A Demon!**	John 8:48-59

1 The Jews answered, and said to Him, "Do we not rightly say that You are a Samaritan, and that You have a demon?"

2 Jesus answered, "I do not have a demon; but I honor My Father, and you dishonor Me.

3 "I do not seek My own glory; there is One who seeks and judges. 4 Truly, truly, I say to you, if anyone keeps My Word, he will not see death in this age."

5 The Jews said to Him, "Now we know that You have a demon! Abraham died, and the prophets also; and You say, 'If anyone keeps My Word he will not taste death in this age.' 6 Surely You are not greater than our father Abraham, who died? The prophets also died. Whom do You make Yourself out to be?"

7 Jesus answered, "If I glorify Myself, My glory is nothing; it is My Father who glorifies Me, of whom you say, 'He is our God'. 8 And you have not come to know Him, but I know Him; and if I say that I do not know Him then I will be a liar like you. 9 But I do know Him, and I keep His Word.

10 "Your father Abraham rejoiced to see My day, and he saw it, and was glad." 11 So the Jews said to Him, "You are not yet fifty years old, and You have seen Abraham?"

12 Jesus said to them, "Truly, truly, I say to you, that before Abraham was born, I am."

13 Therefore they picked up stones to throw at Jesus, but He hid Himself, and went out of the Temple.

Act 3 - Healing A Man Born Blind

Scene 631   **Jesus Cures A Man Who Was Born Blind**

Jerusalem, *Judea*   a Sabbath, October / 32 CE   *John 9:1-12*

1 As Jesus passed by, He saw a man who had been born blind, and His disciples asked Him, "Rabbi, who sinned, this man or his parents, that he would be born blind?"

2 Jesus answered, "It was neither that this man sinned, nor his parents, but it was so that the works of God might be displayed in him. 3 We must work the works of Him who sent Me while it is day, because night is coming when no one can work. 4 While I am in the world, I am the Light of the world."

5 When Jesus had said this, He spat on the ground, and made clay of the spittle, and applied the clay to the eyes of the blind man. 6 And Jesus said to him, "Go, and wash in the pool of Siloam" (which is translated as *sent*).

7 So the man went away and washed, and he came back seeing. 8 Therefore the neighbors, and those who had seen him as a beggar, were saying, "Is this not the one who used to sit and beg?" 9 Some were saying, "This is he," and others were saying, "No, but he is like him." 10 He himself kept saying, "I am the one!" 11 So they were saying to him, "How then were your eyes opened?"

12 He answered, "The man who is called Jesus made clay, and anointed my eyes; and He said to me, 'Go to Siloam, and wash.' 13 So I went away and washed, and I received sight!"

14 They asked him, "Where is He?" He said, "I do not know."

Scene 632   **The Pharisees Question The Man and His Parents**

John 9:13-23

1 Now it was a Sabbath on the day when Jesus made the clay, and opened the eyes of the man who had been born blind, so they brought him to the Pharisees. 2 When the Pharisees asked him how he had received his sight, he said to them, "Jesus applied clay to my eyes, and I washed, and now I see."

3 Therefore, some of the Pharisees were saying, "This man is not from God, because He does not keep the Sabbath." 4 But others were saying, "How can a man who is a sinner perform such signs?" And there was a division among them. 5 So they said to the man again, "What do you say about Him, since He opened your eyes?" He said, "He is a prophet."

6 The Jews did not believe that he had been born blind and had received sight, until they called the man's parents, and questioned them, saying, "Is this your son, and was he born blind? How then, does he now see?"

7 His parents answered them, and said, "We know that this is our son, and that he was born blind. But how he now sees, we do not know; or who opened his eyes, we do not know. 8 He is of age; ask him, and he will speak for himself." 9 His parents said this because they were afraid of the Jews, for the Jews had agreed that if anyone confessed Jesus to be the Christ, he was to be put out of the synagogue. 10 For this reason his parents said, "He is of age; ask him."

Scene 633   **They Question The Man A Second Time**

Jerusalem, *Judea*   a Sabbath, October / 32 CE   *John 9:24-34*

1 So for a second time the Pharisees called the man who had been born blind, and they said to him, "Give glory to God! We know that this man Jesus is a sinner."

2 The man answered, "Whether He is a sinner, I do not know. One thing I do know, is that though I was blind, now I see."

3 So they said to him, "What did He do to you? How did He open your eyes?"

4 He answered them, "I told you already, and you did not listen; why do you want to hear it again? Do you also want to become His disciples?"

5 The Pharisees reviled him, and said, "You are His disciple, but we are disciples of Moses! 6 We know that God has spoken to Moses, but as for this man, we do not know where He is from."

7 The man answered them, "Well, here is an amazing thing, that you do not know where He is from, and yet He opened my eyes! 8 We know that God does not hear sinners, but if anyone is God-fearing and does His will, He hears them. 9 Since the beginning of time, it has never been heard that anyone opened the eyes of a person born blind. 10 If this man were not from God, He could do nothing."

11 They answered him, "You were born entirely in sins, and you are teaching us?" So they put him out.

Scene 634   **Do You Believe In The Son of Man?**   *John 9:35-41*

1 Jesus heard that they had put him out; and finding him, Jesus asked, "Do you believe in the Son of Man?"

2 The man answered, "Who is He, Lord, that I may believe in Him?"

3 Jesus said to him, "You have both seen Him, and He is the One who is talking with you."

4 He said, "Lord, I believe!" And he worshiped Him.

5 Jesus said, "For judgment I came into this world, so that those who do not see may see, and that those who see may become blind."

6 The Pharisees who were with Jesus heard these things, and they said to Him, "Are we also blind?"

7 He said to them, "If you were blind you would have no sin, but since you say, 'We see,' your sin remains."

Act 4 - The Good Shepherd

Scene 641   **I Am The Door of The Sheep**
         Jerusalem, *Judea*   a Sabbath, October / 32 CE   *John 10:1-10*

---

1 "Truly, truly, I say to you, he who does not enter into the fold of the sheep by the door, but climbs in some other way, is a thief and a robber. 2 But he who enters by the door is the shepherd of the sheep. 3 To him the doorkeeper opens; and the sheep hear his voice, and he calls them by name, and leads them out.

4 "When he puts them out, he goes ahead of them, and the sheep follow him because they know his voice. 5 They will not follow a stranger, but will flee from him, because they do not know the voice of strangers."

6 Jesus spoke this figure of speech to them, but they did not understand what He was saying. 7 So Jesus said to them again, "Truly, truly, I say to you, I am the door of the sheep. 8 All who came before Me were thieves and bandits, and the sheep did not hear them. 9 I am the door. If anyone enters through Me, he will be saved; and he will go in and go out, and find pasture.

10 "The thief comes only to steal, and kill, and destroy; but I have come so that they may have life, and have it abundantly."

Scene 642   **I Am The Good Shepherd**   *John 10:11-16*

---

1 "I am the good shepherd; the good shepherd lays down His life for the sheep. 2 He who is a hired hand, and is not a shepherd nor the owner of the sheep, when he sees the wolf coming he leaves the sheep and flees; and the wolf scatters the sheep, and snatches them. 3 He flees because he is a hired hand, and is not really concerned about the sheep.

4 "I am the good shepherd, and I know My own and My own know Me, even as The Father knows Me, and I know The Father; 5 and I lay down My life for the sheep.

6 "And I have other sheep which are not of this fold, and I must bring them also. 7 They will hear My voice, and they will become one flock, with one shepherd."

Scene 643   **I Lay Down My Life to Take It Again**   *John 10:17-21*

---

1 "For this reason The Father loves Me, because I lay down My life so that I may take it again. 2 No one has taken it from Me, but I lay it down on My own initiative. 3 I have authority to lay it down, and I have authority to take it up again. This commandment I received from My Father."

4 A division occurred again among the Jews because of these words. Many of them were saying, "He has a demon and is insane! Why do you listen to Him?"

5 Others were saying, "These are not the sayings of one who is demon-possessed. 6 A demon cannot open the eyes of the blind, can he?"

Scene 644   **Repent And Bear Fruit, or Perish**

Jerusalem, *Judea*   a Sabbath, October / 32 CE   *Luke 13:1-9*

1 Now on the same occasion there were some present who reported to Jesus about the Galileans whose blood Pilate had mixed with their sacrifices.

2 Jesus said to them, "Do you suppose that these Galileans were greater sinners than all other Galileans, because they suffered this fate? 3 I tell you, no; but unless you repent, you will all likewise perish.

4 "Or do you suppose that those eighteen on whom the tower of Siloam fell and killed, were worse culprits than all the men who live in Jerusalem? 5 I tell you, no, but unless you repent, you will all likewise perish!"

6 Then Jesus began telling this parable: "A man had a fig tree which had been planted in his vineyard, and he came looking for fruit on it, and did not find any. 7 He said to the keeper of the vineyard, 'Behold, for three years I have come looking for fruit on this fig tree without finding any. Cut it down. Why does it even use up the ground?'

8 "The vine-keeper answered him, 'Let it alone, sir, for this year also, until I dig around it and put in fertilizer; and if it bears fruit next year, fine; but if not, I will cut it down.' "

Act 5 - The Feast of Dedication

Scene 651   **Depart From Me, All You Evildoers!**

Judea   December / 32 CE   *Luke 13:22-33 / John 10:22*

1 The Feast of the Dedication was near, and Jesus was passing through from one city and village to another, teaching, and proceeding on His way to Jerusalem.

2 Someone said to Him, "Lord, are there just a few who are being saved?"

3 Jesus said to them, "Strive to enter through the narrow door, for many I tell you, will seek to enter, and will not be able. 4 When the head of the house gets up and shuts the door, then you will stand outside, and knock on the door, saying, 'Lord, open up to us!' 5 And He will answer, and say to you, 'I do not know where you are from.'

6 "Then you will say, 'We ate and drank in Your presence, and You taught in our streets'; 7 and He will say, 'I tell you, I do not know where you are from. Depart from Me, all you evildoers!'

8 "In that place there will be weeping, and gnashing of teeth, when you see Abraham and Isaac and Jacob, and all the prophets in the Kingdom of God, but yourselves being thrown out. 9 They will come from the east and the west, and from the north and south, and will recline at the table in the Kingdom of God. 10 And behold, some who are last will be first, and some who are first will be last."

11 At that time some Pharisees approached Jesus, and said to Him, "Leave here and go away, for Herod wants to kill You."

12 But Jesus said to them, "Go and tell that fox: 'Behold, I cast out demons and perform cures today and tomorrow, and the third day I reach My goal.' 13 Nevertheless, I must journey on today and tomorrow, and the next day, for it cannot be that a prophet would perish outside of Jerusalem."

Scene 652   **I And The Father Are One**

The Temple, Jerusalem, *Judea*   Feast of Dedication, December / 32 CE   *John 10:23-30*

1 It was winter, and Jesus was walking in the Temple, in the portico of Solomon. 2 The Jews gathered around Him, and were saying to Him, "How long will You keep us in suspense? If You are the Christ, tell us plainly."

3 Jesus answered them, "I told you, and you do not believe. 4 The works that I do in My Father's Name, these testify of Me; but you do not believe, because you are not of My sheep.

5 "My sheep hear My voice, and I know them, and they follow Me. 6 I give eternal life to them, and they will never perish; and no one will snatch them out of My hand.

7 "My Father, who has given them to Me, is greater than all, and no one is able to snatch them out of The Father's hand. 8 I and The Father are One."

Scene 653   **The Jews Try To Stone Jesus For Blasphemy**
John 10:31-42

1 The Jews picked up stones again to stone Jesus.

2 He answered them, "I showed you many good works from The Father; for which of them are you stoning Me?"

3 The Jews answered Him, "We do not stone You for a good work, but for blasphemy - because You, being a man, make Yourself out to be God."

4 Jesus answered them, "Has it not been written in your Law, 'I said, you are gods'? 5 If he called them gods to whom the Word of God came, and the Scripture cannot be broken, do you say of Him whom The Father sanctified and sent into the world, 'You are blaspheming,' because I said, 'I am the Son of God'?

6 "If I do not do the works of My Father, then do not believe Me; 7 but if I do them, even though you do not believe Me, believe the works, so that you may know and understand that The Father is in Me, and that I am in The Father."

8 Therefore, they were seeking again to seize Jesus, but He eluded their grasp. 9 And He went away again beyond the Jordan, to the place where John was first baptizing, and He stayed there.

10 Many came to Jesus, and they were saying, "While John performed no sign, yet everything that he said about this man was true!" 11 And many believed in Jesus there.

Act 6 - The Resurrection of Lazarus

Scene 661   **Jesus Hears That Lazarus Has Died**

Galilee   winter / 33 CE   *John 11:1-16~, ~16*

---

1 Now Lazarus, from the village of Bethany, was sick. 2 He was the brother of Martha, and her sister Mary. 3 So the sisters sent word to Jesus, saying, "Lord, he whom You love is sick."

4 When Jesus heard this, He said, "This sickness is not to end in death, but for the glory of God, so that the Son of God may be glorified by it."

5 Now Jesus loved Martha and her sister, and Lazarus, yet when He heard that Lazarus was sick, He stayed for two more days in the place where He was.

6 After two days, Jesus said to His apostles, "Let us go to Judea again."

7 The apostles said to Him, "Rabbi, the Jews were just now seeking to stone You, and You are going there again?"

8 Jesus answered, "Are there not twelve hours in the day? If anyone walks in the day he does not stumble, because he sees the light of this world. 9 But if anyone walks in the night he stumbles, because the light is not in him."

10 Then Jesus said to them, "Our friend Lazarus has fallen asleep, and I go so that I may waken him."

11 The apostles said to Him, "Lord, if he has fallen asleep, he will recover." 12 Now they thought that Jesus was speaking of literal sleep, but He had spoken of his death.

13 So Jesus said to them plainly, "Lazarus is dead; and I am glad for your sakes that I was not there, so that you may believe. 14 Now, let us go to him."

15 Then Thomas, who is called Didymus, said to his fellow apostles, "Let us also go, so that we may die with Him!"

Scene 662   **I Am The Resurrection and The Life**

Bethany, Judea   winter / 33 CE   *John 11:18-29, 31*

---

1 Many came to console Martha and Mary concerning their brother; but when Martha heard that Jesus was coming she went to meet Him, while Mary stayed at the house. 2 Bethany was near Jerusalem, about two miles away.

3 When they met, Martha said to Jesus, "Lord, if You had been here, my brother would not have died. 4 Yet even now, I know that whatever You ask of God, God will give You."

5 Jesus said to her, "Your brother will rise again."

6 Martha said, "I know that he will rise again, in the resurrection on the last day."

7 Jesus said to her, "I am the resurrection, and the life. 8 He who believes in Me will live, even if he dies; and everyone who lives and believes in Me will never die. 9 Do you believe this?"

10 She said to Him, "Yes, Lord. I have believed that You are the Christ, the Son of God, even He who comes into the world."

11 After Martha had said this, she went and secretly called her sister Mary, saying, "The Teacher is here, and is calling for you." 12 When Mary heard this

she got up quickly, and went to Him.

13 When those who were consoling Mary in the house saw that she got up quickly and went out, they followed her, supposing that she was going to the tomb, to weep there.

Scene 663   **Mary Goes To Meet Jesus**   *John 11:30, 32-37*

1 Now Jesus had not yet come into the village, but was still in the place where Martha had met Him.

2 When Mary came to where Jesus was, she fell at His feet, saying, "Lord, if You had been here, my brother would not have died."

3 When Jesus saw her weeping, and the Jews who came with her also weeping, He was deeply moved in spirit, and troubled.

4 He asked, "Where have you laid him?" They said to Him, "Lord, come and see."

5 Jesus wept, so the Jews were saying, "See how He loved him!" 6 But some of them said, "Could not this man, who opened the eyes of the blind, not also have kept Lazarus from dying?"

Scene 664   **Jesus Calls Lazarus Forth From The Tomb**
Bethany, *Judea*   *John 11:17, 38-46*

1 When Jesus arrived, He found that Lazarus had already been in the tomb for four days. 2 The tomb was a cave, and there was a stone lying against it.

3 Being again deeply moved within, Jesus came to the tomb, and said, "Remove the stone."

4 Martha, the sister of the deceased, said to Him, "Lord, by this time there will be a stench, for he has been dead for four days."

5 Jesus said to her, "Did I not say to you that if you believe you will see the glory of God?" So they removed the stone.

6 Then Jesus raised His eyes, and said, "Father, I thank You that You have heard Me. 7 I know that You always hear Me, but because of the people standing around I said it, so that they may believe that You sent Me."

8 After Jesus had said this, He cried out with a loud voice, "Lazarus, come forth!" 9 And the man who had died came forth, bound hand and foot with wrappings, and a cloth was wrapped around his face.

10 Jesus said to them, "Unbind him, and let him go."

11 Many of the Jews who had come to Mary saw what Jesus did, and they believed in Him; 12 but some of them went to the Pharisees, and told them what Jesus had done.

Scene 665   **The Pharisees Plot To Kill Jesus**
Jerusalem, *Judea*   *John 11:47-54*

1 Then the chief priests and the Pharisees gathered the Council together, and they were saying, "What are we doing? For this man is performing many signs. 2 If we let Him go on like this, all men will believe in Him, and then the Romans will come and take away both our place, and our nation."

Scene 665 - *continued*

3 But one of them, Caiaphas, who was the High Priest that year, said to them, "You know nothing at all; nor do you take into account that it is expedient for us that one man die for the people, and that the whole nation not perish."

4 Now he did not say this on his own initiative, but being the High Priest that year, he had prophesied that Jesus was going to die for the nation; 5 and not only for the nation, but in order that He might also gather together into one the children of God who are scattered abroad. 6 So from that day, they planned together to kill Jesus.

7 Therefore, Jesus no longer continued to walk publicly among the Jews, but He went away from there to a city called Ephraim, in the country near the wilderness, and He stayed there with His apostles.

Act 7 - Further Teachings

Scene 671   **Teachings On Divorce**

Judea   early spring / 33 CE   *Matthew 19:1-8 / Mark 10:1-9*

---

1 When Jesus arrived in the region of Judea beyond the Jordan, large crowds gathered together and followed Him again; 2 and according to His custom, He once more began to teach them, and He healed them.

3 Then some Pharisees came to Jesus, and testing Him they began to question Him, asking, "Is it lawful for a man to divorce his wife, for any reason?"

4 He answered, and said to them, "What did Moses command you?"

5 They said, "Moses permitted a man to write his wife a certificate of divorce, and send her away."

6 Jesus said to them, "Because of your hardness of heart Moses wrote you this commandment, which permitted you to divorce your wives; but from the beginning, it has not been this way.

7 "Have you not read that from the beginning of creation, God who created them made them male and female, 8 and said, 'For this reason a man shall leave his father and mother and be joined to his wife, and the two shall become one flesh'? So they are no longer two, but one flesh. 9 What therefore God has joined together, let no man separate."

Scene 672   **Teachings On Adultery**

Matthew 19:9-11 / Mark 10:10-12 / Luke 16:18

---

1 In the house, His disciples began questioning Jesus about this.

2 He said to them, "Everyone who divorces his wife, except for immorality, and marries another woman, commits adultery against her.

3 "And if a woman divorces her husband, and marries another man, she is committing adultery. 4 And he who marries one who is divorced from a husband commits adultery."

5 The disciples said to Jesus, "If the relationship of a man with his wife is like this, it is better not to marry."

6 Jesus said to them, "Not all men can accept this statement, but only those to whom it has been given."

Scene 673   **A Word About Eunuchs**   *Matthew 19:12*

1 And Jesus said, "There are eunuchs who were born that way from their mother's womb, and there are eunuchs who were made eunuchs by men, 2 and there are also eunuchs who made themselves eunuchs for the sake of the Kingdom of Heaven.

3 "Let he who is able to accept this, accept it."

Scene 674   **Let The Children Come To Me**
Matthew 19:13-15 / Mark 10:13-16 / Luke 18:15-17

1 Then they were bringing some children and even their babies to Jesus, so that He might touch them, and pray.

2 When the disciples saw it, they began rebuking them; 3 but when Jesus saw this, He was indignant, and He said to them, "Permit the children, and do not hinder them from coming to Me; for the Kingdom of Heaven belongs to such as these!

4 "Truly I say to you, whoever does not receive the Kingdom of God like a child, will not enter it at all."

5 Then Jesus took the young children in His arms, and He began blessing them.

6 After laying His hands on them, He departed from there.

Scene 675   **What Must I Do To Obtain Eternal Life?**
Matthew 19:16-22 / Mark 10:17-22 / Luke 18:18-23

1 As Jesus was setting out on a journey, a young ruler came up and knelt before Him, and questioned Him, saying, "Good Teacher, what shall I do that I may obtain eternal life?"

2 Jesus said to him, "Why do you call Me good? There is only One who is good; no one is good except God alone. 3 But if you wish to enter into life, keep the commandments."

4 He said to Him, "Which ones?"

5 Jesus said, "You know the commandments: Do not commit murder;' 6 'Do not commit adultery;' 7 'Do not steal;' 8 'Do not bear false witness;' 9 'Do not defraud;' 10 'Honor your father and your mother;' 11 and, 'You shall love your neighbor as yourself.' "

12 The young ruler said to Him, "Teacher, I have kept all these things from my youth up. What am I still lacking?"

13 When Jesus heard this, He felt a love for him, and said to him, "One thing that you still lack, if you wish to be complete; go and sell all that you possess, and distribute it to the poor, and you will have treasure in Heaven; 14 and come, follow Me."

15 But when the young ruler heard these words he became very sad; and he went away grieving, for he was one who owned much property, and was extremely rich.

Scene 676   **It Is Hard For The Wealthy To Enter The Kingdom**

Judea   early spring / 33 CE   *Matthew 19:23-26 / Mark 10:23-27 / Luke 18:24-27*

1 Jesus looked around, and said to His disciples, "How hard it is for those who are wealthy to enter the Kingdom of God! 2 Truly I say to you, it is hard for a rich man to enter the Kingdom of Heaven."

3 The disciples were amazed at His words, so Jesus said to them again, "Children, how hard it is to enter the Kingdom of God. 4 Again I say to you, it is easier for a camel to go through the eye of a needle, than for a rich man to enter the Kingdom of God."

5 When the disciples heard this, they were even more astonished; and they said to Him, "Then who can be saved?"

6 Looking at them, Jesus said, "With people this is impossible, but not with God, for all things are possible with God."

Scene 677   **What Will There Be For Us?**

Matthew 19:27-30 / Mark 10:28-31 / Luke 18:28-30

1 Then Peter said to Jesus, "Behold, we have left our homes and everything, and followed You; what then, will there be for us?"

2 Jesus said to them, "Truly, I say to you who have followed Me, in the regeneration, when the Son of Man will sit on His glorious throne, then you also shall sit upon twelve thrones, judging the twelve tribes of Israel.

3 "And I say to you, that there is no one who has left house or farm, or wife or brothers or sisters, or father or mother or children, for the sake of the gospel of the Kingdom of God, and for My sake, who will not receive many times as much; 4 now, in the present age - houses and farms, and brothers and sisters, and mothers and children, along with persecutions - 5 and in the age to come, they will inherit eternal life.

6 "But many who are the first will be the last, and the last will be first."

Scene 678   **The Generous Landowner**   *Matthew 20:1-16*

1 Jesus said, "For the Kingdom of Heaven is like a landowner who went out early in the morning to hire laborers for his vineyard. 2 When he had agreed with the laborers for a denarius for the day, he sent them into his vineyard.

3 "At about the third hour, he went out and saw others standing idle in the market place; and he said to them, 'You also go into the vineyard, and whatever is right I will give you.' And so they went. 4 Again he went out about the sixth hour and the ninth hour, and did the same thing.

5 "At about the eleventh hour, he went out and found others standing around, and he said to them, 'Why have you been standing here idle all day?' 6 They said to him, 'Because no one hired us.' He said to them, 'You too go into the vineyard.'

7 "When evening came, the vineyard owner said to his foreman, 'Call the laborers and pay them their wages, beginning with the last group to the first.'

8 "When those hired about the eleventh hour came, they each received a denarius. 9 When those who were hired first came, they thought that they would receive more, but each of them also received a denarius.   *continued >*

10 "When they received it, they grumbled at the landowner, saying, 'These last men have worked only one hour, and you have made them equal to us who have borne the burden, and the scorching heat of the day.'

11 "But he answered, and said to them, 'Friend, I am doing you no wrong. Did you not agree with me for a denarius? Take what is yours and go; 12 but I wish to give to this last man the same as to you. 13 Is it not lawful for me to do what I wish with what is my own? Or is your eye envious because I am generous?'

14 "So the last shall be first, and the first last."

Scene 679   **The Unworthy Slaves**   *Luke 17:7-10*

1 "Which of you having a slave plowing or tending sheep, will say to him when he has come in from the field, 'Come immediately, and sit down to eat'? 2 But will he not say to him, 'Prepare something for me to eat, and properly clothe yourself, and serve me while I eat and drink; and then afterward you may eat and drink'? 3 He does not thank the slave because he did the things which were commanded, does he?

4 "So you too, when you do all the things which are commanded of you, say, 'We are unworthy slaves, for we have done only that which we should have done.' "

```
┌─────────────────────────────────────────────┐
│        Act 8 - The Road To Jerusalem          │
└─────────────────────────────────────────────┘
```

Scene 681   **Shall We Command Fire From Heaven?**

Samaria   late March / 33 CE   *Luke 9:51-56*

1 When the days were approaching for His ascension, Jesus was determined to go to Jerusalem, and He sent messengers ahead of Him. 2 They went and entered a village of the Samaritans to make arrangements for Jesus, but the Samaritans did not receive Him, because He was traveling to Jerusalem.

3 When His apostles James and John saw this, they said, "Lord, do You want us to command fire to come down from heaven, and consume them?"

4 But Jesus turned and rebuked them, and said, "You do not know what kind of spirit you are of; 5 for the Son of Man did not come to destroy men's lives, but to save them." 6 And they went on to another village.

Scene 682   **The Ten Lepers of Samaria**   *Luke 17:11-19*

1 While on the way to Jerusalem, Jesus was passing from Galilee into Samaria. 2 As He entered a village, ten leprous men who stood at a distance met Him; and they raised their voices, saying, "Jesus, Master! Have mercy on us!"

3 When Jesus saw them, He said to them, "Go and show yourselves to the priests." 4 And as they were going, they were cleansed.

5 When one of them saw that he had been healed, he returned, glorifying God with a loud voice. 6 And he came and fell on his face at Jesus' feet, and gave thanks to Him. And he was a Samaritan.

7 Jesus said, "Were there not ten cleansed? But where are the other nine?

continued >

8 "Did no one return to give glory to God, except this foreigner?"

9 And Jesus said to him, "Stand up and go. Your faith has made you well."

Scene 683   **What Will Happen To The Son of Man**
Samaria   late March / 33 CE   *Matthew 20:17-19 / Mark 10:32-34 / Luke 18:31-34*

1 On the road to Jerusalem Jesus was walking ahead of them. They were amazed, and those who followed were fearful.

2 On the way, Jesus took the twelve apostles aside by themselves, and He began to tell them again what was going to happen to Him. 3 He said, "Behold, we are going up to Jerusalem, and all the things which are written through the prophets about the Son of Man will be accomplished. 4 He will be delivered to the chief priests and the scribes, and they will condemn Him to death.

5 "Then they will hand Him over to the Gentiles, who will mock and mistreat Him, and spit on Him, and scourge Him; and after they have scourged Him they will crucify Him, and kill Him; 6 and on the third day He will rise again."

7 But the apostles understood none of these things, because the meaning of this statement was hidden from them, and they did not understand the things that He said.

Scene 684   **To Sit On My Right and On My Left**
Matthew 20:20-24 / Mark 10:35-41

1 Then the mother of James and John, the two sons of Zebedee, came up to Jesus with her sons, bowing down, and making a request of Him. 2 They said, "Teacher, we want You to do for us whatever we ask of You."

3 He said to them, "What do you want Me to do for you?"

4 They said, "Grant us that in Your Kingdom, we may sit in Your glory, one on Your right, and one on Your left."

5 But Jesus answered, and said to them, "You do not know what you are asking. Are you able to drink the cup that I am about to drink; or to be baptized with the baptism with which I am baptized?"

6 They said to Him, "We are able."

7 So Jesus said to them, "Then the cup that I drink you shall drink, and you shall be baptized with the baptism with which I am baptized. 8 But to sit on My right and on My left, this is not Mine to give, but it is for those for whom it has been prepared by my Father."

9 Hearing this, the ten began to feel indignant with the two brothers, James and John.

Scene 685   **The Greatest Is The One Who Serves**
Matthew 20:25-28 / Mark 10:42-45

1 Jesus called them to Himself, and said to them, "You know that those who are recognized as the rulers of the Gentiles lord it over them, and their great men exercise authority over them. 2 But it is not this way among you; for whoever wishes to become great among you shall be your servant, and whoever wishes to be first among you shall be the slave of all.

3 "For even the Son of Man did not come to be served, but to serve, and to give His life as a ransom for many."

Scene 686   **Jesus Restores The Sight of Bartimaeus**
Jericho, *Judea*   late March / 33 CE   *Matthew 20:29-34 / Mark 10:46-52 / Luke 18:35-43*

1 As Jesus was approaching Jericho with His disciples, and a large crowd following Him, a blind beggar named Bartimaeus, the son of Timaeus, was sitting by the road begging. 2 Hearing a crowd going by, he began to inquire what this was. They told him that Jesus of Nazareth was passing by.

3 When he heard that it was Jesus, Bartimaeus began to cry out, and say, "Lord Jesus, son of David, have mercy on me!" 4 Those who led the way were sternly telling him to be quiet, but he kept crying out all the more, "Lord! Son of David! Have mercy on me!"

5 Jesus stopped, and said, "Call him here." 6 So they called the blind man, saying to him, "Take courage and stand up, He is calling for you."

7 Throwing aside his cloak, he jumped up and came to Jesus.

8 When Bartimaeus came near, Jesus asked him, "What do you want Me to do for you?" 9 The blind man said, "Lord, I want to regain my sight."

10 Moved with compassion, Jesus touched his eyes, and said to him, "Go, receive your sight. Your faith has made you well." 11 Immediately Bartimaeus regained his sight, and he began following Jesus on the road, glorifying God.

12 When all the people saw it, they gave praise to God.

Scene 687   **The Salvation of Zaccheus**   *Luke 19:1-10*

1 As Jesus was passing through Jericho, a rich, chief tax collector named Zaccheus was trying to see who Jesus was, but he was unable to because of the crowd, and because he was small in stature. 2 So he ran ahead, and climbed up into a sycamore tree in order to see Jesus, who was about to pass by that way.

3 When Jesus came to the place, He looked up, and said to him, "Zaccheus, hurry and come down, for today I must stay at your house."

4 Zaccheus hurried and came down, and he gladly received Jesus.

5 When the crowd saw it, they all began to grumble, saying, "He has gone to be the guest of a man who is a sinner."

6 Zaccheus stopped, and said to Jesus, "Behold Lord, half of my possessions I will give to the poor; 7 and if I have defrauded anyone of anything, I will give them back four times as much."

8 Jesus said to him, "Today salvation has come to this house, because he is also a son of Abraham; 9 for the Son of Man has come to seek and to save that which was lost."

Scene 688   **The Parable of The Good and Faithful Servants**
Judea   late March / 33 CE   *Matthew 25:14-30 / Luke 19:11-28*

1 While they were listening to these things, Jesus told them a parable, because He was near Jerusalem, and they supposed that the Kingdom of God was going to appear immediately.

2 He said, "It is just like a nobleman about to go on a journey to a distant country, to receive a kingdom for himself, and then return. 3 And he called his slaves, and entrusted his possessions to them. 4 To one of them he gave five gold coins, and to another he gave two gold coins, and to another one, each

Scene 688 - *continued*

according to his ability. 5 And he said to them, 'Do business with this until I come back,' and went on his journey. 6 But his citizens hated him, and they sent a delegation after him, saying, 'We do not want this man to reign over us!'

7 "Immediately the one who had received the five gold coins went and traded with them, and he gained five more gold coins. 8 In the same manner, the one who had received the two gold coins gained two more. 9 But he who received the one coin went away, and he dug a hole in the ground, and hid his master's money.

10 "After a long time, the master of those slaves received the kingdom, and returned. 11 Then he ordered that the slaves to whom he had given the money be called to him, so that he might know what business they had done, and to settle accounts with them.

12 "The one who had received the five gold coins came, and he brought five more gold coins, saying, 'Master, you entrusted five gold coins to me, and see, I have gained five more coins.'

13 "His master said to him, 'Well done, good and faithful slave! Because you have been faithful with a few little things, I will put you in charge of many things; you are to be in authority over ten cities. Enter into the joy of your master!'

14 "The second slave, who had received the two gold coins, came and said, 'Master, you entrusted two gold coins to me. See, I have gained two more coins!'

15 "His master said to him, 'Well done, good and faithful slave! You were faithful with a few things, I will put you in charge of many things; you are to be over five cities. Enter into the joy of your master!'

16 "When the one who had received the one gold coin came, he said, 'Master, I knew you to be a hard and exacting man; you reap where you did not sow, and gather where you did not lay down; and I was afraid of you, and I hid your money in the ground. 17 See, you have what is yours. Here is your coin, which I kept hidden in a handkerchief.'

18 "But his master answered, and said to him, 'By your own words I will judge you, you wicked, lazy, and worthless slave! 19 If you knew that I am an exacting man, reaping where I did not sow, and taking up what I did not lay down, then you should have put my money in the bank, and on my arrival I would have received my money back with interest.'

20 "Then he said to the bystanders, 'Take the gold coin away from him, and give it to the one who has the ten coins.'

21 "They said to him, 'But master, he has ten gold coins already.'

22 "But he said, 'I tell you that to everyone who has, more shall be given, and he will have an abundance. 23 But from the one who does not have, even what he does have shall be taken away from him. 24 Throw that worthless slave out into the outer darkness; in that place there will be weeping, and gnashing of teeth.

25 'And these enemies of mine, who did not want me to reign over them, bring them here, and slay them in my presence.' "

26 After Jesus said these things, He continued on to Jerusalem.

Act 9 - Anointed For Burial

Scene 691   **Mary Anoints Jesus With Perfume**

Bethany, *Judea*   Saturday evening, March 28th / 33 CE

Matthew 26:6-7 / Mark 14:3 / John 11:55 - 12:3

1 Now the Passover was near, and many from the country went up to Jerusalem to purify themselves before the feast. 2 They were looking for Jesus, and were saying to one another as they stood in the Temple, "What do you think? Will He come to the feast at all?"

3 Now the chief priests and the Pharisees had given orders, that if anyone knew where Jesus was he was to report it, so that they might seize Him. 4 Jesus therefore, six days before the Passover, came to Bethany where Lazarus was, whom He had raised from the dead.

5 While Jesus was in Bethany, they made a supper for Him at the home of Simon the leper. 6 Martha was serving, and Lazarus was one of those reclining at the table with Him.

7 Then Mary came to Jesus with an alabaster vial of a pound of very costly perfume of pure nard; and she broke the vial, and poured it over His head as He reclined at the table. 8 Then she anointed His feet, and wiped His feet with her hair; and the house was filled with the fragrance of the perfume.

Scene 692   **The Disciples Question The Waste**

Matthew 26:8-13 / Mark 14:4-9 / John 12:4-11

1 When some of the apostles saw this, they were indignant, and said to one another, "Why has this perfume been wasted, for it might have been sold for a high price?" And they were scolding her.

2 Judas Iscariot, the apostle who was intending to betray Jesus, said, "Why was this perfume not sold for over three hundred denarii, and the money given to the poor?" 3 Now he said this not because he was concerned about the poor people, but because he was a thief, and as he had the money box, he used to pilfer what was put into it.

4 But Jesus, aware of this, said to them, "Leave her alone, and let her keep it. 5 Why do you bother the woman? For she has done a good deed to Me. 6 For you always have the poor with you, and whenever you wish you can do good to them; but you do not always have Me.

7 "She has done what she could, for when she poured this perfume she anointed My body, to prepare Me beforehand, for the day of My burial.

8 "Truly I say to you, wherever this gospel is preached in the whole world, what this woman has done will also be spoken of, in memory of her."

9 When the large crowd learned that Jesus was there, they came not only for His sake, but so that they might also see Lazarus, whom He had raised from the dead. 10 So the chief priests planned to also put Lazarus to death, because on account of him many of the Jews were going away, and believing in Jesus.

CHAPTER 7 - THE FINAL WEEK

Act 1 - Sunday - Arrival In Jerusalem

Scene 711   **The Lord Has Need of Your Donkey**

Bethphage, *Judea*   Sunday, March 29th / 33 CE

Matthew 21:1-3, 6 / Mark 11:1-3 / Luke 19:29-31 / John 12:12~

1 The next day, they approached Jerusalem from Bethany, and came to Bethphage, near the Mount of Olives.

2 Jesus sent two of his apostles, and said to them, "Go into the village ahead of you, and immediately as you enter you will find a donkey tied there, and a colt with her, on which no one has ever yet sat. 3 Untie it, and bring it here to Me. 4 And if anyone asks you, 'Why are you untying it?' you shall say, 'The Lord has need of it,' and he will immediately send it back here."

5 The two apostles went and did just as Jesus had instructed them.

Scene 712   **Jesus Rides On The Colt**

Matthew 21:4-5, 7 / Mark 11:4-7 / Luke 19:32-35 / John 12:14-15

1 So those who were sent went, and they found a colt outside in the street, tied at the door just as Jesus had told them, and they untied it.

2 As they were untying the colt, its owners said to them, "What are you doing? Why are you untying the colt?" 3 The apostles spoke to them just as Jesus had told them, and said, "The Lord has need of it;" and they gave them permission.

4 So they brought the young donkey to Jesus, and they laid their coats on it, and He sat on it. 5 This took place to fulfill what was spoken through the prophets, as it is written: "Say to the daughter of Zion: 'Fear not! Behold, your King is coming to you, gentle, and mounted on a donkey, even on a colt, the foal of a beast of burden.' "

Scene 713   **The Approach To Jerusalem**

Matthew 21:8 / Mark 11:8 / Luke 19:36 / John 12:~12-13~

1 When the large crowd who had come to the feast heard that Jesus was coming to Jerusalem, they went out to meet Him.

2 As He was going, many in the crowd were spreading their coats on the road, and others took leafy branches which they had cut from the palm trees, and they spread them on the road.

Scene 714   **Hosanna, To The Son of David!**

Bethphage, *Judea*   *Matthew 21:9 / Mark 11:9-10 / Luke 19:37-40 / John 12:~13, 16-19*

1 As Jesus was approaching near the descent of the Mount of Olives, the whole crowd of His disciples began to praise God joyfully with a loud voice, for all the miracles which they had seen.

2 Those who went ahead of Him, and those who followed, began to shout, "Hosanna, to the son of David! 3 Blessed is He who comes in the Name of the

Lord, even the King of Israel! 4 Blessed is the coming Kingdom of our father David! 5 Peace in Heaven, and Hosanna in the highest!"

6 Some of the Pharisees in the crowd said to Jesus, "Teacher, rebuke Your disciples!"

7 But He answered, "I tell you, if these become silent, then the stones will cry out!"

8 These things His disciples did not understand at first, but when Jesus was glorified then they remembered that these things were written of Him, and that they had done these things to Him.

9 So the people who were with Jesus when He called Lazarus out of the tomb, and raised him from the dead, continued to testify about Him. 10 For this reason also the people went to meet Him, because they heard that He had performed this sign.

11 So the Pharisees said to one another, "You see that you are not doing any good; look, the whole world has gone after Him."

Scene 715	**Jesus Weeps For Jerusalem**	*Luke 19:41-44*

1 As Jesus approached Jerusalem and saw the city, He wept over it, saying, "If only you had known in this day the things which make for peace. But now they have been hidden from your eyes.

2 "For the days will come upon you when your enemies will throw up a barricade against you, and surround you, and hem you in on every side; 3 and they will level you to the ground, and your children within you; and they will not leave in you one stone upon another, 4 because you did not recognize the time of your visitation."

Scene 716	**Jesus Enters Jerusalem**
	Jerusalem, *Judea* *Matthew 21:10-11 / Mark 11:11~, 15~*

1 When they came to Jerusalem, Jesus entered the city; and all of the people were stirred, and saying, "Who is this?" 2 And the crowds were saying, "This is the Prophet Jesus, from Nazareth in Galilee."

Scene 717	**Jesus Cleanses The Temple, The Final Time**
	The Temple, Jerusalem, *Judea* Sunday, March 29th / 33 CE
	Matthew 21:12-13 / Mark 11:~11~, ~15-18 / Luke 19:45-46

1 Jesus entered the Temple, and began to drive out all those who were buying and selling in the Temple. 2 He overturned the tables of the money changers, and the seats of those who were selling doves; and He would not permit anyone to carry merchandise through the Temple.

3 Then Jesus began to teach, and He said to them, "It is written, 'My house shall be called a house of prayer for all the nations', but you have made it a robbers' den!"

4 When the chief priests and the scribes heard this, they began seeking how to destroy Him; but they were afraid of Him, for the whole crowd was astonished at His teaching.

Scene 718   **Healing In The Temple**   *Matthew 21:14-17 / Mark 11:~11*

1 The blind and the lame came to Jesus in the Temple, and He healed them. 2 But when the chief priests and the scribes saw the wonderful things that He had done, and the children in the Temple who were shouting, "Hosanna to the Son of David!" they became indignant, and they said to Him, "Do You hear what these children are saying?"

3 Jesus said to them, "Yes. Have you never read, 'Out of the mouth of infants and nursing babies You have prepared praise for Yourself'?"

4 Then, after looking around at everything, since it was late, Jesus left with the twelve, and they went out of the city to Bethany, and spent the night there.

Act 2 - Monday

Scene 721   **Jesus Curses A Fig Tree**

east of Jerusalem, *Judea*   Monday, March 30th / 33 CE
Matthew 21:18-22 / Mark 11:12-14, 20-24

1 The next day, they left Bethany in the morning, and were returning to the city. 2 Jesus became hungry, and seeing a lone fig tree in leaf at a distance by the road, He went to see if perhaps He would find any fruit on it.

3 When He came to the tree, He found nothing on it but only leaves, for it was not the season for figs. 4 Jesus said to it, "May no one ever eat fruit from you again!" And His apostles were listening.

5 As they were passing by, they saw the fig tree withered from the roots up. 6 Peter said to Jesus, "Rabbi, look, the fig tree which You cursed has withered!" 7 Seeing this, the apostles were amazed, and asked, "How did the fig tree wither all at once?"

8 Jesus answered, and said to them, "Have faith in God. 9 Truly I say to you, if you have faith, and do not doubt, you will not only do what was done to this fig tree, but even if you say to this mountain, 'Be taken up and cast into the sea,' and do not doubt in your heart, but believe that what you say is going to happen, then it will be granted to you, and it will happen.

10 "Therefore I say to you, all things for which you ask in prayer, believing that you will receive them, they will be granted to you."

Scene 722   **Who Gave You This Authority?**

The Temple, Jerusalem, *Judea*   *Matthew 21:23-27 / Mark 11:27-33 / Luke 20:1-8*

1 When they came to Jerusalem, Jesus entered the Temple, and was teaching the people.

2 While He was preaching the gospel, the chief priests and the scribes, with the elders of the people, came and confronted Him. 3 And they began saying to Him, "Tell us, by what authority are You doing these things; or who is the one who gave You the authority to do these things?"

4 Jesus answered, and said to them, "I will also ask you a question, which if you answer Me, then I will tell you by what authority I do these things. 5 The baptism of John was from what source - from Heaven, or from men? Answer Me."   *continued >*

6 They began reasoning among themselves, saying, "If we say, 'From Heaven,' He will say to us, 'Then why did you not believe him?' 7 But if we say, 'From men,' we fear that the people will stone us to death, for they are all convinced that John was a real prophet." 8 So they answered Jesus, and said, "We do not know where it came from."

9 And Jesus said to them, "Then neither will I tell you by what authority I do these things."

Scene 723   **Who Did The Will of His Father?**

The Temple, Jerusalem, *Judea*   *Matthew 21:28-32*

1 "What do you think? A man had two sons, and he came to the first one, and said, 'Son, go work today in the vineyard.' 2 He answered, 'I will not'; but afterward he regretted it, and went.

3 "Then the man came to his second son, and he said the same thing. 4 The son answered, 'I will, sir', but he did not go.

5 "Which of the two did the will of his father?" They said, "The first."

6 Jesus said to them, "Truly I say to you, that the tax collectors and prostitutes will get into the Kingdom of God before you; 7 for John came to you in the way of righteousness, and you did not believe him; but the tax collectors and prostitutes did believe him; 8 and you, seeing this, did not even feel remorse afterward, so as to believe him."

Scene 724   **The Parable of The Evil Vine-Growers**

Matthew 21:33-46 / Mark 12:1-12~ / Luke 20:9-19

1 Then Jesus began to tell them a parable: "Listen to this: There was a landowner who planted a vineyard, and he put a wall around it, and dug a vat under the wine press, and built a tower. 2 Then he rented it out to vine-growers, and went away on a journey for a long time.

3 "At the harvest time, the landowner sent a slave to the vine-growers, so that they would give him some of the produce of the vineyard. 4 But the vine-growers took the slave and beat him, and sent him away empty-handed.

5 "Again the landowner proceeded to send another slave, and they also beat him, wounded him in the head, treated him shamefully, and sent him away empty-handed.

6 "So the landowner sent a third slave; and this one they also wounded, and cast out. 7 And he sent another, and that one they stoned and killed.

8 "Then the landowner sent a large group of slaves, and they did the same thing to them, beating some and killing others.

9 "The owner of the vineyard said, 'What shall I do?'

10 "He had one more to send, a beloved son; so last of all he sent his son to them, saying, 'I will send my beloved son, perhaps they will respect him.'

11 "But when the vine-growers saw the son, they reasoned among themselves, and said to one another, 'This is the heir; come, let us kill him and seize his inheritance, so that it will be ours!' 12 So they took the son, and threw him out of the vineyard, and killed him.   *continued >*

Scene 724 - *continued*

13 "Therefore, when the owner of the vineyard comes, what will he do to those vine-growers? 14 He will come and destroy those wretches, and then he will rent out the vineyard to other vine-growers, who will pay him the proceeds at the proper seasons."

15 When the people heard this, they said to Jesus, "May it never be!"

16 But He looked at them, and said, "What then is this that is written; have you never read this Scripture? 17 'The stone which the builders rejected has become the chief corner stone. This came about from the Lord, and it is marvelous in our eyes.' 18 Therefore, I say to you, that the Kingdom of God will be taken away from you, and given to a people producing the fruit of it.

19 "And, 'Everyone who falls on that stone will be broken to pieces; but on whomever it falls, it will scatter them like dust!' "

20 When the scribes, the chief priests, and the Pharisees heard this parable, they understood that Jesus was speaking against them, and they tried to lay hands on Him that very hour; 21 but when they sought to seize Him they feared the people, because they considered Him to be a prophet.

Scene 725	**To Serve Me, You Must Follow Me**	
The Temple, Jerusalem, *Judea*	Monday, March 30th / 33 CE	*John 12:20-26*

1 Then some Greeks from among those who were going up to worship at the feast came to Philip, and they said to him, "Sir, we wish to see Jesus."

2 Philip went and told Andrew, and the two of them came and told Jesus.

3 Jesus said to them, "The hour has come for the Son of Man to be glorified! 4 Truly, truly, I say to you, unless a grain of wheat falls into the earth and dies, it remains alone; but if it dies, it bears much fruit.

5 "He who loves his life will lose it; and he who hates his life in this world will keep it, and live eternally.

6 "If anyone serves Me, he must follow Me; and where I am, there My servant will be also. 7 If anyone serves Me, The Father will honor him."

Scene 726	**A Voice From Heaven**	*John 12:27-33*

1 "Now My soul has become troubled. And what shall I say, 'Father, save Me from this hour'? But I have come for this hour. 2 Father, glorify Your Name!"

3 Then a voice came out of heaven: "I have both glorified it, and will glorify it again."

4 So the crowd of people who stood by and heard it were saying that it had thundered; others were saying, "An angel has spoken to Him."

5 Jesus answered, and said, "This voice has not come for My sake, but for your sakes.

6 "Now judgment is upon this world, and now the ruler of this world will be cast out! 7 And I, if I am lifted up from the earth, will draw all men to Myself." 8 Jesus was saying this to indicate the kind of death by which He was going to die.

Scene 727   **Believe In The Light**

The Temple, Jerusalem, *Judea*   Monday, March 30th / 33 CE   *John 12:34-43*

---

1 The crowd answered Jesus, "We have heard out of the Law that the Christ is to remain forever, so how can You say, 'The Son of Man must be lifted up'? 2 Who is this Son of Man?"

3 Jesus said to them, "For a little while longer the Light is among you; 4 walk while you have the Light, so that the darkness will not overtake you. 5 He who walks in darkness does not know where he goes.

6 "While you have the Light, believe in the Light, so that you may become sons of Light."

7 After Jesus spoke these things, He went away, and hid Himself from them, because although He had performed so many signs before them, they did not believe in Him. 8 This was to fulfill the word which Isaiah the prophet spoke: "Lord, who has believed our report? And to whom has the arm of the Lord been revealed?"

9 For this reason they could not believe, for Isaiah also said, "He has blinded their eyes, and He hardened their heart, so that they would not see with their eyes, and perceive with their heart, and return, and I would heal them." 10 These things Isaiah said because he saw His glory, and spoke of Him.

11 Nevertheless, many of the rulers also believed in Jesus, but because of the Pharisees they were not confessing Him, for fear that they would be put out of the synagogue; for they loved the approval of men more than the approval of God.

Scene 728   **Believe In Me, and The One Who Sent Me**

Luke 19:47-48 / John 12:44-50

---

1 Jesus cried out, and said, "He who believes in Me, does not believe in Me, but in Him who sent Me. 2 He who sees Me, sees the One who sent Me.

3 "I have come as Light into the world, so that everyone who believes in Me will not remain in darkness.

4 "If anyone hears My sayings, and does not keep them, I do not judge him; for I did not come to judge the world, but to save the world.

5 "He who rejects Me, and does not receive My sayings, has one who judges him - the Word which I spoke is what will judge him, on the last day. 6 For I did not speak on My own initiative, but The Father Himself who sent Me has given Me a commandment as to what to say, and what to speak.

7 "I know that His commandment is eternal life, therefore the things that I speak, I speak just as The Father has told Me."

8 Jesus was teaching daily in the Temple, and the chief priests and the scribes, and the leading men among the people were trying to destroy Him; 9 but they could not find anything that they might do to Him, because all the people were hanging on to every word that He said.

Act 3 - Tuesday

Scene 731   **Be Prepared For The Wedding Feast**
The Temple, Jerusalem, *Judea*   Tuesday, March 31st / 33 CE
Matthew 22:1-14 / Luke 14:16-24; 17:20-21

1 Having been questioned by the Pharisees as to when the Kingdom of God was coming, Jesus answered them, and said, "The Kingdom of God is not coming with signs to be observed; nor will they say, 'Look, here it is!' or, 'There it is!' for behold, the Kingdom of God is in your midst."

2 Then He spoke to them in parables again, saying, "The Kingdom of Heaven may be compared to a king who gave a big wedding feast for his son, and he invited many guests.

3 "At the dinner hour, he sent out his slaves to say to those who had been invited, 'Come to the wedding feast, for everything is ready now.' 4 But they paid no attention, and they went on their way, and were unwilling to come.

5 "Again the king sent out other slaves saying, 'Tell those who have been invited, "Behold, I have prepared my dinner; my oxen and my fattened livestock are all butchered, and everything is ready. Come to the wedding feast!" '

6 "But they all began to make excuses. The first one said, 'I have bought a piece of land, and I need to go and look at it; please consider me excused.' 7 Another one said, 'I have bought five yoke of oxen, and I am going to try them out; please consider me excused.' 8 Another one said, 'I have married a wife, and for that reason I cannot come;' and another went to his business. 9 The rest seized his slaves, and mistreated them, and killed them.

10 "When the slave came back and reported this to his master, the king became enraged; and he sent his armies who destroyed those murderers, and set their city on fire.

11 "Then the king said to his slaves, 'The wedding is ready, but those who were invited are not worthy; therefore, go out at once into the streets and the lanes of the city, and invite the poor and the crippled, and the blind and the lame, here to the wedding feast.'

12 "The slave said, 'Master, what you commanded has been done, and there is still room.'

13 "The king said to the slave, 'Go out into the highways and along the hedges, and compel them to come in, so that my house may be filled; for I tell you, none of those who were invited, shall taste my dinner.'

14 "His slaves went out into the streets, and gathered together all that they found, both good and evil, and the wedding hall was filled with dinner guests.

15 "When the king came in to look over the dinner guests, he saw a man there who was not dressed in wedding clothes, and he said to him, 'Friend, how did you come in here without wedding clothes?' And the man was speechless.

16 "Then, the king said to his servants, 'Bind him hand and foot, and throw him into the outer darkness; in that place there will be weeping, and gnashing of teeth!' 17 For many are called, but few are chosen."

Scene 732   **The Pharisees Plot To Trap Jesus**

Jerusalem, *Judea*   *Matthew 22:15-16~ / Mark 12:~12-13 / Luke 20:20*

---

1 Then the Pharisees left Jesus and went away, and they plotted together how they might trap Him in what He said. So they watched Him.

2 Then they sent spies to Him - some of their disciples who pretended to be righteous, along with the Herodians - in order that they might catch Him in some statement, so that they could deliver Him to the rule and authority of the Governor.

Scene 733   **Is It Lawful To Pay Taxes To Caesar?**

The Temple, Jerusalem, *Judea*   *Matthew 22:~16-22 / Mark 12:14-17 / Luke 20:21-26*

---

1 The spies came to Jesus, and they questioned Him, saying, "Teacher, we know that You are truthful, and that You speak and teach correctly, and teach the way of God in truth, because You defer to no one, and are not partial to any. 2 Tell us then, what do you think? Is it lawful for us to pay taxes to Caesar, or not? Shall we pay, or shall we not pay?"

3 But Jesus, knowing their hypocrisy perceived their malice, and said to them, "Why are you testing Me, you hypocrites? Show Me the coin used for the poll-tax."

4 They brought Him a denarius; and He asked them, "Whose likeness and inscription does it have?"

5 They said to Him, "Caesar's."

6 Then Jesus said to them, "Then render to Caesar the things that are Caesar's, and to God the things that are God's."

7 Hearing this, they were amazed at His answer, and became silent.

8 And being unable to catch Him in a saying in the presence of the people, they left Him and went away.

Scene 734   **In The Next Life, Whose Wife Will She Be?**

The Temple, Jerusalem, *Judea*   *Matthew 22:23-33 / Mark 12:18-27 / Luke 20:27-40*

---

1 On that day, some of the Sadducees (who say that there is no resurrection) came to Jesus, and began to question Him, saying, "Teacher, Moses wrote for us that if a man dies and leaves behind a wife, and having no children is childless, his brother, as next of kin should marry his wife, and raise up children for his brother.

2 "Now there were seven brothers; and the first one married a wife, and died, and having no children he left his wife to his brother. 3 So the second brother married her, and he also died leaving behind no children; and the third one likewise married her, and so in the same way all seven died, leaving no children. 4 Finally, last of all, the woman died.

5 "In the resurrection therefore, when they rise again, which one of the seven will she be the wife of, for all seven had married her?"

6 Jesus answered, and said to them, "You are mistaken, because you do not understand the Scriptures, nor the power of God.   *continued >*

Scene 734 - *continued*

7 "The sons of this age marry and are given in marriage, but those who are considered worthy to attain to that age, and the resurrection, when they rise from the dead, they neither marry, nor are they given in marriage; 8 because they cannot die anymore, because they are like angels in Heaven, and are sons of God, being sons of the resurrection.

9 "But regarding the fact that the dead are raised, have you not read the passage about the burning bush in the book of Moses, where God said to him, 'I am the God of Abraham, and the God of Isaac, and the God of Jacob'? 10 Now, He is not the God of the dead, but of the living, for all live to Him. You are greatly mistaken."

11 When the crowds heard this, they were astonished at His teaching.

12 Some of the scribes said, "Teacher, You have spoken well;" for they did not have the courage to question Jesus any longer about anything.

Scene 735	**The Greatest Commandment**
The Temple, Jerusalem, *Judea*	*Matthew 22:34-40 / Mark 11:19; 12:28-34 / Luke 21:37*

1 When the Pharisees heard that Jesus had silenced the Sadducees, they gathered themselves together.

2 One of the scribes, a lawyer, came and heard them arguing, and recognizing that Jesus had answered them well, he asked Him a question, to test Him.

3 He asked, "Teacher, what is the great commandment in the Law? Which commandment is the foremost of all?"

4 Jesus answered, "The foremost is: 'Hear, O Israel! The Lord our God is One Lord'; 5 and 'you shall love the Lord your God with all your heart, and with all your soul, and with all your mind, and with all your strength.' 6 This is the great and foremost commandment.

7 "And the second, is this: 'You shall love your neighbor as yourself.' 8 There is no other commandment greater than these, because on these two commandments depend the whole Law, and the Prophets."

9 The scribe said to Him, "Right, Teacher! You have truly stated that He is One, and that there is no one else besides Him; 10 and that to love Him with all your heart, and with all your mind, and with all your strength, and to love one's neighbor as yourself, is worth much more than all burnt offerings and sacrifices."

11 When Jesus saw that he had answered intelligently, He said to him, "You are not far from the Kingdom of God."

12 After that, no one would venture to ask Jesus any more questions.

13 Now during the day He was teaching in the Temple, but when evening came they would go out of the city, and spend the night on the Mount of Olives.

Act 4 - Wednesday - Woe To The Pharisees

Scene 741   **How Is The Christ The Son of David?**
The Temple, Jerusalem, *Judea*   Wednesday, April 1st / 33 CE
Matthew 22:41-46 / Mark 12:35-37 / Luke 20:41-44; 21:38

1 All the people would get up early in the morning, and come to the Temple to listen to Jesus.

2 As He taught in the Temple, while the Pharisees were gathered together, Jesus asked them a question: "What do you think about the Christ; whose son is He?"

3 They said to Him, "The son of David."

4 Then Jesus said to them, "How is it that the scribes say that the Christ is David's son? 5 For in the book of Psalms, David himself in the Holy Spirit calls him 'Lord,' saying, 'The Lord said to my Lord, "Sit at My right hand, until I make Your enemies a footstool beneath Your feet." 6 Therefore, if David himself calls Him 'Lord,' how is He his son?"

7 The large crowd enjoyed listening to Jesus, but no one was able to answer Him a word, and nor did anyone dare to ask Him another question from that day on.

Scene 742   **Beware of The Scribes and The Pharisees**
Matthew 23:1-13 / Mark 12:38-39 / Luke 20:45-46

1 While the crowd of people were listening, Jesus spoke to His disciples.

2 In His teaching He was saying: "The scribes and the Pharisees have seated themselves in the chair of Moses, therefore all that they tell you, do and observe; 3 but do not do according to their deeds, for they say things, and do not do them.

4 "They tie up heavy burdens, and lay them on men's shoulders, but they themselves are unwilling to move them with so much as a finger. 5 They do all their deeds to be noticed by men, for they broaden their phylacteries, and lengthen the tassels of their garments.

6 "So beware of the scribes who like to walk around in long robes, and love respectful greetings in the market places, and the chief seats in the synagogues, and the places of honor at banquets, and being called Rabbi by men.

7 "But do not be called Rabbi; for One is your Teacher, and you are all brothers.

8 "Do not call anyone on earth your father, for you have One Father, who is in Heaven.

9 "Do not be called leaders; for One is your Leader, that is, Christ. 10 The greatest among you shall be your servant, and whoever exalts himself shall be humbled, and whoever humbles himself shall be exalted.

11 "But woe to you, scribes and Pharisees! Hypocrites, because you shut off the Kingdom of Heaven from people; for you yourselves do not enter in, and nor do you allow those who are entering to go in."

Scene 743   **The Hypocrisy Of The Scribes and The Pharisees**

The Temple, Jerusalem, *Judea*   *Matthew 23:14-24 / Mark 12:40 / Luke 20:47*

1 "Woe to you, scribes and Pharisees! Hypocrites, because you devour widows' houses, and for appearance's sake you make long prayers; therefore you will receive greater condemnation!

2 "Woe to you, scribes and Pharisees! Hypocrites, because you travel around on land and sea to make one proselyte; and when he becomes one, you make him twice as much a son of hell as yourselves!

3 "Woe to you, blind guides who say, 'Whoever swears by the Temple, that is nothing, but whoever swears by the gold of the Temple is obligated.' 4 You fools and blind men! Which is more important; the gold, or the Temple that sanctified the gold?

5 "And you say, 'Whoever swears by the altar, that is nothing, but whoever swears by the offering on it, he is obligated.' 6 You blind men! Which is more important; the offering, or the altar that sanctifies the offering?

7 "Therefore, whoever swears by the altar, swears by both the altar and by everything on it. 8 And whoever swears by the Temple, swears by both the Temple and by Him who dwells within it. 9 And whoever swears by Heaven, swears by both the throne of God, and by Him who sits upon it.

10 "Woe to you, scribes and Pharisees, hypocrites! For you tithe mint and dill and cummin, and have neglected the weightier provisions of the law: justice and mercy and faithfulness. 11 These are the things you should have done, without neglecting the others.

12 "You blind guides who strain out a gnat, and swallow a camel!"

Scene 744   **First, Clean The Inside of The Cup**   *Matthew 23:25-28*

1 "Woe to you, scribes and Pharisees! Hypocrites, because you clean the outside of the cup and of the dish, but inside you are full of robbery and self-indulgence! 2 You blind Pharisee! First clean the inside of the cup and the dish, so that the outside of it may become clean also.

3 "Woe to you, scribes and Pharisees! Hypocrites, because you are like whitewashed tombs, which on the outside appear beautiful, but inside they are full of dead men's bones, and all uncleanness. 4 So you too appear outwardly righteous to men, but inside you are full of hypocrisy and lawlessness."

Scene 745   **You Shed The Blood of The Prophets**

The Temple, Jerusalem, *Judea*   *Matthew 23:29-36 / Luke 11:47-51*

1 "Woe to you, scribes and Pharisees! Hypocrites, because you build the tombs of the prophets, and adorn the monuments of the righteous, and it was your fathers who killed them!

2 "You say, 'If we had been living in the days of our fathers, we would not have been partners with them in shedding the blood of the prophets.' 3 So you are witnesses, and testify against yourselves, that you are the sons of those who murdered the prophets, and that you approve of the deeds of your fathers, because it was they who killed them, and you build their tombs!

4 "For this reason, the wisdom of God said, 'Behold, I am sending to you prophets and apostles, wise men and scribes; some of them you will scourge in your synagogues, and persecute from city to city. 5 Some of them you will kill, and some you will crucify, so that upon this generation may fall the guilt of all the righteous blood of all the prophets shed on the earth, since the foundation of the world; 6 from the blood of righteous Able, to the blood of Zechariah, the son of Berechiah, whom you murdered beside the altar in the House of God.'

7 "Yes, truly I say to you, all these things will be charged against this generation. Fill up, then, the measure of the guilt of your fathers!

8 "You serpents! You brood of vipers! How will you escape the sentence of hell?"

Scene 746   **A Second Lament For Jerusalem**

Matthew 23:37-39 / Luke 13:34-35

1 "O Jerusalem, Jerusalem, the city that kills the prophets, and stones those who are sent to her! 2 How often I wanted to gather your children together, just the way that a hen gathers her brood of chicks under her wings; but you were unwilling, and you would not have it. 3 Behold, your house is being left to you desolate.

4 "And I say to you, that you will not see Me from now on, until the time comes when you say, 'Blessed is He who comes in the Name of the Lord!' "

Scene 747   **The Greatest Contributor To The Treasury**

The Temple, Jerusalem, *Judea*   *Mark 12:41-44 / Luke 21:1-4*

1 Jesus sat down opposite the treasury, and began observing how the people were putting their money into the treasury. 2 He saw the many rich people putting in their large sums, and He saw a poor widow come and put in two small copper coins, which amount to a cent.

0 Calling His disciples to Him, Jesus said to them, "Truly I say to you, that this poor widow put into the treasury more than all of the other contributors; for they all put into the offering out of their surplus, but she, out of her poverty, put in all she owned, all that she had to live on."

Act 5 - Wednesday - The End of The Age

Scene 751   **The Temple Will Be Destroyed**

The Temple, Jerusalem, *Judea*   Wednesday, April 1st / 33 CE

Matthew 24:1-2 / Mark 13:1-2 / Luke 21:5-6

---

1 Jesus came out of the Temple and was leaving, when some of His apostles began talking about the Temple, and saying that it was adorned with beautiful stones and votive gifts.

2 One of them said to Jesus, "Teacher, behold! What wonderful stones, and what wonderful buildings!"

3 Jesus said to them, "As for all these great buildings which you are looking at, truly I say to you, the days will come when there will not be left one stone upon another here, which will not be torn down."

Scene 752   **The Signs of The End of The Age**

Mount of Olives, Jerusalem, *Judea*   *Matthew 24:3-8 / Mark 13:3-8 / Luke 21:7-11*

---

1 As Jesus was sitting on the Mount of Olives, opposite the Temple, His apostles Peter, James, John and Andrew came to Him, and they questioned Him privately, saying, "Teacher, tell us when will these things happen, 2 and what will be the sign of Your coming, and of the end of the age, when all these things are going to take place?"

3 Jesus answered, and began to say to them, "See to it that no one misleads you, for many will come in My Name, saying, 'I am the Christ!' and, 'The time is near!' and will mislead many, so do not go after them."

4 Then Jesus continued by saying to them, "You will be hearing of wars and rumors of wars. When you hear of wars and disturbances do not be frightened, for these things must take place first, but the end does not follow immediately. 5 For nation will rise against nation, and kingdom against kingdom; and in various places there will be great earthquakes and famines, and plagues; 6 and there will also be terrors, and great signs from heaven.

7 "But all these things are only the beginning of birth pangs."

Scene 753   **Your Testimony When They Persecute You**

Mount of Olives, Jerusalem, *Judea*   *Matthew 24:9~ / Mark 13:9, 11 / Luke 21:12-15*

---

1 "Be on your guard, because before all of these things, they will lay their hands on you, and they will persecute you. 2 Then they will deliver you to tribulation in the courts, and you will be flogged in the synagogues and prisons.

3 "And they will bring you to stand before governors and kings, for My sake. This will lead to an opportunity for your testimony to them. 4 So when they arrest you and hand you over, do not worry beforehand about what you are to say, but say whatever is given to you in that very hour; for it is not you who speaks, but it is the Holy Spirit.

5 "So do not prepare a defense for yourself beforehand, for I will give you speech and wisdom which none of your opponents will be able to refute, or resist."

Scene 754   **You Will Be Hated Because Of My Name**
Mount of Olives, Jerusalem, *Judea*   *Matthew 24:~9-14 / Mark 13:10, 12-13 / Luke 21:16-19*

1 "Many false prophets will arise and mislead many; and because lawlessness has increased, most people's love will grow cold.

2 "At that time, many will fall away and hate one another, and you will be betrayed. 3 Brother will betray brother to death, and a father his child; and children will rise up against their parents, and relatives, and friends; 4 and they will put some of you to death.

5 "You will be hated by all because of My Name, and yet not one hair of your head will perish. 6 By your endurance you will gain your lives, and the one who endures to the end will be saved.

7 "This gospel of the Kingdom must first be preached in the whole world, as a testimony to all the nations, and then the end will come."

Scene 755   **Do Not Turn Back!**
Matthew 24:15-22 / Mark 13:14-20 / Luke 17:31-33; 21:20-24

1 "When you see Jerusalem surrounded by armies, then recognize that her desolation is near.

2 "And when you see the abomination of desolation, which was spoken of by Daniel the prophet, standing in the Holy Place where it should not be (let the reader understand), then those who are in Judea must flee to the mountains, and those who are in the city must leave, and those who are in the country must not enter the city, 3 because these are days of vengeance, so that all of the things which are written will be fulfilled.

4 "On that day, the one who is on the housetop, and whose goods are in the house, must not go down or go in to get anything out of his house. 5 And likewise, whoever is in the field must not turn back to get his coat. 6 Remember Lot's wife; whoever seeks to keep his life will lose it, and whoever loses his life will preserve it.

7 "But woe to those who are pregnant, and to those who are nursing babies in those days, for there will be great distress upon the land, and wrath to this people! 8 They will fall by the edge of the sword, and be led captive into all the nations; 9 and Jerusalem will be trampled under foot by the Gentiles, until the times of the Gentiles are fulfilled.

10 "But pray that your flight may not happen in the winter, or on a Sabbath; 11 for those days will be a time of great tribulation, such as has not occurred since the beginning of the creation of the world which God created until now, nor ever will.

12 "And unless the Lord had shortened those days, no life would have been saved; but for the sake of the elect whom He chose, those days will be cut short."

Scene 756   **False Christs Will Arise**

Mount of Olives, Jerusalem, *Judea*   Wednesday, April 1st / 33 CE
Matthew 24:23-27 / Mark 13:21-23 / Luke 17:22-24

---

1 Then Jesus said to His apostles, "The days will come when you will long to see one of the days of the Son of Man, and you will not see it. 2 And then if anyone says to you, 'Behold, here is the Christ,' or 'Look, He is there!' do not believe him, and do not go and run away after them; 3 for false Christs and false prophets will arise, and will show great signs and wonders, so as to lead astray if possible, even the elect. 4 But take heed! Behold, I have told you everything in advance.

5 "So if they say to you, 'Behold, He is in the wilderness,' do not go out; or, 'Behold, He is in the inner rooms,' do not believe them. 6 For just as the lightning comes from the east, and flashes even to the west, so will the coming of the Son of Man be in His day."

Scene 757   **Signs In The Sun, Moon and Stars**

Matthew 24:29-31 / Mark 13:24-27 / Luke 21:25-28

---

1 "Immediately after the tribulation of those days, there will be signs in the sun, and the moon, and the stars. 2 The sun will be darkened, and the moon will not give its light; 3 and the stars will be falling from heaven, for the powers that are in the heavens will be shaken.

4 "And on the earth, dismay among nations who are perplexed at the roaring of the sea and the waves, with men fainting from fear at the expectation of the things which are coming upon the world.

5 "Then the sign of the Son of Man will appear in the sky, and all the tribes of the earth will mourn. 6 And they will see the Son of Man coming in the clouds of heaven, with great power and glory!

7 "Then He will send forth His angels with a great trumpet, and they will gather together His elect from the four winds, from the farthest end of the earth to the farthest end of Heaven.

8 "But when you see these things begin to take place, straighten up, and lift up your heads, because your redemption is drawing near!"

Act 6 - Wednesday - The Return

Scene 761   **The Parable of The Fig Tree**

Mount of Olives, Jerusalem, *Judea*   Wednesday, April 1st / 33 CE
Matthew 24:32-39 / Mark 13:28-32 / Luke 17:25-30; 21:29-33

---

1 Then Jesus said to them, "Now learn a parable. Behold the fig and all trees: as soon as it puts forth its leaves you see it, and know for yourselves that summer is now near. 2 Even so, when you see all these things happening, recognize that the Kingdom of God is near, and He is right at the door.

3 "Truly I say to you, this generation will not pass away until all these things take place 4 Heaven and earth will pass away, but My words will not pass away.   *continued >*

5 "But of that day and hour, no one knows - not even the angels in Heaven, nor the Son - but The Father alone. 6 But first, He must suffer many things, and be rejected by this generation.

7 "For the coming of the Son of Man will be just like it happened in the days of Noah; for in those days before the flood, they were eating and they were drinking, and they were marrying and being given in marriage, until the day that Noah entered the ark. 8 And they did not understand until the flood came, and took them all away.

9 "The same thing happened in the days of Lot: They were eating and they were drinking, they were buying and they were selling, they were planting and they were building; 10 but on the day that Lot went out from Sodom, it rained fire and brimstone from heaven, and destroyed them all.

11 "So it will be just the same, on the day that the Son of Man is revealed."

Scene 762   One Will Be Taken, and The Other Will Be Left
Mount of Olives, Jerusalem, *Judea*   *Matthew 24:28, 40-42 / Mark 13:33 / Luke 17:34-37*

1 "I tell you, on that night there will be two people in one bed; one will be taken, and the other will be left. 2 There will be two men in the field; one will be taken, and the other will be left. 3 Two women will be grinding at the same mill; one will be taken, and the other will be left."

4 They asked Him, "Where, Lord?"

5 Jesus said, "Wherever the corpse is, there the vultures will also be gathered. 6 Therefore take heed, and keep on the alert, for you do not know when the appointed day of your Lord will come."

Scene 763   Be On The Alert!
Matthew 24:43-44 / Mark 13:34-37 / Luke 12:39-40; 21:34-36

1 "Be on guard, so that your hearts will not be weighed down with dissipation and drunkenness, and the worries of this life, and that day come upon you suddenly like a trap; for it will come upon all those who dwell on the face of all the earth.

2 "It is like a man going away on a journey, who upon leaving his house he puts his slaves in charge, assigning to each one his task; and he commanded the door keeper to stay on the alert. 3 But be sure of this, that if the head of the house had known at what hour of the night the thief was coming, he would have been on the alert, and he would not have allowed his house to be broken into.

4 "Therefore, be on the alert! For you do not know when the master of the house is coming, whether in the evening, at midnight, or when the rooster crows, or in the morning - in case he should come suddenly, and find you asleep. 5 For this reason you also must be ready, for the Son of Man is coming at an hour when you do not expect that He will.

6 "So keep on the alert at all times, praying that you may have the strength to escape all of these things that are about to take place, and to stand before the Son of Man. 7 What I say to you, I say to all: 'Be on the alert!' "

Scene 764   **Be Dressed In Readiness**

Mount of Olives, Jerusalem, *Judea*   *Matthew 24:45-51 / Luke 12:35-38, 41-48*

1 "Be dressed in readiness, and keep your lamps lit! 2 Be like men who are waiting for their master when he returns from the wedding feast, so that they may immediately open the door to him when he comes and knocks. 3 Blessed are those slaves whom the master will find on the alert when he comes! 4 Truly I say to you, that he will gird himself to serve, and have them recline at the table; and he himself will come and wait on them. 5 So whether he comes in the second watch, or even in the third, and finds them ready, blessed are those slaves!"

6 Peter said, "Lord, are You addressing this parable to us, or to everyone else as well?"

7 Jesus said, "Who then is the faithful and sensible steward, whom his master will put in charge of his household servants, to give them their food and rations at the proper time? 8 Blessed is that slave whom his master will find so doing when he comes! Truly I say to you, that he will put him in charge of all his possessions.

9 "But if that evil slave says in his heart, 'My master will not be coming for a long time', and he begins to beat his fellow slaves, both men and women, and to eat and get drunk with drunkards, 10 then the master of that slave will come on a day when he does not expect him, and at an hour which he does not know, and he will cut him in pieces, and assign him a place with the hypocrites and the unbelievers; in that place there will be weeping, and gnashing of teeth.

11 "And that slave who knew his master's will, and did not get ready, or act in accordance with it, will receive many lashes; 12 but the one who did not know it, and committed deeds worthy of a flogging, will receive only a few. 13 From everyone who has been given much, much will be required; and to whom they entrusted much, of him they will ask even more."

Scene 765   **The Lamps of The Ten Virgins**   *Matthew 25:1-13*

1 "At that time, the Kingdom of Heaven may be compared to ten virgins, who took their lamps and went out to meet the bridegroom. 2 Five of them were foolish and five were prudent; for when the foolish took their lamps, they took no oil with them, but the prudent took oil in flasks along with their lamps.

3 "Now while the bridegroom was delaying, they all got drowsy, and began to sleep. 4 But at midnight there was a shout, 'Behold, the bridegroom! Come out to meet him!'

5 "When the ten virgins rose and trimmed their lamps, the foolish said to the prudent, 'Give us some of your oil, for our lamps are going out!'

6 "But the prudent answered, 'No, there will not be enough for us and you too. Go instead to the dealers, and buy some for yourselves.' 7 While they were going away to make the purchase the bridegroom came, and those who were ready went in with him to the wedding feast; and the door was shut.

8 "Later, the other virgins also came, saying, 'Lord, lord, open up to us!' But he answered, 'Truly I say to you, I do not know you.'

9 "Be on the alert then, because you do not know the day, or the hour.'"

Scene 766   **Separating The Sheep From The Goats**
Mount of Olives, Jerusalem, *Judea*   *Matthew 25:31 - 26:2 / Mark 14:1~ / Luke 22:1*

1 "When the Son of Man comes in His glory, and all the angels with Him, then He will sit on His glorious throne. 2 All the nations will be gathered before Him, and He will separate them one from another, as the shepherd separates the sheep from the goats; 3 and He will put the sheep on His right, and the goats on the left.

4 "Then the King will say to those on His right, 'Come, you who are blessed of My Father, inherit the Kingdom prepared for you from the foundation of the world! 5 For I was hungry, and you gave Me something to eat; I was thirsty, and you gave Me something to drink; I was a stranger, and you invited Me in; I was sick, and you visited Me; I was in prison, and you came to Me.'

6 "Then the righteous will answer Him, 'Lord, when did we see You hungry, and feed You; or thirsty, and give You something to drink? 7 When did we see You a stranger and invite You in; or naked, and clothe You. 8 Or when did we see You sick or in prison, and come to You?'

9 "The King will answer, and say to them, 'Truly I say to you, to the extent that you did it to one of these brothers of Mine, even the least of them, you did it to Me.'

10 "Then He will say to those on His left, 'Depart from Me accursed ones, into the eternal fire which has been prepared for the Devil and his angels! 11 For I was hungry, and you gave Me nothing to eat; I was thirsty, and you gave Me nothing to drink; 12 I was a stranger, and you did not invite Me in; naked, and you did not clothe Me; sick and in prison, and you did not visit Me.'

13 "Then they will say, 'Lord, when did we see You hungry or thirsty, or a stranger, or naked, or sick, or in prison, and not take care of You?'

14 "And He will answer them, 'Truly I say to you, that to the extent that you did not do it to one of the least of these, you did not do it to Me.' 15 These will go away into eternal punishment, but the righteous into eternal life."

16 When Jesus had finished all of these words, He said to His apostles, "You know that the Feast of Unleavened Bread and the Passover are two days away, and the Son of Man is going to be handed over for crucifixion."

Scene 767   **Judas Plots With The Jews To Betray Jesus**
The Temple, Jerusalem, *Judea*   Wednesday, April 1st / 33 CE
Matthew 26:3-5, 14-16 / Mark 14:~1-2, 10-11 / Luke 22:2-6 / John 13:2

1 The chief priests and the scribes, [with] the elders of the people were gathered together in the court of the High Priest, named Caiaphas; and they plotted together seeking how they might seize Jesus by stealth, and put Him to death. 2 But they were afraid of the people, and said, "Not during the festival, otherwise a riot might occur."

3 Then Satan entered into the heart of one of the twelve, Judas, the son of Simon Iscariot. 4 And he went to the chief priests to discuss how he might betray Jesus to them.

5 Judas said, "What will you give me to betray Him to you?"   *continued >*

Scene 767 - *continued*

6 They were glad when they heard this, and agreed to give him money; and they weighed out thirty pieces of silver to him.

7 So Judas consented, and from then on he began looking for a good opportunity to betray Jesus to them, away from the crowds.

Act 7 - Thursday - The Last Supper

Scene 771   **Preparing The Venue**

Jerusalem, *Judea*   Thursday, April 2nd / 33 CE
Matthew 26:17-19 / Mark 14:12-16 / Luke 22:7-13 / John 13:1

---

1 Now on the first day of Unleavened Bread, on which the Passover lamb was to be sacrificed, His apostles came to Jesus, and asked Him, "Where do you want us to go and prepare for You to eat the Passover?"

2 Jesus sent two of His apostles, Peter and John; and He said to them, "Go and prepare it for us to eat in the city. 3 When you have entered the city, a certain man will meet you carrying a pitcher of water; follow him, 4 and say to the owner of the house that he enters, 'The Teacher says to you, "My time is near. I am to keep the Passover at your house. 5 Where is the guest room in which I may eat the Passover with My disciples?" ' 6 And he himself will show you a large upper room, furnished and ready; prepare it for us there."

7 Peter and John did as Jesus directed them, and they went into the city and found everything just as He had told them; and they prepared the Passover.

8 Now before the Passover Feast, Jesus, knowing that His hour had come when He would depart out of this world and go to The Father, having loved His own who were in the world, He loved them to the end.

Scene 772   **The Last Supper Begins**

A house in Jerusalem, *Judea*   Thursday evening, April 2nd / 33 CE
Matthew 26:20 / Mark 14:17 / Luke 22:14-16, 24-30

---

1 When it was evening, and the hour had come, Jesus came and reclined at the table with His twelve apostles.

2 He said to them, "I have earnestly desired to eat this Passover with you before I suffer, for I say to you, that I shall not eat it again until it is fulfilled in the Kingdom of God."

3 And a dispute arose among them, as to which one of them was to be regarded as the greatest.

4 Jesus said to them, "The kings of the Gentiles lord it over them, and those who have authority over them are called 'Benefactors.' 5 But it is not this way with you, for the one who is the greatest among you must become like the youngest, and the leader like the servant. 6 For who is greater, the one who reclines at the table, or the one who serves? Is it not the one who reclines at the table? 7 But I am among you as the One who serves.

8 "You are those who have stood by Me in My trials, and just as My Father has granted Me a Kingdom, I grant that you may eat and drink at My table, in My Kingdom; 9 and you will sit on thrones, judging the twelve tribes of Israel."

Scene 773　　**Jesus Washes His Apostles' Feet**　　*John 13:3-20; 15:3*

1 Jesus, knowing that The Father had given all things into His hands, and that He had come forth from God, and was going back to God, got up from supper, and He laid aside His garments, and girded Himself with a towel. 2 Then He poured water into the basin, and began to wash His apostles' feet, and to wipe them with the towel with which He was girded.

3 When Jesus came to Simon, Peter said to Him, "Lord, do You wash my feet?"

4 Jesus answered him, "What I do you do not realize now, but you will understand later."

5 Peter said to Him, "Never shall You wash my feet!"

6 Jesus answered, "If I do not wash you, you have no part with Me."

7 Peter said to Him, "Lord, then wash not only my feet, but also my hands, and my head."

8 Jesus said to him, "He who has bathed is completely clean, and needs only to wash his feet. 9 And you are already clean, because of the Word which I have spoken to you; but not all of you." 10 Jesus knew the one who was betraying Him, and for this reason He said, "Not all of you are clean."

11 When He had washed their feet, Jesus took His garments, and reclined at the table again.

12 Then He said to them, "Do you know what I have done to you? 13 You call Me Teacher and Lord; and you are right, for so I am. 14 If I, the Lord and the Teacher, have washed your feet, then you should also wash one another's feet; for I gave you an example that you should do as I did to you.

15 "Truly, truly, I say to you, a slave is not greater than his master, and nor is one who is sent greater than the one who sent him. 16 If you know these things, you are blessed if you do them!

17 "I do not speak of all of you. I know the ones whom I have chosen; but it is that the Scripture may be fulfilled: 'He who eats My bread has lifted up his heel against Me.' 18 From now on, I am telling you before it comes to pass, so that when it does occur, you may believe that I am He.

19 "Truly, truly, I say to you, he who receives whomever I send receives Me; and he who receives Me, receives the One who sent Me."

Scene 774　　**One of You Will Betray Me**
Matthew 26:21-24 / Mark 14:18-21 / Luke 22:21-23 / John 13:21-22

1 After Jesus had said this, as they were reclining at the table and eating, He became troubled in His spirit; and He testified, saying, "Truly, truly, I say to you, that one of you will betray Me - one who is eating with Me."

2 They all began to be deeply grieved, and they each one by one began to say to Him, "Surely not I, Lord?"

3 Jesus answered, and said to them, "It is one of the twelve. 4 Behold, he who dips his hand with Mine in the bowl is the one who will betray Me. 5 For indeed, the Son of Man is going to go just as it has been written of Him - 6 but woe to that man by whom He is betrayed! It would have been good for that man if he had not been born."　　　　*continued >*

Scene 774 - *continued*

7 The apostles began looking at one another, at a loss to know of whom He was speaking. 8 And they began to discuss among themselves which one of them it might be who was going to do this thing.

Scene 775   **Judas Is Revealed**
A house in Jerusalem, *Judea*   Thursday evening, April 2nd / 33 CE
Matthew 26:25 / John 13:23-32

1 Reclining there on Jesus' bosom was the apostle whom Jesus loved, so Simon Peter gestured to him, and said, "Tell us of whom He is speaking."

2 He, leaning back on Jesus' bosom, asked Him, "Who is it, Lord?"

3 Jesus answered, "It is the one for whom I shall dip the morsel, and give it to him." 4 So when He had dipped the morsel, He gave it to Judas, the son of Simon Iscariot.

5 Judas said, "Surely it is not I, Rabbi." Jesus answered him, "You have said it."

6 After the morsel, Satan entered into Judas. Therefore Jesus said to him, "What you do, do quickly."

7 No one reclining at the table knew why Jesus said this to him, but some were supposing that because Judas had the money box, He was saying to him, "Buy the things we need for the feast," or that he should give something to the poor.

8 So after receiving the morsel Judas immediately went out, and it was night.

9 After he had gone out, Jesus said, "Now is the Son of Man glorified, and God is glorified in Him! And God will glorify Him in Himself, and will glorify Him immediately."

Scene 776   **The Blood of The New Covenant**
Thursday evening, April 2nd / 33 CE   *Matthew 26:26-29 / Mark 14:22-25 / Luke 22:17-20*

1 While they were eating, Jesus took some bread; and after giving a blessing of thanks, He broke the bread, and gave it to the apostles.

2 And He said, "Take it, and eat. This is my body which is given for you. Do this in remembrance of Me."

3 After they had eaten, Jesus took the cup; and in the same way, after He had given thanks, He gave it to the apostles, saying, "Take this, and share it among yourselves. Drink from it, all of you."

4 As they all drank from it, Jesus said to them, "This cup is My blood of the new covenant, which is poured out for you and for many, for the forgiveness of sins.

5 "Truly I say to you, I will not drink of this fruit of the vine again, until that day when the Kingdom of God comes, and I drink it new with you, in My Father's Kingdom."

Scene 777   **My New Commandment: Love One Another**   *John 13:34-35*

1 "A new commandment I give to you, that you love one another; even as I have loved you, that you also love one another.

2 "By this all men will know that you are My disciples, if you have love for one another."

Scene 778   **Peter, You Will Deny Me Three Times**
Matthew 26:31-35 / Mark 14:27-31 / Luke 22:31-34 / John 13:33, 36-38

1 "Little children, I am with you for only a little while longer. 2 You will seek Me, and as I said to the Jews, I now say also to you; 'Where I am going, you cannot come.' "

3 Simon Peter said to Jesus, "Lord, where are You going?"

4 Jesus answered, "Where I go, you cannot follow Me now, but you will follow later."

5 Peter said to Him, "Lord, why can I not follow You now?"

6 Jesus said to them, "You will all fall away because of Me this night, for it is written; 'I will strike down the shepherd, and the sheep of the flock shall be scattered!' 7 But after I have been raised, I will go ahead of you to Galilee."

8 Peter said to Him, "Even though all may fall away because of You, I will never fall away."

9 Jesus said to him, "Simon, Simon, behold! Satan has demanded permission to sift you like wheat; but I have prayed for you, that your faith may not fail. 10 And you, when you have turned again, strengthen your brothers."

11 But Peter said, "Lord, I am ready to go with You both to prison and to death! I will lay down my life for You."

12 Jesus answered, and said him, "Will you lay down your life for Me? 13 Truly, truly, I say to you Peter, that this very night, a rooster will not crow until you yourself have denied that you know Me, three times."

14 But Peter kept insisting, "Even if I have to die with You, I will not deny You!" 15 And all the apostles were saying the same thing.

Scene 779   **Two Swords Are Enough**   *Luke 22:35-38*

1 Jesus said to them, "When I sent you out without money belt or bag or sandals, you did not lack anything, did you?" They said, "No, nothing."

2 Then He said to them, "But now, whoever has a money belt is to take it along, likewise also a bag. 3 And whoever has no sword is to sell his coat and buy one. 4 For I tell you, that this which is written must be fulfilled in Me, 'And He was numbered with transgressors'; for that which refers to Me has its fulfillment."

5 They said, "Lord, look, here are two swords." And He said to them, "It is enough."

Act 8 - The Holy Spirit and The Father

Scene 781   **I Am The Way, and The Truth, and The Life**

A house in Jerusalem, *Judea*   Thursday evening, April 2nd / 33 CE   *John 14:1-12*

---

1 "Do not let your heart be troubled. Believe in God, and believe also in Me.

2 "In My Father's house are many places to dwell; if it were not so, I would have told you, because I go to prepare a place for you. 3 And if I go and prepare a place for you, I will come again and receive you to Myself, so that where I am, there you may be also. 4 And you know the way to where I am going."

5 Thomas said to Him, "Lord, we do not know where You are going. How do we know the way?"

6 Jesus said to him, "I am the way, and the truth, and the life; no one comes to The Father but through Me. 7 If you had known Me, you would have known My Father also. From now on you know Him, and have seen Him."

8 Philip said, "Lord, show us The Father, and it is enough for us."

9 Jesus said to him, "Have I been with you this long, and yet you have not come to know Me, Philip? 10 He who has seen Me has seen The Father.

11 "How can you say, 'Show us The Father'? Do you not believe that I am in The Father, and that The Father is in Me? 12 The words that I say to you, I do not speak on My own initiative, but The Father abiding in Me does His works. 13 Believe Me, that I am in The Father, and that The Father is in Me; otherwise believe because of the works themselves.

14 "Truly, truly, I say to you, he who believes in Me, the works that I do, he will do also. 15 And greater works than these he will do, because I go to The Father."

Scene 782   **The Holy Spirit Helper**   *John 14:13-26*

---

1 "Whatever you ask in My Name, that I will do, so that The Father may be glorified in the Son. 2 If you ask anything of Me in My Name, I will do it

3 "If you love Me, you will keep My commandments, 4 and I will ask The Father, and He will give you another Helper, that He may be with you forever, that is the Spirit of Truth; 5 whom the world cannot receive, because it does not see Him, or know Him; but you know Him, because He abides with you, and will be in you. 6 I will not leave you as orphans, I will come to you.

7 "After a little while, the world will no longer see Me, but you will see Me; and because I live you will also live. 8 In that day, you will know that I am in My Father, and that you are in Me, and I am in you.

9 "He who has My commandments, and keeps them, is the one who loves Me; 10 and he who loves Me will be loved by My Father; and I will love him, and will disclose Myself to him."

11 Judas Thaddaeus said to Him, "Lord, what has happened that You are going to disclose Yourself to us, and not to the world?"

12 Jesus answered, and said to him, "If anyone loves Me, he will keep My Word, and My Father will love him; 13 and We will come to him, and make Our abode with him.   *continued >*

14 "He who does not love Me does not keep My words; and the Word which you hear is not Mine, but The Father's who sent Me.

15 "These things I have spoken to you while I am abiding with you, but the Helper, the Holy Spirit whom The Father will send in My Name, He will teach you all things, and bring to your remembrance all that I have said to you."

Scene 783   **I Go Away, and I Will Come To You**   *John 14:27-31~*

1 "Peace I leave with you! My peace I give to you, but not as the world gives do I give to you.

2 "Do not let your heart be troubled, nor let it be fearful. 3 You have heard that I said to you, 'I go away, and I will come to you.' 4 If you loved Me, you would have rejoiced because I go to The Father, for The Father is greater than I.

5 "Now I have told you before it happens, so that when it happens, you may believe.

6 "I will not speak much more with you now, for the ruler of the world is coming, and he has no part of Me. 7 But so that the world may know that I love The Father, I do exactly as The Father has commanded Me."

Scene 784   **Abide In My Love, and Bear Fruit**   *John 15:1-11*

1 "I am the true vine, and My Father is the vinedresser. 2 Every branch in Me that does not bear fruit, He takes away; 3 and every branch that bears fruit He prunes, so that it may bear more fruit.

4 "Abide in Me, as I abide in you. As the branch cannot bear fruit of itself unless it abides in the vine, so neither can you bear fruit unless you abide in Me.

5 "I am the vine, and you are the branches. 6 He who abides in Me, and I in him, bears much fruit; for apart from Me, you can do nothing. 7 If anyone does not abide in Me, he is thrown away as a branch and dries up, and is gathered and cast into the fire, where they are burned.

8 "If you abide in Me, and My words abide in you, ask whatever you wish, and it will be done for you. 9 My Father is glorified by this, that you bear much fruit, and so prove to be My disciples.

10 "Just as The Father has loved Me, I have also loved you. Abide in My love!

11 "If you keep My commandments you will abide in My love, just as I have kept My Father's commandments, and abide in His love.

12 "These things I have spoken to you so that My joy may be in you, and that your joy may be made full!"

Scene 785   **My Commandment Again: Love One Another**

A house in Jerusalem, *Judea*   Thursday evening, April 2ⁿᵈ / 33 CE   *John 15:12-17*

1 "This is My commandment; that you love one another, just as I have loved you! 2 Greater love has no one than this, that one would lay down his life for his friends. 3 You are My friends, if you do what I command you.

4 "No longer do I call you slaves, for the slave does not know what his master is doing; but I have called you friends, for all of the things that I have heard from My Father, I have made them known to you.

5 "You did not choose Me, but I chose you, and appointed you, so that you would go and bear fruit, and that your fruit would remain; 6 so that whatever you ask of The Father in My Name, He will give to you.

7 "This I command you; that you love one another."

Scene 786   **The World Hates Me and My Father**   *John 15:18-25*

1 "If the world hates you, know that it has hated Me before it hated you. 2 If you were of the world, the world would love its own; 3 but because you are not of the world, but I chose you out of the world, because of this the world hates you.

4 "Remember the Word that I said to you; 'A slave is not greater than his master.' 5 If they have persecuted Me, then they will also persecute you; 6 and if they have kept My word, then they will also keep yours. 7 All these things they will do to you for My name's sake, because they do not know the One who sent Me. 8 If I had not come and spoken to them, they would not have sin, but now they have no excuse for their sin.

9 "The one who hates Me also hates My Father. 10 If I had not done among them the works which no one else did, then they would not have sin; but now they have both seen Me, and hated Me, and My Father as well. 11 But they have done this to fulfill the word that is written in their Law; 'They hated Me without a cause.' "

Scene 787   **More About The Holy Spirit of Truth**   *John 15:26 - 16:15*

1 "When the Helper comes, whom I will send to you from The Father - that is the Spirit of Truth who proceeds from The Father - He will testify about Me.

2 "And you will also testify, because you have been with Me from the beginning. 3 These things I have spoken to you, so that you may be kept from stumbling, 4 because they will make you outcasts from the synagogue, and an hour is coming when everyone who kills you will think that he is offering service to God. 5 These things they will do because they do not know The Father, or Me. 6 But I have spoken these things to you, so that when their time comes, you may remember that I told you of them.

7 "These things I did not say to you at the beginning, because I was with you, but now I am going to Him who sent Me; 8 and none of you asks Me, 'Where are You going?'

9 "Now, because I have said these things to you, sorrow has now filled your heart. 10 But I tell you the truth, it is to your advantage that I go away, for if I do not go away then the Helper will not come to you; however, if I go, then I will send Him to you.   *continued >*

11 "And when He comes, He will convict the world concerning sin, and right-eousness, and judgment. 12 Concerning sin, because they do not believe in Me; 13 and concerning righteousness, because I go to The Father, and you will no longer see Me; 14 and concerning judgment, because the ruler of this world has been judged.

15 "I have many more things to say to you, but you cannot bear them now; but when the Spirit of Truth comes, He will guide you into all of the truth, 16 for He will not speak on His own initiative, but whatever He hears He will speak; and He will disclose to you what is to come. 17 He will glorify Me, for He will take of Mine, and will disclose it to you.

18 "All things that The Father has are Mine, therefore I said that He will take what is Mine, and disclose it to you."

Scene 788   **I Am Going To The Father**   *John 16:16-33*

---

1 "After a little while, you will no longer see Me; and again after a little while, then you will see Me."

2 Some of His apostles said to one another, "What is this thing He is telling us, 'After little while and you will not see Me; and again after a little while, then you will see Me'; and, 'because I go to The Father'? 3 What is this that He says, 'A little while'? We do not know what He is talking about."

4 Jesus knew that they wished to question Him, and He said to them, "Are you deliberating together about this, that I said, 'A little while, and you will not see Me; and again a little while, and you will see Me'? 5 Truly, truly, I say to you, that you will weep and lament, but the world will rejoice; and you will grieve, but your grief will be turned into joy!

6 "Whenever a woman is in labor she has pain, because her hour has come; 7 but when she gives birth to the child, she no longer remembers the anguish, because of the joy that a child has been born into the world. 8 Therefore, you will also have grief now, but I will see you again, and your heart will rejoice; and no one will take your joy away from you. 9 In that day you will not question Me about anything.

10 "Truly, truly, I say to you, if you ask The Father for anything in My Name, He will give it to you. 11 Until now, you have not asked for anything in My Name; ask and you will receive, so that your joy may be made full.

12 "These things I have spoken to you in figurative language, but an hour is coming when I will no longer speak to you in figurative language, but I will tell you plainly of The Father.

13 "In that day you will ask in My Name, and I do not say to you that I will request of The Father on your behalf, for The Father Himself loves you, because you have loved Me, and have believed that I have come forth from The Father. 14 I came forth from The Father, and have come into the world, and now I am leaving the world, and going back to The Father."

15 His apostles said, "Ah, now You are speaking plainly, and are not using a figure of speech. 16 Now we know that You know all things, and have no need for anyone to question You; by this we believe that You have come from God."

continued >

Scene 788 - *continued*

17 Jesus answered them, "Do you now believe? 18 Behold, the hour has come for each of you to be scattered on his own, and to leave Me alone; 19 and yet I am not alone, because The Father is with Me.

20 "These things I have spoken to you so that in Me you may have peace. 21 In the world you have tribulation, but take courage, I have overcome the world."

Scene 789   **Jesus Prays To The Father**
A house in Jerusalem, *Judea*   Thursday evening, April 2nd / 33 CE
Matthew 26:30 / Mark 14:26 / Luke 22:39 / John 14:~31; 17:1 - 18:1~

1 After Jesus spoke these things, He raised His eyes to heaven, and said, "Father, the hour has come! Glorify Your Son, so that the Son may glorify You; 2 even as You gave Him authority over all flesh, that to all whom You have given Him, He may give eternal life.

3 "This is eternal life, that they may know You, the only true God, and Jesus Christ, whom You have sent.

4 "I glorified You on the earth, having accomplished the work which You have given Me to do. 5 Now Father, glorify Me together with Yourself, with the glory which I had with You before the world was.

6 "I have manifested Your Name to the men whom You gave Me out of the world; they were Yours, and You gave them to Me, and they have kept Your Word.

7 "Now they have come to know that everything You have given Me is from You, for I have given to them the words which You gave to Me; 8 and they received them, and have truly understood that I came forth from You, and they believe that You sent Me.

9 "I ask on their behalf, I do not ask on behalf of the world, but of those whom You have given Me, for they are Yours. 10 All things that are Mine are Yours, and Yours are Mine; and I have been glorified in them!

11 "I am no longer in the world, and yet they themselves are in the world, and I come to You.

12 "Holy Father, keep them in Your Name - the Name which You have given to Me - that they may be one, even as We are.

13 "While I was with them, I kept them in Your Name which You have given to Me; 14 and I guarded them, and not one of them perished except the son of perdition, so that the Scripture would be fulfilled.

15 "And now I come to You; and these things I speak in the world, so that they may have My joy made full within themselves.

16 "I have given them Your Word, and the world has hated them, because they are not of the world, even as I am not of the world. 17 I do not ask You to take them out of the world, but to keep them from the evil one.

18 "They are not of the world, even as I am not of the world. 19 Sanctify them in the truth; Your Word is truth!   *continued >*

20 "As You sent Me into the world, I have also sent them into the world.

21 "For their sakes I sanctify Myself, that they themselves may also be sanctified in truth.

22 "I do not ask on behalf of these alone, but also for those who believe in Me through their word, that they may all be one; 23 even as You, Father, are in Me, and I am in You, that they may also be in Us, so that the world may believe that You sent Me.

24 "The glory which You have given Me, I have given to them, that they may be one, just as We are one; I in them, and You in Me, that they may be perfected in unity; 25 so that the world may know that You sent Me, and loved them, even as You have loved Me.

26 "Father, I also desire that those whom You have given Me, be with Me where I am, so that they may see My glory which You have given Me; for You loved Me before the foundation of the world.

27 "O righteous Father! Although the world has not known You, yet I have known You; and these have known that You sent Me. 28 And I have made Your Name known to them, and will make it known, so that the love with which You have loved Me may be in them, and I in them."

29 After Jesus had spoken these words, He said, "Get up, and let us go from here."

30 After singing a hymn, He went out and proceeded, as was His custom, to the Mount of Olives; and His apostles followed Him.

CHAPTER 8 - ARREST, TRIALS & CRUCUIFIXION

Act 1 - Jesus Is Arrested At Gethsemane

Scene 811   **The First Agonized Prayer of Jesus**

Garden of Gethsemane, Mount of Olives, Jerusalem, *Judea*
late Thursday evening, April 2nd / 33 CE
Matthew 26:36-39 / Mark 14:32-36 / Luke 22:40-44 / John 18:~1-2

---

1 Jesus went forth with His apostles through the Kidron ravine, and came to a place called Gethsemane where there was a garden, into which they entered. 2 Now Judas Iscariot, who was betraying Him, also knew the garden, for Jesus had often met there with His apostles.

3 When they arrived at the place, Jesus said to them, "Sit here, while I go over there and pray. And pray that you may not enter into temptation."

4 Jesus took with Him Peter, and James and John, the two sons of Zebedee.

5 Then He began to be very distressed and troubled; and He said to them, "My soul is deeply grieved, to the point of death. 6 Remain here, and keep watch with Me."

7 Then Jesus withdrew about a stone's throw beyond them, and fell down to the ground on His face.

8 And He began to pray, that if it were possible, the hour might pass Him by; saying, "Abba. My Father. All things are possible for You. 9 If You are willing, remove this cup, and let it pass from Me; yet not as I will, but what You will be done."

10 Then an angel from Heaven appeared to Jesus, strengthening Him.

11 And being in agony, He was praying very fervently; and His sweat became like drops of blood, falling down upon the ground.

Scene 812   **Jesus Prays A Second Time**

Matthew 26:40-42 / Mark 14:37-39 / Luke 22:45-46

---

1 When Jesus rose from prayer, He came to the apostles, and found them sleeping from sorrow.

2 He said to Peter, "Simon, are you asleep? Why are you sleeping? Could you men not keep watch with Me for one hour?

3 "Get up! Keep watching, and praying that you may not enter into temptation; 4 the spirit is willing, but the flesh is weak."

5 Then Jesus went away a second time, and He prayed again, saying the same words; "My Father, if this cannot pass unless I drink it, Your will be done."

Scene 813   **The Third Prayer of Jesus In The Garden**

Garden of Gethsemane, Mount of Olives, Jerusalem, *Judea*

late Thursday evening, April 2nd / 33 CE   *Matthew 26:43-46 / Mark 14:40-42*

1 Again Jesus came and found them sleeping, for their eyes were very heavy; and they did not know what to answer Him.

2 And again He left them, and went away and prayed for a third time, saying the same thing once more.

3 Then Jesus came to the three apostles, and He said to them, "Are you still sleeping and resting? It is enough! 4 Behold, the hour has come, and the Son of Man is being betrayed into the hands of sinners.

5 "Get up, and let us be going! Behold, the one who betrays Me is at hand!"

Scene 814   **Judas Leads The Authorities To Jesus**

Matthew 26:47-49 / Mark 14:43-45 / Luke 22:47-48 / John 18:3-5~, 6-9

1 Immediately, while Jesus was still speaking, behold, the one of the twelve called Judas came there, preceding a large crowd of the chief priests and the Pharisees, with the scribes and the elders of the people, along with the Roman cohort and officers. 2 They were carrying lanterns and torches, and swords and clubs.

3 Now Judas Iscariot, who was betraying Jesus, had given them a signal, saying, "Whomever I kiss, He is the One. Seize Him, and lead Him away under guard."

4 Upon arriving, Judas immediately approached Jesus, and said, "Hail, Rabbi!" and kissed Him.

5 Jesus said to him, "Judas, are you betraying the Son of Man with a kiss?"

6 So Jesus, knowing all the things that were coming upon Him, said to them, "Whom do you seek?"

7 They answered Him, "Jesus the Nazarene." He said to them, "I am He."

8 When He said to them, "I am He," they drew back, and fell to the ground.

9 So again Jesus asked them, "Whom do you seek?" And again they said, "Jesus the Nazarene."

10 Jesus answered, "I told you that I am He; so if you seek Me, let these go on their way," 11 to fulfill the Word which He spoke, "Of those whom You have given to Me, I lost not one."

Scene 815   **Peter Defends Jesus With A Sword**

Garden of Gethsemane, Mount of Olives, Jerusalem, *Judea*
around midnight Thursday, April 2ⁿᵈ / 33 CE
Matthew 22:50-54 / Mark 14:46-47 / Luke 22:49-51 / John 18:~5, 10-11

1 Judas the betrayer was standing with the crowd, and Jesus said to him, "Friend, do what you have come for."

2 Then they came and laid hands on Jesus, and seized Him.

3 When those who were around Jesus saw what was happening, they said, "Lord, shall we defend You?"

4 Then Simon Peter, having a sword, drew it and struck Malchus, the slave of the High Priest, and cut off his right ear.

5 But Jesus said, "Stop! No more of this!" 6 And He touched the slave's ear, and healed him.

7 Then Jesus said to Peter, "Put your sword back in its sheath, for all those who take up the sword shall perish by the sword.

8 "The cup which The Father has given to Me, shall I not drink it? 9 Or do you not think that I can appeal to My Father, and He will at once put at My disposal more than twelve legions of angels? 10 But how then will the Scriptures be fulfilled, which say that it must happen this way?"

Scene 816   **Jesus Is Arrested**

Garden of Gethsemane, Mount of Olives   around midnight Thursday, April 2ⁿᵈ / 33 CE
Matthew 22:55-56 / Mark 14:48-52 / Luke 22:52-53 / John 18:12

1 Then Jesus said to the crowds and the chief priests, with and the elders and the officers of the Temple who had come out against Him, "Have you come with swords and clubs to arrest Me, as you would against a robber? 2 Every day I used to sit with you in the Temple teaching, and you did not lay hands on Me. 3 But all of this has taken place to fulfill the Scriptures of the prophets; this hour, and the power of darkness, are yours."

4 So the Roman cohort and the commander, with the attendants of the Jews arrested Jesus, and bound Him. 5 Then all the apostles left Him, and fled.

6 A young man was following Him, wearing nothing but a linen sheet over his naked body; and they seized him, but he pulled free of the linen sheet, and escaped naked.

Act 2 - Jesus Is Accused By The High Priest

Scene 821　　　　　**First, To The House of Annas**

House of Annas, Jerusalem, *Judea*　　　early Friday morning, April 3rd / 33 CE

Matthew 26:57 / Mark 14:53 / Luke 22:54~ / John 18:13-14, 19-24

---

1 Having arrested Jesus, those who seized Him led Him away, and brought Him to the house of Annas first, for he was the father-in-law of Caiaphas, who was the High Priest that year.

2 When Annas questioned Jesus about His disciples, and about His teaching, Jesus answered him, "I have spoken openly to the world. 3 I always taught in the synagogues and in the Temple, where all the Jews come together, and I spoke nothing in secret. 4 Why do you question Me? Question those who have heard what I spoke. They know what I said."

5 When Jesus had said this, one of the attendants standing nearby struck Him, and said, "Is that the way You answer the High Priest?"

6 Jesus answered him, "If I have spoken wrongly, testify of the wrong; but if rightly, why do you strike Me?"

7 Then Annas sent Him bound to Caiaphas the High Priest, where all the chief priests, with the elders and the scribes, were gathered together.

8 Now Caiaphas was the one who had advised the Jews that it was expedient for one man to die on behalf of the people.

Scene 822　　　　　**Then To The High Priest, Caiaphas**

Palace of Caiaphas, Jerusalem, *Judea*　　　early Friday morning, April 3rd / 33 CE

Matthew 26:58-63~ / Mark 14:~54, 55-61~ / Luke 22:~54 / John 18:15-16

---

1 Simon Peter was following Jesus at a distance, and so was another apostle. 2 Since that apostle was known to the High Priest, he entered with Jesus into the court of the High Priest, but Peter was standing outside at the door. 3 So the apostle who was known to the High Priest went and spoke to the doorkeeper, and they brought Peter into the courtyard.

4 Peter entered, and sat down with the attendants to see the outcome.

5 Meanwhile, the chief priests and the whole Council kept trying to obtain testimony against Jesus, so that they might put Him to death; 6 but they did not find any, even though many false witnesses came forward and gave testimony against Him, but their testimony was not consistent.

7 But later on, two people came forward who gave false testimony against Him, saying, "We heard this man state, 'I will destroy this Temple of God made with hands, and in three days I will build another, made without hands.' " 8 So, not even in this respect was their testimony consistent.

9 Then the High Priest stood up and came forward, and he questioned Jesus, saying, "Do You not answer? What is it that these men are testifying against You?"

10 But Jesus kept silent, and He did not answer.

Scene 823   **Peter's First Denial of Jesus**

Palace of Caiaphas, Jerusalem, *Judea*   early Friday morning, April 3ʳᵈ / 33 CE
Matthew 26:69-70 / Mark 14:~54, 66-68 / Luke 22:55-57 / John 18:17-18

1 Now after the servants and the attendants who were standing outside in the middle of the courtyard had kindled a charcoal fire, they sat down together, for it was cold and they were warming themselves.

2 Peter was also sitting among them and warming himself, when a servant-girl of the High Priest who kept the door came.

3 Seeing Peter, as he sat warming himself in the firelight, she looked intently at him, and said to him, "You too were with Jesus the Galilean. You are not also one of His disciples, are you?"

4 But Peter denied it before them all, saying, "Woman, I am not. I neither know nor understand what you are talking about. I do not know Him."

5 And Peter went out onto the porch.

Scene 824   **Peter's Second Denial**

Matthew 26:71-72 / Mark 14:69-70~ / Luke 22:58 / John 18:~25-26

1 When Peter had gone out through the gateway and onto the porch, another servant-girl of the High Priest, being a relative of the one whose ear Peter had cut off, saw him, and said, "You are one of them too! Did I not see you in the garden with Him?"

2 And she said to the bystanders who were there, "This man was with Jesus of Nazareth!"

3 And again Peter denied it with an oath, and said, "I am not! I do not know the man."

Scene 825   **Jesus Is Charged With Blasphemy**

Palace of Caiaphas, Jerusalem, *Judea*   *Matthew 26:~63-66 / Mark 14:~61-64*

1 Again the High Priest questioned Jesus, and said to Him, "I adjure You by the living God, that You tell us: Are You the Christ, the Son of God?"

2 Jesus said to him, "You have said it yourself; I am. 3 Nevertheless, I tell you that hereafter you shall see the Son of Man sitting at the right hand of Power, and coming with the clouds of Heaven."

4 Then the High Priest tore his robes, and said, "He has blasphemed! 5 What further need do we have of witnesses? Behold, you have now heard the blasphemy. 6 What do you think? How does it seem to you?"

7 And they all condemned Jesus, and answered, "He deserves death."

Scene 826   **Jesus Is Beaten**

Matthew 26:67-68 / Mark 14:65 / Luke 26:63-65

1 Then the men who were holding Jesus in custody were mocking Him, and some began to spit in His face. 2 And they blindfolded Him, and beat Him with their fists.

3 Then the attendants slapped Him in the face, and said to Him, "Prophesy to us, You Christ! Who is the one who hit You?"

4 And they were saying many other blasphemous things against Him.

Scene 827   **Peter Denies Jesus The Third Time**
Matthew 26:73-75 / Mark 14:~70-72 / Luke 22:59-62 / John 18:25~, 27

1 After about an hour had passed, Simon Peter was again standing and warming himself in the courtyard, so the bystanders said to him, "You are not also one of His disciples, are you?"

2 Another man came up and began to insist, saying to Peter, "Surely you were with Him, for you too are a Galilean - even the way you talk gives you away."

3 Then Peter began to curse and swear, and he denied it again, and said, "I do not know this man that you are talking about!" 4 And immediately, while he was still speaking, a rooster crowed.

5 And the Lord turned, and looked at Peter; and Peter remembered the word of the Lord - how Jesus had made the remark to him: "Before a rooster crows today, you will deny Me three times."

6 And Peter went out, and he began to weep bitterly.

Act 3 - Jesus Is Questioned By The Sanhedrin

Scene 831   **The Sanhedrin Council Condemns Jesus**
Sanhedrin Council Chamber, The Temple, Jerusalem, *Judea*
early Friday morning, April 3rd / 33 CE   *Matthew 27:1 / Mark 15:1~ / Luke 22:66-71*

1 Early in the morning, when it was day, all the chief priests and the scribes assembled with the whole Council of the elders of the people; and immediately they held a consultation.

2 Then they led Jesus into their Council chamber, and said, "If You are the Christ, tell us."

3 He said to them, "If I tell you, you will not believe; and if I ask you a question, you will not answer. 4 But from now on, the Son of Man will be seated at the right hand of the power of God."

5 They all asked, "Are You the Son of God, then?"
And Jesus said to them, "Yes, I am."

6 Then they said, "What further need do we have of testimony? For we have heard it for ourselves, from His own mouth!"

7 And they conferred together to put Jesus to death.

Scene 832   **The Jews Take Jesus To The Roman Governor**
The Praetorium, Jerusalem, *Judea*   early Friday morning, April 3rd / 33 CE
Matthew 27:2 / Mark 15:~1 / Luke 23:1 / John 18:28

---

1 Then the whole body of them got up, and they bound Jesus; 2 and they led Him away from Caiaphas, and brought Him to the Praetorium, and delivered Him to Pilate, the Roman Governor.

3 It was early, and they themselves did not enter into the Praetorium so that they would not be defiled, but might eat the Passover.

Act 4 - Questioned By The Romans

Scene 841   **Pilate Hears The Accusation Against Jesus**

The Praetorium, Jerusalem, *Judea*   early Friday morning, April 3rd / 33 CE

Luke 23:2 / John 18:29-33~

1 Pilate, the Roman Governor of Judea, went out to the Jews, and he said to them, "What accusation do you bring against this man?"

2 They answered, and said to him, "If this man were not an evildoer, we would not have delivered Him to you."

3 Pilate said to them, "Take Him yourselves, and judge Him according to your law."

4 The Jews said to him, "We are not permitted to put anyone to death"; to fulfill the word which Jesus spoke, signifying by what kind of death He was about to die.

5 Then they began to accuse Jesus, saying, "We found this man misleading our nation, and forbidding us to pay taxes to Caesar; 6 and saying that He Himself is the Messiah, a King."

7 When Pilate heard this, he entered into the Praetorium again, and summoned Jesus.

Scene 842   **Are You The King of The Jews?**

Matthew 27:11 / Mark 15:2 / Luke 23:3 / John 18:~33-38~

1 When Jesus stood before the Governor, Pilate asked Him, "Are You the King of the Jews?"

2 Jesus answered him, "Are you asking this on your own initiative, or did others tell you about Me?"

3 Pilate answered, "I am not a Jew, am I? 4 Your own nation and the chief priests have delivered You to me. What have You done?"

5 Jesus answered, "My Kingdom is not of this world. 6 If My Kingdom were of this world then My servants would be fighting so that I would not be handed over to the Jews; but as it is, My Kingdom is not of this realm."

7 Therefore Pilate said to Him, "So You are a king?"

8 Jesus answered him, "It is as you say, that I am a King. 9 For this I have been born, and for this I have come into the world; to testify to the truth. 10 Everyone who is of the truth hears My voice."

11 Pilate said to Him, "What is truth?"

Scene 843   **Pilate Finds No Guilt In Jesus**

Matthew 27:12-14 / Mark 15:3-5 / Luke 23:4-7 / John 18:~38

1 After Pilate said this, he went out again to the Jews, and said to the chief priests and the crowds, "I find no guilt in this man."

2 Then the chief priests began to accuse Jesus harshly, and while He was being accused by the chief priests and the elders, He did not answer.

3 So Pilate questioned Jesus again, and said to Him, "Do You not hear how many things they testify about You, and the charges that they brings against

You? Do You not answer?"

4 But Jesus made no further reply, and He did not answer him with regard to even a single charge; so the Governor was quite amazed.

5 But the Jews kept insisting, saying, "He stirs up the people, teaching all over Judea, starting from Galilee, even as far as this place!"

6 When Pilate heard this, he asked whether Jesus was a Galilean; and when he learned that He belonged to Herod's jurisdiction, Pilate sent Him to Herod, who himself was also in Jerusalem at that time.

Scene 844   **Herod, Tetrarch of Galilee, Questions Jesus**

Hasmonean Palace, Jerusalem, *Judea*   early Friday morning, April 3rd / 33 CE
Luke 23:8-12

1 Now Herod, the Tetrarch of Galilee, was very glad when he saw Jesus, for he had wanted to see Him for a long time, because he had been hearing about Him, and he was hoping to see some sign performed by Him.

2 Herod questioned Jesus at some length, while the chief priests and the scribes were standing there, and accusing Him vehemently; but Jesus did not answer him.

3 Then Herod with his soldiers, after treating Jesus with contempt and mocking Him, dressed Him in a gorgeous robe, and sent Him back to Pilate.

4 Now Herod and Pilate became friends with one another that very day, for they had previously been enemies with each other.

Scene 845   **We Romans Find No Guilt In This Man**

The Praetorium, Jerusalem, *Judea*   *Luke 23:13-16*

1 Then Pilate summoned the chief priests, and the rulers of the Jews, and the people; and he said to them all, "You brought this man to me as one who incites the people to rebellion. 2 And behold, having examined Him before you, I have found no guilt in this man regarding the charges which you make against Him. 3 No, and nor has Herod, for he has sent Him back to us.

4 "And behold, since nothing deserving of death has been done by Him, I will punish Him, and release Him."

```
Act 5 - Jesus Is Sentenced To Die
```

Scene 851   **Shall I Release For You Jesus, or Barabbas?**

The Praetorium, Jerusalem, *Judea*   Friday morning, April 3rd / 33 CE
Matthew 27:15-18, 20-21 / Mark 15:6-11 / Luke 23:17-19 / John 18:39-40

1 Now at the Passover Feast, the Governor was accustomed to release to the people any one prisoner whom they requested. 2 At that time they were holding a notorious prisoner named Barabbas, a robber who had been imprisoned with the insurrectionists who had committed murder in an insurrection in the city. 3 So when the people were gathered together, the crowd began asking Pilate to do for them as they had been accustomed.   *continued >*

Scene 851 - *continued*

4 Pilate answered them, saying, "Do you wish me to release for you the King of the Jews?"

5 But they cried out all together, saying, "Not this Man! Away with this man, and release for us Barabbas!"

6 Now Pilate was aware that the chief priests had handed Jesus over because of envy, so he asked them, "Whom do you want me to release for you? Barabbas, or Jesus who is called Christ?"

7 The chief priests and the elders stirred up and persuaded the crowds to ask Pilate to release Barabbas for them, and to put Jesus to death.

8 So the Governor asked them again, "Which of the two do you want me to release for you?" And they said, "Barabbas!"

Scene 852   **The Jews Cry Out To Crucify Jesus**

The Praetorium, Jerusalem, *Judea*   Friday morning, April 3rd / 33 CE
Matthew 27:19, 22-23 / Mark 15:12-14 / Luke 23:20-23

1 Then Pilate said to them, "And what shall I do with Jesus, who is called Christ; whom you call the King of the Jews?"

2 They all shouted back, "Crucify Him!"

3 While Pilate was sitting on the judgment seat, his wife sent him a message, saying, "Have nothing to do with that righteous Man, for last night I suffered greatly in a dream because of Him!"

4 Pilate, wanting to release Jesus, addressed the crowd again, but they kept on calling out, "Crucify! Crucify Him."

5 So Pilate said to them the third time, "Why, what evil has He done? 6 I have found in Him no reason demanding of death, therefore I will punish Him, and release Him."

7 But they were insistent, and with loud voices kept shouting even more, "Crucify Him!" And their voices began to prevail.

Scene 853   **Pilate Sentences Jesus To Die**

Matthew 27:24-26~ / Mark 15:15~ / Luke 23:24-25

1 When Pilate saw that he was accomplishing nothing, but rather that a riot was starting, he took water and washed his hands in front of the crowd, saying, "I am innocent of this Man's blood; see to that yourselves."

2 And all the people said, "His blood shall be upon us, and upon our children!"

3 Wishing to satisfy the crowd, Pilate then pronounced sentence that their demand be granted; and he released Barabbas for them, the man who had been thrown into prison for insurrection and murder, 4 and he delivered Jesus to their will.

The Gospel of Jesus Christ

Scene 854   **The Soldiers Mock and Scourge Jesus**

The Praetorium, Jerusalem, *Judea*   Friday morning, April 3rd / 33 CE
Matthew 27:~26~, 27-30 / Mark 15:~15~, 16-19 / John 19:1-3

1 Then Pilate had Jesus scourged; and after scourging Him the soldiers of the Governor took Jesus into the Praetorium palace, and they gathered together the whole Roman cohort around Him.

2 Then the soldiers stripped Jesus, and dressed Him in purple, and they put a scarlet red robe on Him. 3 After twisting together a crown of thorns, they put it on His head, and a reed in His right hand.

4 Then they began to come up and mock Jesus, bowing down and kneeling before Him, and saying, "Hail, King of the Jews!"

5 And they slapped Him in the face, and spat on Him; and they took the reed and began to beat Him on His head with it.

Scene 855   **Pilate Tries Again To Release Jesus**   *John 19:4-13*

1 Then Pilate came out, and said to the crowd, "Behold, I am bringing Him out to you, so that you may know that I find no guilt in Him."

2 When Jesus came out, wearing the crown of thorns and the scarlet robe, Pilate said to them, "Behold, the Man!"

3 When the chief priests and the attendants saw Him, they cried out saying, "Crucify! Crucify!"

4 Pilate said to them, "Take Him yourselves and crucify Him, for I find no guilt in Him."

5 The Jews answered him, "We have a law, and by that law He ought to die, because He made Himself out to be the Son of God."

6 When Pilate heard this statement, he became more afraid; and he entered into the Praetorium again, and said to Jesus, "Where are You from?" But Jesus gave him no answer.

7 So Pilate said to Him, "Do You not speak to me? Do You not know that I have authority to release You, and I have authority to crucify You?"

8 Jesus answered, "You would have no authority over Me unless it had been given to you from above; 9 for this reason, he who delivered Me to you has greater sin."

10 As a result of this, Pilate made efforts to release Jesus, but the Jews cried out saying, "If you release this Man, you are no friend of Caesar! Everyone who makes himself out to be a king opposes Caesar."

11 When Pilate heard these words, he brought Jesus out, and sat down on the judgment seat, at a place called The Pavement, which is *Gabbatha* in Hebrew.

Scene 856   **Jesus Is Handed Over To Be Crucified**

The Praetorium, Jerusalem, *Judea*   Friday morning, April 3ʳᵈ / 33 CE
Matthew 17:~26 / Mark 15:~15 / John 19:14-16

1 Now it was the day of preparation for the Passover, and at about the sixth hour Pilate said to the Jews, "Behold, your King."

2 So they cried out, "Away with Him! Away with Him! Crucify Him!"

3 Pilate asked them, "Shall I crucify your King?"

4 The chief priests answered, "We have no king but Caesar."

5 So Pilate handed Jesus over to be crucified.

Scene 857   **Judas The Betrayer Hangs Himself**

Jerusalem, *Judea*   Friday morning, April 3ʳᵈ / 33 CE   *Matthew 27:3-10*

1 When Judas, who had betrayed Jesus, saw that He had been condemned, he felt remorse; 2 and he returned the thirty pieces of silver to the chief priests and the elders, saying, "I have sinned by betraying innocent blood."

3 But they said to him, "What is that to us? See to that yourself."

4 So Judas threw the pieces of silver into the Temple sanctuary, and departed; 5 and he went away and hanged himself.

6 The chief priests took the pieces of silver, and said, "It is not lawful to put them into the Temple treasury, since it is the price of blood."

7 So they conferred together; and with the money they bought the Potter's Field, as a burial place for strangers. 8 For this reason, that field has been called "The Field of Blood" to this day.

9 Then, that which was spoken through Zechariah the prophet was fulfilled: "And I took the thirty pieces of silver, the price of the one whose value had been set by the sons of Israel, 10 and I gave them for the Potter's Field, as the Lord directed me."

Act 6 - The Crucifixion of Jesus Christ

Scene 861   **Simon of Cyrene Carries The Cross of Jesus**

Jerusalem, *Judea*   Friday morning, April 3ʳᵈ / 33 CE
Matthew 27:31-32 / Mark 15:20-21 / Luke 23:26, 32 / John 19:17~

1 After the soldiers had mocked Jesus, they took the scarlet robe off of Him, and put His own garments back on. 2 Then they led Him away to crucify Him; and He went out, bearing His own cross.

3 As they were coming out, to bear His cross, they seized and pressed into service a passer-by coming in from the country, a man of Cyrene named Simon, the father of Alexander and Rufus. 4 And they placed the cross on him to carry behind Jesus.

5 Two others also, who were criminals, were being led away to be put to death with Jesus.

Scene 862   **The Walk To Golgotha**

      Jerusalem, *Judea*   Friday morning, April 3rd / 33 CE   *Luke 23:27-31*

1 Following Jesus was a large crowd of people, and of women who were mourning and lamenting for Him.

2 Turning to them, Jesus said, "Daughters of Jerusalem, do not weep for Me, but weep for yourselves, and for your children. 3 For behold, the days are coming when they will say, 'Blessed are the barren, and the wombs that never bore, and the breasts that never nursed!' 4 Then they will begin to say to the mountains, 'Fall on us,' and to the hills, 'Cover us!'

5 "So, if they do these things when the tree is green, what will happen when it is dry?"

Scene 863   **Jesus Is Crucified**

      Golgotha, Jerusalem, *Judea*   around 9:30 am, Friday morning, April 3rd / 33 CE

      Matthew 27:33-34 / Mark 15:22-24~, 25~ / Luke 23:33~, 34~, 35-36 / John 19:~17

1 Then they came to the place called Golgotha in Hebrew, which means, "The Place of a Skull".

2 The people stood by, looking on while the rulers were sneering at Jesus, saying, "He saved others, let Him save Himself, if this is the Christ of God, His Chosen One."

3 The soldiers also mocked Him, and coming up to Jesus, they tried to give Him sour wine to drink, mixed with myrrh and gall; but after tasting it, He was unwilling to drink.

4 And Jesus said, "Father, forgive them; for they do not know what they are doing."

5 And they crucified Him at the third hour.

Scene 864   **The Soldiers Divide His Clothing**

      Golgotha, Jerusalem, *Judea*   Friday morning, April 3rd / 33 CE

      Matthew 27:35-36 / Mark 15:~24, ~25 / Luke 23:~34, 37 / John 19:23-25~

1 After they had crucified Jesus, the soldiers divided His outer garments among themselves, and they made four parts, a part to every soldier, and also the tunic. 2 Since the tunic was woven in one piece and seamless, they said to one another, "Let us not tear it, but cast lots for it, to decide whose it shall be."

3 The soldiers did these things to fulfill the Scripture: "They divided My outer garments among themselves, and for My clothing they cast lots."

4 Then the soldiers sat down, and began to keep watch over Him.

5 And they were saying, "If You are the King of the Jews, save Yourself!"

Scene 865   **Jesus Is Crucified Between Two Criminals**

Golgotha, Jerusalem, *Judea*   *Matthew 27:38 / Mark 15:27-28 / Luke 23:~33 / John 19:18*

1 There at that time, they crucified two criminals with Him; one on His right, and the other on His left, with Jesus in between. 2 And the Scripture was fulfilled which says, "He was numbered with transgressors."

Scene 866   Pilate's Inscription of The Charge Against Jesus

Golgotha, Jerusalem, *Judea*   *Matthew 27:37 / Mark 15:26 / Luke 23:38 / John 19:19-22*

1 Pilate wrote an inscription of the charge against Jesus, and they put it on the cross, up above His head. 2 It was written in Hebrew, Latin, and Greek, and it read: "THIS IS JESUS THE NAZARENE, THE KING OF THE JEWS."

3 Many of the Jews read this inscription, for the place where Jesus was crucified was near the city.

4 The chief priests were saying to Pilate, "Do not write, 'The King of the Jews', but that He said, 'I am the King of the Jews.' "

5 Pilate answered, "I have written what I have written."

Scene 867   Jesus Entrusts His Mother To John   *John 19:~25-27*

1 Standing by the cross of Jesus were His mother, and His mother's sister, and Mary the wife of Cleopas, and Mary Magdalene.

2 When Jesus saw His mother, and the disciple whom He loved standing nearby, He said to His mother, "Woman, behold, your son!"

3 Then He said to the apostle, "Behold, your mother."

4 And from that hour, John took her into his own household.

Scene 868   Let This Christ Save Himself!

Matthew 27:39-43 / Mark 15:29-32~

1 Those passing by were hurling abuse at Jesus, wagging their heads, and saying, "Ha! You who are going to destroy the Temple, and rebuild it in three days! 2 If You are the Son of God, save Yourself, and come down from the cross!"

3 In the same way, the chief priests also, along with the scribes and the elders, were mocking Him among themselves, and saying, "He saved others, but He cannot save Himself? 4 He is the King of Israel; let this Christ come down from the cross, so that we may see, and we will believe in Him!

5 "He trusts in God, so let God rescue Him now, if He delights in Him; for He said, 'I am the Son of God.' "

Scene 869   The Last Words of The Two Criminals

Matthew 27:44 / Mark 15:~32 / Luke 23:39-43

1 One of the criminals who had been crucified with Jesus was also insulting Him with the same words, and saying, "Are You not the Christ? Save Yourself, and us!"

2 But the other one answered, and rebuking him said, "Do you not fear even God, since you are under the same sentence of condemnation? 3 And we indeed are suffering justly, for we are receiving what we deserve for our deeds; but this man has done nothing wrong."

4 And he said, "Jesus, remember me when You come into Your Kingdom!"

5 And Jesus said to him, "Truly, I say to you, that today you shall be with Me in Paradise."

Act 7 - The Death of Jesus Christ

Scene 871   **Darkness Falls Over The Land**

Golgotha, Jerusalem, *Judea*   roughly noon to 3:00 pm, Friday afternoon, April 3rd / 33 CE
Matthew 27:45-47, 49 / Mark 15:33-35, ~36 / Luke 23:44-45~

1 Now when the sixth hour came the sun was obscured, and darkness fell over the whole land until the ninth hour.

2 At about the ninth hour, Jesus cried out with a loud voice, and said, "Eloi, eloi, lama sabachthani?" which is translated, "My God, My God! Why have You forsaken Me?"

3 When some of the bystanders who were standing there heard this, they began saying, "Behold, He is calling for Elijah." 4 And the rest of them said, "Let us see whether Elijah will come to take Him down, and save Him."

Scene 872   **Jesus Dies On The Cross**

Golgotha, Jerusalem, *Judea*   around 3:00 pm, Friday afternoon, April 3rd / 33 CE
Matthew 27:48, 50 / Mark 15:36~, 37 / Luke 23:46 / John 19:28-30

1 After this, knowing that all things had now been accomplished, to fulfill the Scripture Jesus said, "I am thirsty."

2 A jar full of sour wine was standing there, and immediately someone ran and taking a sponge he filled it with the sour wine, put it on a reed of hyssop, and brought it up to His mouth, and gave Him a drink.

3 After Jesus had received the sour wine, He cried out again with a loud voice, and said, "It is finished. Father, into Your hands I commit My Spirit."

4 Having said this, Jesus breathed His last, bowed His head, and yielded up His Spirit.

Scene 873   **An Earthquake At The Death of Jesus**

Jerusalem, *Judea*   around 3:00 pm, Friday afternoon, April 3rd / 33 CE
Matthew 27:51, 54-56 / Mark 15:38-41 / Luke 23:~45, 47-49

1 And behold, the earth shook, and the rocks were split; and the veil of the Temple was torn in two, from top to bottom.

2 When those who were keeping guard over Jesus saw the way that He breathed His last, and the earthquake, and the things that were happening, they became very frightened, and began praising God.

3 And the centurion, who was standing right in front of Jesus, said, "Truly this righteous man was the Son of God!"

4 After all the crowds who came together for this spectacle observed what had happened, they began to return to their homes, beating their breasts.

5 All of His acquaintances and many other women were there, looking on from a distance, and seeing these things. 6 Among them was Mary Magdalene, and Mary the mother of Jesus, and Salome, the mother of the sons of Zebedee. 7 When Jesus was in Galilee they used to follow Him, while ministering to Him.

8 And there were many other women who had accompanied Him from Galilee to Jerusalem.

Scene 874   **The Body of Jesus Is Taken Down**
Golgotha, Jerusalem, *Judea*   late Friday afternoon   *Mark 15:~42 / John 19:31-34, 36-37*

1 Then, because it was the Jewish day of preparation, that is, the day before the Sabbath, so that the bodies would not remain on the cross during the Sabbath (and that was a high Sabbath day), the Jews asked Pilate that their legs might be broken, and their bodies be taken away.

2 So the soldiers came and broke the legs of the first criminal, and of the other one who was crucified with Him; 3 but when they came to Jesus, they saw that He was already dead, and so they did not break His legs.

4 One of the soldiers pierced His side with a spear, and immediately blood and water came out.

5 These things came to pass to fulfill the Scripture, "Not a bone of Him shall be broken." 6 And another Scripture which says, "They shall look upon Me, whom they have pierced."

Act 8 - Jesus Is Laid In Joseph's Tomb

Scene 881   **Joseph Asks Pilate For The Body of Jesus**
The Praetorium, Jerusalem, *Judea*   late Friday afternoon, April 3rd / 33 CE
Matthew 27:57-58 / Mark 15:42~, 43-45 / Luke 23:50-52, 54 / John 19:38~

1 When it was the evening of the preparation day for the Sabbath, a rich man named Joseph, from Arimathea, came to the Praetorium. 2 He was a prominent member of the Jewish Council of elders; a good and righteous man, who had not consented to their plan and action. 3 He himself was waiting for the Kingdom of God, and had become a disciple of Jesus, but a secret one for fear of the Jews.

4 Joseph gathered up his courage, and he went in before Pilate, and he asked that he might take away the body of Jesus.

5 Pilate wondered if Jesus was dead by this time, and summoning a centurion, he questioned him as to whether He was already dead.

6 Ascertaining this from the centurion, Pilate granted permission that the body be given to Joseph.

Scene 882   **The Body of Jesus Is Placed In Joseph's Tomb**
The Garden Tomb, Jerusalem, *Judea*   late Friday afternoon
Matthew 27:59-61 / Mark 15:46-47 / Luke 23:53, 55-56 / John 19:~38-42

1 Joseph brought a clean linen cloth, and he came and took away the body of Jesus down. 2 Nicodemus, who had first come to Jesus by night, also came, bringing a mixture of myrrh and aloes, about a seventy-five pounds in weight.

3 So they took the body of Jesus, and wrapped it in the linen cloth with the spices, as is the burial custom of the Jews.

4 Now, in the place where Jesus was crucified there was a garden, and in the garden was Joseph's new tomb which had been hewn out of the rock, in which no one had ever yet been laid. 5 Therefore, since the Sabbath was about to begin, and the tomb was nearby, they laid Jesus there. 6 Then they rolled a large stone against the entrance of the tomb, and went away.   continued >

7 Now the women who had come out of Galilee with Jesus were sitting opposite the grave, looking at the tomb, and to see how his body was laid. 8 Mary Magdalene was there, and Mary the mother of Jesus.

9 Then they returned, and prepared spices and perfumes; 10 and on the Sabbath they rested, according to the commandment.

Scene 883   **Roman Soldiers Guard The Tomb**
The Garden Tomb, Jerusalem, *Judea*   Friday evening, April 3rd / 33 CE
Matthew 27:62-66

1 On that day, after the sun had set, the chief priests and the Pharisees gathered together with Pilate, and they said, "Sir, we remember that when He was still alive, that deceiver said, 'After three days, I will rise again.' 2 Therefore, give orders for the grave to be made secure until the third day, otherwise His disciples may come and steal Him away, and say to the people, 'He has risen from the dead,' and the last deception will be worse than the first."

3 Pilate said to them, "You have a guard. Go, and make it as secure as you know how."

4 So they went and made the grave secure; and along with the guard, they set a seal on the stone.

Act 9 - The Resurrection of Jesus Christ

Scene 891   **An Earthquake At The Resurrection of Jesus**
The Garden Tomb, Jerusalem, *Judea*   early Sunday morning, April 5th / 33 CE
Matthew 27:52-53; 28:2-4

1 And behold, a severe earthquake occurred, for an angel of the Lord descended from heaven. 2 He came and rolled away the stone, and sat upon it. 3 His appearance was like lightning, and his clothing as white as snow; 4 and the guards shook for fear of him, and became like dead men.

5 And the tombs were opened; and many bodies of the saints who had fallen asleep were raised, and coming out of the tombs after His resurrection, they entered the holy city, and appeared to many.

Scene 892   **The Soldiers Are Paid To Lie**
Jerusalem, *Judea*   *Matthew 28:11-15*

1 Some of the guards went into the city, and reported to the chief priests all that had happened. 2 When the chief priests had assembled with the elders, they consulted together.

3 Then they gave a large sum of money to the soldiers, and said to them, "You are to say, 'His disciples came by night, and stole Him away while we were asleep.' 4 And if this should come to the Governor's ears, we will win him over, and keep you out of trouble."

5 The guards took the money, and did as they had been instructed; and this story was widely spread among the Jews, as it is to this day.

CHAPTER 9 - APPEARANCES AND ASCENSION

Act 1 - Sunday Morning

Scene 911   **The Women Arrive At The Tomb**

The Garden Tomb, Jerusalem, *Judea*   early Sunday morning, April 5th / 33 CE
Matthew 28:1 / Mark 16:1-4 / Luke 24:1-2 / John 20:1

1 When the Sabbath was over, as it began to dawn very early on the first day of the week, while it was still dark, Mary Magdalene, and Mary the mother of Jesus, with Joanna and Salome, came to the tomb, bringing the spices which they had prepared, so that they might anoint the body of Jesus.

2 They were saying to one another, "Who will roll away the stone from the entrance of the tomb for us?"

3 And looking up, they saw that the stone had already been rolled away from the tomb, although it was extremely large.

Scene 912   **Two Angels Greet The Women At The Tomb**

The Garden Tomb, Jerusalem, *Judea*   early Sunday morning, April 5th / 33 CE
Matthew 28:5-8 / Mark 16:5-8 / Luke 24:3-9~

1 When they entered the tomb, they did not find the body of the Lord Jesus.

2 While they were perplexed about this, behold, a man suddenly stood near them in dazzling clothing; 3 and they saw another young man sitting at the right, wearing a white robe.

4 The women were terrified, and they bowed their faces to the ground.

5 The angel said to them, "Do not be afraid, for I know that you are looking for Jesus, the Nazarene who has been crucified. 6 Why do you seek the living among the dead? 7 He is not here, for He has risen, just as He said.

8 "Remember how He spoke to you while He was still in Galilee, saying that the Son of Man must be delivered into the hands of sinful men, and be crucified, and then rise again on the third day?

9 "Behold, see the place where they laid Him.

10 "Now go quickly, and tell His apostles and Peter that He has risen from the dead. 11 And behold, He is going ahead of you to Galilee, and there you will see Him, just as He told you."

12 The women remembered His words, and they quickly fled from the tomb with fear and great joy; and they ran to report it to the apostles.

13 And they said nothing to anyone, for trembling and astonishment gripped them.

Scene 913   **The Women Tell The Apostles**

Jerusalem, *Judea*   early Sunday morning, April 5th / 33 CE   *Luke 24:~9-11 / John 20:2*

1 Mary Magdalene, and Mary the mother of Jesus, and the other women who were with them, went and reported all these things to the eleven apostles, and to all the rest. 2 But these words appeared to them as nonsense, and they would not believe them.

continued >

3 So Mary came to Simon Peter and John, the other apostle whom Jesus loved, and she said to them, "They have taken the Lord out of the tomb, and we do not know where they have laid Him."

Scene 914   **Peter and John Run To The Tomb**

The Garden Tomb, Jerusalem, *Judea*   early Sunday morning, April 5th / 33 CE

Luke 24:12 / John 20:3-10

---

1 Then Simon Peter and John got up, and they ran to the tomb. 2 They were running together, but John ran faster than Peter, and came to the tomb first. 3 Stooping and looking in, John saw only the linen wrappings lying there, but he did not go in.

4 Peter came following him, and he entered the tomb. 5 And he saw the linen wrappings lying there, but the facecloth which had been on Jesus' head was not lying with the linen wrappings, but was rolled up in a place by itself.

6 Then John also entered the tomb, and he saw, and he believed; 7 for they did not yet understand the Scripture, that He must rise again from the dead.

8 And they went away, marveling at what had happened.

Scene 915   **Jesus Appears To Mary Magdalene**

The Garden Tomb, Jerusalem, *Judea*   *Matthew 28:9-10 / Mark 16:9-11 / John 20:11-18*

---

1 Now, after Jesus had risen early on the first day of the week, He appeared first to Mary Magdalene, from whom He had cast out seven demons. 2 She had returned to the tomb, and was standing outside, weeping.

3 As she wept, she stooped and looked into the tomb; and she saw the two angels in white, sitting one at the head, and one at the feet, of where the body of Jesus had been lying.

4 One of them said to her, "Woman, why are you weeping?"

5 Mary answered, "Because they have taken away my Lord, and I do not know where they have laid Him." 6 When Mary said this, she turned around and saw Jesus standing there; but she did not know that it was Jesus.

7 Jesus said to her, "Woman, why are you weeping? Whom do you seek?"

8 Supposing Him to be the gardener, she said to Him, "Sir, if you have removed Him, tell me where you have laid Him, and I will come and take Him away."

9 And behold, Jesus greeted her, and said, "Mary!"

10 She turned, and said to Him, "Rabboni!" which means "Teacher" in Hebrew; and she took hold of His feet and worshiped Him.

11 Jesus said to her, "Stop clinging to Me, for I have not yet ascended to The Father; 12 but go to My brethren, and say to them, 'I ascend to My Father and your Father, to My God and your God.' "

13 Then Jesus said to her, "Do not be afraid. Go and take word to My brethren to leave for Galilee, and there they will see Me."

14 Mary went and reported this to the apostles, while they were mourning and weeping.

15 She said, "I have seen the Lord!" and she told them the things that He had said to her. 16 But when they heard that Jesus was alive, and had been seen by her, they refused to believe it.

Act 2 - Appearances To The Apostles

Scene 921   **Jesus Walks To Emmaus With Two Disciples**

west of Jerusalem, *Judea*   Sunday afternoon, April 5th / 33 CE

Mark 16:12 / Luke 24:13-29

1 Later that day, Jesus appeared in a different form to two of them while they were walking through the country, on their way to a village named Emmaus, which was about seven miles from Jerusalem.

2 They were talking with each other about all the things that had taken place, and while they were talking, Jesus Himself approached, and began traveling with them; 3 but their eyes were prevented from recognizing Him.

4 He said to them, "What are you two discussing, as you walk?" And they stood still, looking sad.

5 One of them, named Cleopas, answered and said to Him, "Are You the only one visiting Jerusalem who is unaware of the things which have happened here in these days?" 6 Jesus said to them, "What things?"

7 They said, "The things about Jesus the Nazarene, who was a Prophet mighty in Word and deed, in the sight of God, and all the people; 8 and how the chief priests and our rulers delivered Him to the sentence of death, and crucified Him. 9 But we were hoping that it was He who was going to redeem Israel. 10 Indeed, besides all of this, it is the third day since these things have happened.

11 "Also some women from among us amazed us. When they were at the tomb early in the morning, and did not find His body, they came saying that they had seen a vision of angels, who said that Jesus was alive! 12 Then some of those who were with us went to the tomb, and they found it exactly as the women had said; but they did not see Him."

13 Jesus said to them, "O foolish men, and slow of heart to believe in all that the prophets have spoken. 14 Was it not necessary for the Christ to suffer these things, and to enter into His glory?"

15 Then, beginning with Moses, and all the prophets, Jesus explained to them the things concerning Himself in all of the Scriptures.

16 As they approached the village where they were going, Jesus acted as though He were going farther, and so they urged Him, saying, "Stay with us, for it is getting toward evening, and the day is now nearly over."

17 So He went in, and stayed with them.

Scene 922   **They Finally Recognize Jesus**

Emmaus, *Judea*   Sunday, late afternoon, April 5th   *Mark 16:13~ / Luke 24:30-33~*

1 When Jesus had reclined at the table with them, He took the bread and blessed it; and breaking it, He began giving it to them.

2 Then behold, their eyes were opened, and they recognized Him; and He vanished from their sight.

3 They said to one another, "Were not our hearts burning within us while He was speaking to us on the road, and explaining the Scriptures to us?"

4 And they got up that very hour, and returned to Jerusalem.

Scene 923   **Jesus Appears To The Ten Apostles**
a house, Jerusalem, *Judea*   Sunday evening, April 5th / 33 CE
Mark 16:~13-14~ / Luke 24:~33-37 / John 20:19

1 When it was evening that day, the first day of the week, the doors were shut where the apostles and those who were with them were, for fear of the Jews.

2 The two men found them gathered together as they were reclining at the table, and they reported to them, saying, "The Lord really has risen, and appeared to Simon." 3 And they began to relate their experiences on the road, and how they recognized Jesus by the breaking of the bread. 4 But those who were gathered did not believe them.

5 While they were telling these things, Jesus Himself came, and appeared to them. 6 He stood in their midst, and said to them, "Peace be with you!"

7 But they were frightened, and thought that they were seeing a spirit.

Scene 924   **Jesus Proves That His Body Is Real**
a house, Jerusalem, *Judea*   Sunday evening   *Mark 16:~14 / Luke 24:38-43 / John 20:20*

1 Jesus said to them, "Why are you troubled, and why do doubts arise in your hearts? 2 See My hands, and My feet - that it is I Myself. 3 Touch Me, and see; for a spirit does not have flesh and bones, as you see that I have."

4 And when Jesus had said this, He showed them both His hands, and His feet, and His side. 5 The apostles rejoiced when they saw the Lord.

6 While they still could not believe it, because of their joy and amazement, Jesus said to them, "Have you anything here to eat?"

7 They gave Him a piece of broiled fish; and He took it, and ate it before them.

8 Then Jesus reproached them for their unbelief and hardness of heart, because they had not believed those who had seen Him after He had risen.

Scene 925   **Jesus Bestows The Holy Spirit On The Apostles**
a house, Jerusalem, *Judea*   Sunday evening   *John 20:21-25*

1 Then, Jesus said to them again, "Peace be with you! As The Father has sent Me, I also send you."

2 When He had said this, He breathed on them, and said to them, "Receive the Holy Spirit. 3 If you forgive the sins of any, their sins have been forgiven; and if you retain the sins of any, they have been retained."

4 But Thomas, the one of the twelve called Didymus, was not with them when Jesus came, so later they said to him, "We have seen the Lord!"

5 But Thomas said to them, "Unless I see the imprint of the nails in His hands, and put my finger into the place of the nails, and put my hand into His side, I will not believe."

Scene 926   **Jesus Manifests Himself To Thomas**

Jerusalem, *Judea*   Monday, April 13th / 33 CE   *John 20:26-29*

1 Eight days later, the apostles were inside again, and Thomas was with them. 2 Although the doors were shut, Jesus came and stood in their midst, and said to them, "Peace be with you!"

3 Then He said to Thomas, "Reach here with your finger, and see My hands. And put your hand into My side; and do not doubt, but believe."

4 Thomas said to Him, "My Lord, and my God!"

5 Jesus said, "You have believed because you have seen Me, but blessed are those who did not see, and yet believe."

6 This is the third time that Jesus was manifested to the apostles, after He was raised from the dead.

Act 3 - Reunion In Galilee

Scene 931   **Jesus Meets His Apostles At The Mountain**

Galilee   mid April / 33 CE   *Matthew 28:16-17*

1 The eleven apostles proceeded to the mountain which Jesus had designated in Galilee.

2 When they saw Jesus they worshiped Him, but some were doubtful.

Scene 932   **Appearance At The Sea of Galilee**

near Tiberius, Sea of Galilee, *Galilee*   late April / 33 CE   *John 21:1-6*

1 After this, Jesus manifested Himself again to His apostles, at the Sea of Galilee; and He manifested Himself in this way: 2 Simon Peter, and Thomas, and Nathanael, and the sons of Zebedee, and two of His other apostles were together.

3 Peter said to them, "I am going fishing," and they said, "We will come with you." 4 So they went out in the boat, but that night they did not catch anything.

5 When the day was breaking, Jesus stood on the beach; yet they did not know that it was Jesus.

6 He said to them, "Children, do you have anything to eat?" They answered Him, "No."

7 Jesus said, "Cast the net on the right side of the boat, and you will find a catch."

8 So they cast the net, and they were not able to haul it in because of the great number of fish.

Scene 933   **A Catch of One Hundred and Fifty-Three Fish**

near Tiberius, Sea of Galilee, *Galilee*   *John 21:7-14*

1 John said to Peter, "It is the Lord!"

2 When Peter heard that it was the Lord, he put on his garment (for he was naked), and threw himself into the sea.

3 The other apostles came in the little boat dragging the net full of fish, for they were not far from the land, but about a hundred yards away.

4 When they got onto the land they saw a charcoal fire already laid, with fish placed on it, and bread.

5 Jesus said to them, "Bring some of the fish that you have caught."

6 Peter drew the net to land, full of one hundred and fifty-three large fish; and although there were so many, the net was not torn.

7 Jesus said to them, "Come and have breakfast." 8 None of the apostles ventured to ask Him, "Who are You?" knowing that it was the Lord.

9 Jesus came and took the bread, and He gave it to them, along with the fish.

Scene 934   **Peter, Tend My Sheep**   *John 21:15-23*

1 When they had finished breakfast, Jesus said to Peter, "Simon, son of John; do you love Me more than these?"

2 Peter said to Him, "Yes, Lord; You know that I love You!"

3 Jesus said to him, "Tend My lambs."

4 Then Jesus said to Peter a second time, "Simon, son of John, do you love Me?"

5 Peter said to Him, "Yes, Lord; You know that I love You."

6 He said to him, "Shepherd My sheep."

7 Then Jesus said to him a third time, "Simon, son of John, do you love Me?"

8 Peter was grieved because Jesus said to him the third time, "Do you love Me?" and he said to Him, "Lord, You know all things; You know that I love You!"

9 Jesus said to him, "Tend My sheep. 10 Truly, truly, I say to you, when you were younger, you used to gird yourself and walk wherever you wished; but when you grow old, you will stretch out your hands, and someone else will gird you, and bring you to where you do not wish to go." 11 Now, Jesus said this to signify by what kind of death Peter would glorify God.

12 When Jesus had spoken this, He said to him, "Follow Me."

13 Turning around, Peter saw John, the apostle whom Jesus loved, following them; the one who had leaned back on His bosom at the supper, and said, "Lord, who is the one who betrays You?" 14 So Peter, seeing him, said to Jesus, "Lord, and what about this man?"

15 Jesus said to Peter, "If I want him to remain until I come, what is that to you? You follow Me."

16 Therefore, this saying went out among the brethren, that John would not die. 17 Yet Jesus did not say that John would not die, but only, "If I want him to remain until I come, what is that to you?"

Scene 935   **The Promise of The Father**
near Tiberius, Sea of Galilee, *Galilee*   late April / 33 CE   *Luke 24:44-49*

1 Jesus said to them, "These are My words which I spoke to you while I was still with you, that all of the things which are written about Me in the Law of Moses, and the Prophets, and the Psalms, must be fulfilled."

2 Then Jesus opened their minds to understand the Scriptures; 3 and He said to them, "Thus it is written, that the Christ would suffer, and rise again from the dead on the third day; 4 and that repentance for the forgiveness of sins would be proclaimed in His Name to all of the nations, beginning from Jerusalem. 5 You are witnesses of these things.

6 "And behold, I am sending forth the promise of My Father upon you, but you are to stay in the city until you are clothed with power from on high!"

```
Act 4 - The Great Commission
```

Scene 941   **Jesus Sends The Eleven To Preach The Gospel**
Jerusalem, *Judea*   Friday, May 15th / 33 CE   *Matthew 28:18-20~ / Mark 16:15-16*

1 Later, Jesus spoke to them, saying, "All authority has been given to Me in Heaven, and on earth.

2 "Go therefore, into all the world, and preach the gospel to all creation; 3 and make disciples of all the nations, baptizing them in the Name of The Father, and of the Son, and of the Holy Spirit.

4 "Teach them to observe all that I have commanded you.

5 "He who has believed, and has been baptized, shall be saved; 6 but he who has disbelieved shall be condemned."

Scene 942   **These Signs Will Accompany You**
Jerusalem, *Judea*   Friday, May 15th / 33 CE   *Matthew 28:~20 / Mark 16:17-18*

1 "These signs will accompany those who have believed: in My Name they will cast out demons; 2 they will speak with new tongues; 3 they will pick up serpents, 4 and if they drink any deadly poison, it will not hurt them; 5 they will lay their hands on the sick, and they will recover.

6 "And behold, I am with you all the days until the end of the age."

Act 5 - The Ascension of Jesus Christ

Scene 951 **Jesus Christ Ascends To Heaven**

Bethany, *Judea* Friday, May 15ᵗʰ / 33 CE *Mark 16:19 / Luke 24:50-53*

1 After the Lord had spoken to the apostles, He led them out as far as Bethany.

2 Then Jesus lifted up His hands, and blessed them.

3 While He was blessing them, He departed from them, and was taken up into Heaven, and sat down at the right hand of God.

4 After worshiping Him, they returned to Jerusalem with great joy, and they were continually in the Temple, praising God.

Scene 952 **They Went Out and Preached Everywhere** *Mark 16:20*

1 Then Jesus sent out through the apostles, from east to west, the sacred and imperishable proclamation of eternal salvation.

2 And they went out and preached everywhere, while the Lord worked with them, and confirmed the Word by the signs that followed.

Act 6 - Epilogue

Scene 961 **Final Words**

John 1:11-13, 16-18; 19:35; 20:30-31; 21:24-25

1 No one has seen God at any time; 2 the only begotten God who is in the bosom of The Father, He has explained Him.

3 He came to His own, and those who were His own did not receive Him. 4 But as many as received Him, to them He gave the right to become children of God, even to those who believe in His Name; 5 who were born not of blood, nor of the will of the flesh, nor of the will of man, but of God. 6 For although the Law was given through Moses, grace and truth came through Jesus Christ. 7 Of His fullness, we have all received, which is grace upon grace.

8 One who has seen is testifying, and he wrote these things; 9 and we know that his testimony is true, and that he is telling the truth, so that you may also believe.

10 And there are many other things which Jesus did, and many other signs which He performed in the presence of the disciples which are not written in this book, 11 which if they were written in detail, I suppose that even the world itself could not contain the books that would be written; 12 but these have been written so that you may believe that Jesus is the Christ, the Son of God; 13 and that by believing, you may have life in His Name.

~ End ~

IMPROVING The SYNOPTIC GOSPEL

This edition of **The Synoptic Gospel** Merged Harmony of the four New Testament Gospels is as complete and accurate as possible at the time of its publication, and **FIVE COLUMN: The Synoptic Gospel**, and the works that are based upon its text, is open to comment, review and criticism. As the many eyes and minds of the group are better than a few, it is hoped that interested people would share their input to help further enhance and refine future editions of this work. Everyone is encouraged to submit their comments, corrections, suggestions and personal Testimonials, using the form at: *synopticgospel.com/feedback*
or email: *feedback@synopticgospel.com*

All input to help improve this unified Synoptic Gospel is greatly appreciated, and may enhance future editions of this work. Thank You!

Reviews: To formally review this work in media visit:
synopticgospel.com/reviews

Website: synopticgospel.com   Youtube: youtube.com/SynopticGospel
facebook.com/SynopticGospel   twitter.com/SynopticGospel

If you purchased this book from Amazon, please help encourage everyone to read this Gospel message, by leaving a positive and honest review at:

Amazon: amazon.com/dp/B010557Q5Q
Goodreads: goodreads.com/book/show/123503652

Thank You!

This concludes the **Standard Edition** of **The Synoptic Gospel**. To see all of the advanced Features that are available in the full version of this work, get the **Complete Edition**, which includes:

1. 340+ References to the Old Testament Scriptures & historical figures
2. 9 Chapter Maps of Israel and of Jerusalem (see *Note 4.3* on page *xi*)
3. The *Table of Chapter Contents* found at the start of each Chapter
4. *Note 5: An Overview of The Four Gospels + Four Gospel Comparison Chart*
5. Seven *Articles* about the Four Gospel Harmony & Merger *FIVE COLUMN*
6. The *Gospel Verse Cross-Reference* (*Appendix*) which shows if a verse from the four original Gospels is part of a synoptic set, and where that verse is located within *FIVE COLUMN* and *The Synoptic Gospel*

Purchase the **Complete Edition** as a PDF file or get the printed book. These features and more are also available in the **FIVE COLUMN** Four Gospel Harmony and Merger, from which the text of this book is reprinted.

Other formats of *The Synoptic Gospel*
Kindle: ISBN 978-0-9939140-3-4   ePub: ISBN 978-1-988271-49-1
Standard PDF: ISBN 978-1-988271-29-7   *Complete* PDF: ISBN 978-1-988271-41-5
Complete Edition - Paperback: ISBN 978-1-988271-44-6
Complete Edition - Hard Cover: ISBN 978-1-988271-83-5
Audiobook Download (.m4b): ISBN 978-1-988271-00-2

Editions of *The Red Letter Gospel: All The Words of Jesus Christ in Red*
Kindle: ISBN 978-1-988271-07-1
ePub: ISBN 978-1-988271-10-1   PDF: ISBN 978-1-988271-06-4
Standard Edition - Paperback: ISBN 978-1-988271-89-7
Complete Edition - Paperback: ISBN 978-1-988271-90-3
Complete Edition - Hard Cover: ISBN 978-1-988271-84-2

Editions of *FIVE COLUMN* - *Verse-By-Verse* (4 Gospel Harmony + Merger)
PDF: ISBN 978-1-998271-92-7
Paperback: ISBN 978-1-988271-79-8   Hard Cover: ISBN 978-1-988271-93-4

Editions of *FIVE COLUMN* - *Word-For-Word* (554 pages)
PDF: ISBN 978-0-993914-06-5   Paperback: ISBN 978-1-988271-01-9
are available at: synopticgospel.com/purchase

Audiobook available! (*iTunes .m4b*)
The Synoptic Gospel: The Story of The Life of Jesus
Hear the entire Gospel Story in under seven hours!   Narrated by: Daniel John
Available for instant **Download** at: *synopticgospel.com/audiobook*